DEMOCRACY
WITHOUT WOMEN

ACKNOWLEDGMENTS

We are grateful to Karen Offen for her historically informed, thorough reading of this translation. We also thank Oscar Kenshur, Michael Berkvam, and Judith Friedlander for their generous commitment of historical, philosophical, and linguistic expertise in reading parts of the manuscript, and Suzanne Jill Levine and Don Ulin for their encouragement. Finally, our thanks go to the American Translators Association for their recognition.

DEMOCRACY WITHOUT WOMEN

Feminism and the Rise of Liberal Individualism in France

BY

CHRISTINE FAURÉ

TRANSLATED BY

Claudia Gorbman
AND
John Berks

INDIANA UNIVERSITY PRESS

Bloomington and Indianapolis

Originally published as *La démocratie sans les femmes*

by Christine Fauré

© 1985 by Presses Universitaires de France

The English language edition of this book was made possible in part by financial assistance received from the French Ministry of Culture and the Lilian Barber Press.

© 1991 by Indiana University Press

The paper used in this publication meets the minimum requirements of American National Standard for Information Sciences—Permanence of Paper for Printed Library Materials, ANSI Z39.48-1984.

Manufactured in the United States of America

Library of Congress Cataloging-in-Publication Data

Fauré, Christine.
    [Démocratie sans les femmes. English]
    Democracy without women : feminism and the rise of liberal individualism in France / by Christine Fauré ; translated by Claudia Gorbman and John Berks.
      p.   cm.
    Translation of: La démocratie sans les femmes.
    Includes bibliographical references and index.
    ISBN 0-253-32155-7 (alk. paper)
    1. Women in public life—France—History. 2. Feminism—France—History. 3. Political science—France—History. I. Title.
HQ1236.5.F8F3813   1991
305.4'2'0944—dc20   90-45845
                                               CIP

1 2 3 4 5   95 94 93 92 91

CONTENTS

FOREWORD

Christine Fauré belongs to the generation of French feminist scholars who came of age politically during the student revolt of 1968. At this time young radicals like herself challenged the Stalinism of the French Communist Party and created new groups, some Trotskyists, others Maoists, defying those who represented the established left.[1] In the early 1970s, Fauré abandoned the students' struggle as well, for she was frustrated by the way it was dominated by men. Joining other women who similarly walked out, she helped found the contemporary women's movement in France.

As a feminist, Fauré remained committed to radical political and social change. Looking for models, she decided to study the efforts of revolutionary women in czarist Russia who had participated in terrorist activities at the turn of the century. Fauré produced two books on the subject in the late 1970s and through these works she began questioning the assumptions she and others had held about the future of women under socialism.[2] Turning next to the life of Alexandra Kollontai, her faith grew even weaker as she read about the way this Russian feminist was silenced in the Soviet Union during the 1920s and then ignored in France for the next fifty years, by Communists and feminists alike.[3]

May 1968 led Fauré and others to reconsider their relationship to Marxism. It also challenged feminists to study the history of liberal theory in France and analyze the role this democratic tradition has given (or not given) women to play in political society. *Democracy without Women* is Fauré's contribution to this new scholarship.

Although some begin the story in the late eighteenth century, Fauré takes us back to the days of Christine de Pizan (1364–1403?). Then she focuses on the works of philosophers written in the sixteenth century when France, as she points out, became a unified nation under François I. Liberal theory, Fauré argues, and its central idea about the abstract individual, dates to this period, when France saw itself for the first time as a single nation.

By the eighteenth century the connection between nationalism and liberalism was indisputable. Progressive theorists of the French Revolution spoke of granting political rights only to those who accepted participation in a single national culture. Before legislating that all men were created equal, they had developed the structures to make everybody the same. Abstract individuals, not distinct ethnic groups, would have their "inalienable" rights protected.

According to scholars like Alison Jaggar, Teresa Brennan, and Carole Pateman, women in the liberal state have been living under two contradictory theories: liberalism and patriarchy; one that celebrates the abstract individual and the other that promotes the traditional family, where women and children fall "naturally" under the authority of men.[4] Recognizing the contradiction, liberal feminists have challenged the state to do away with the archaic patriarchal order and grant women the right to be abstract individuals just as it had granted the right to men. Inspired by the French Revolution, Mary Wollstonecraft made this argument in the late eighteenth century and John Stuart Mill made it again in the mid-nineteenth. This also became the position of Simone de Beauvoir, the greatest liberal feminist thinker of twentieth-century France, and it has influenced the strategies of the National Organization of Women, the dominant branch of the women's movement in the United States today.

Drawing their arguments from liberal theory, many feminists have made a compelling case for women's inclusion in the class of abstract individuals. They reject claims made by others that women are different from men in ways requiring the legal protection of laws. For these feminists no reason exists, in either nature or culture, for excluding women from the privileges and dangers assumed by male citizens of the democratic nation-state.

Determined to establish a place for themselves in the political arena, liberal feminists have rarely worried about challenging their theory's aversion to difference. Like many black political leaders in the civil rights movement, they decided to compromise, arguing that the only hope for ending discrimination was to fight for the right to assimilate: to study, work, and live in an integrated, culturally homogeneous nation. Success in these terms has clearly had its price: women (and blacks) have had to blend in and make a virtue of the notion that they were just like (white) men.

In sum, the symbolic system of almost every culture chooses to elaborate upon the "natural" differences that exist among people—between the sexes, age groups, and, where relevant, races. The Western democratic tradition, however, claims to minimize them. Expressing an ideological commitment to political equality for all members of the nation-state, progressive liberal thinkers created the idea of the abstract individual, of a person who had no distinguishing characteristics before the law. With this vision came policies aimed at eliminating those differences that did still exist, preferably by assimilation, but also, at times, by discrimination, a strategy that went against the spirit of the liberal ideal. As Fauré shows us in this fascinating book, from the very beginning critics saw the contradictions and challenged those who tried to use liberal theory to justify creating a "democracy without women."[5]

Judith Friedlander

DEMOCRACY
WITHOUT WOMEN

INTRODUCTION

Feminism and liberalism! Is there such a thing as liberal feminism or feminist liberalism? Although this connection may seem unlikely at first, it begins to stir your imagination. Male or female, reader or writer, suppose you want to come to grips with recent changes in the status of women in contemporary society, and you feel the need for a personalized approach to questions normally addressed by the objective rules of historical method. This undertaking will be all the easier for you in that there exists absolutely no tradition on the subject. Up to the present, feminism and its history have held a small place indeed in the study of political philosophies.

Female Activist, Female Historian

In your memory you replay the film of the stages you have successively gone through, and the story of these political and social currents starts to materialize.

Initially, your analysis of the feminist movement has turned up little dramatic effect: its actresses rare, its decor uncertain, its storyline questionable. In addition to these hazy beginnings, your research has uncovered an unfortunate tendency toward hagiography: the documents are full of praises and portraits of Women of Times Past. Bibliographies are scant. There is nothing about the history of these women—each "life" rather resembling an insect mounted and pinned—that resembles an act of political birth.

Pursuing your course, you turn toward the study of revolutionary movements, through whose exceptional density you can discern women's collective participation: 1789, 1830, 1848, 1871—the ground no longer slips away beneath your feet. Your prestigious predecessors[1] devoted enthusiastic pages to the women of these revolutions. The heroism of the humblest classes of women becomes real for you now: you can see them at the barricades, firing guns alongside their comrades, in the tribunals defending the principles of political equality judged unacceptable by most men of their times. "In the name of our duties we claim our rights," defiantly proclaims the paper *La Voix des femmes* in 1848, the same year in which so-called universal, masculine suffrage was obtained. Women's protest continued to punctuate and comment on the structural changes in our society. Did these protests issue from a weaker minority than the male minority that presided over the fate of our institutions? You are continually astounded by the fact that women's political voices so often failed to find representation. In this failure to achieve political representation[2] you have observed a rhythm particular to social movements initiated by women rebelling against the unjust condition of their sex. But this explanation, too close to a "naturalizing" concept of social struggles and their actors, no longer satisfies you.

Revolutionary periods privilege rapid means of disseminating information—means that can quickly and effectively strike the imagination and thereby precipitate the course of events. Women in their struggles used these same weapons: proclamations, speeches, numerous (often short-lived) newspapers. Such an investment in the spoken and the written word reminds you of the kinds of media that the feminist movements of the last decade have mobilized: the pamphlet, the street-theater demonstration, a taste for symbolic acts (which has been reactivated in light of the recent discovery of the unconscious). Post-1968 feminists' political style recalls the insurrectionist spirit of the Vésuviennes.[3] But the historian in you, meticulous about chronology, will disapprove of drawing such comparisons across the centuries. Her work of reconstructing the past makes her impervious to the enthusiasm of the activist who is seeking new legitimacy. This deontological prudence points up a new difficulty: the saga of the struggles women have waged to improve their lives bears a complex relation to history. Theirs is an ahistorical oppression as old as the world, yet it is manifested in the form of specific actions through time.

More than in other areas of research, one is faced with a wide range of historical studies and methods (with the exception, however, of studies of women's work, which are firmly anchored in a tradition of Marxist analysis). Owing to the imprecision of this vast field of women's history, there is a risk of merely ending up with the analysis of an innocuous superstructure. One solution for the historian in her research is to adopt a perspective of even greater sympathy than the affinity researchers usually feel for their chosen era; for the pioneering energy necessary in founding a new discipline is hardly compatible with even a benevolent neutrality. But another difficulty remains: the thematic and "sympathetic" approach to the history of women and of feminism unwittingly replicates traditional family relationships. The project of a "sisterly" history must draw on both approaches, inscribing itself in the space of a natural family that mimics the legitimate (i.e., patriarchal) family. Such is the most frequent approach of male and female historians devoted to women's history, making up for the lack of the subject's "rootedness" by the positivity of the historical subject.

Sifting through the anachronistic modes of thought and alien discourses, your approach runs counter to any normal consecration of a new historical field. You discover so few consistencies in the political acts of these struggling women, that you inevitably wish to link their political behavior with better-known notions: socialist feminism, liberal or bourgeois feminism. The feminism we so naively thought to be as constant as the mistletoe on the oak of patriarchy, is replete with variations. Take, for instance, the moralizing tone of nineteenth-century women: foreign to your society and your aspirations for the total liberation of the individual, it appears to you to express an obsolete way of thinking. Who could imagine a pure and simple transposition of these political demands into our time?

Feminism and Socialism: An Undisputed Alliance?

It seems natural to explore the history of socialist movements in order to study the feminist movement. Generally, and without proof, it is the turbulent, neologism-rich imagination of Charles Fourier that is credited with having invented the word "feminism."[4] The utopian Fourier forged a sensible alliance between the socialist ideal and the idea of a necessary transformation in women's condition in the new society: all subsequent desires for social transformation have fed from the common source of Fourier's prehistory of socialist thought.

An account of feminism's vicissitudes in the contexts of socialist or quasi-socialist organizations must incorporate some reflection on the significance of these contexts. The widely recognized intolerance of the working-class avant-garde for women's economic independence allows us to formulate broader hypotheses, based on sectoral studies, regarding the social and political constitution of a modern state and its reproduction.

In most cases, the big names in working-class socialism at the end of the last century proved to be savagely authoritarian as they confronted the advances of women in various sectors of economic production. The more threatened the masculine population felt, the more they based their arguments on the sexual division of labor and social space defined in relation to the family.[5] For them, the working-class woman's role was derived from a functional finalism; it was in her nature to be wife and mother, and thus not to work in the factory. An exemplary statement:

> If the woman considers herself capable of other functions than those we consider natural, we refrain from imposing any constraint on her in this matter. But it is impossible for us to put social forces at the service of institutions we consider to be immoral, and whose practices have given to contemporary women diseases unknown to our grandmothers. These can rightly be counted as one of the most significant causes of the degeneration of the race, initiated by poverty, and aided and abetted by the labor of sewing machines.[6]

Many other examples could be cited; this kind of discourse characterizes a widely shared working-class mentality. Among the travesties that the workers' guilty consciences offered so as to disguise their refusal to have women work alongside them, medical explanations hold a prominent place. These prejudices against women working took a particularly violent turn in what is perhaps the most resonant conflict over labor and the unionization of women, the Couriau affair of 1913. The exclusion of a woman typographer by demand of the Lyons Printer's Union executive committee, and the expulsion of her husband for having allowed his wife to practice her trade, drew attention to the whole union debate on the legitimacy of women's labor in printing at the turn of the century.[7] This brief instance of the difficulties faced by women workers who wished to leave behind their domestic roles and to redefine themselves in the work sphere conveys not only the prejudices of the patriarchal worker, but also a particular representation of the female body: sick, exhausted from too much childbearing. Indeed, could the material situation of the underprivileged classes in the nineteenth century have yielded any other image?

Any historical account of discrimination must exercise caution in its generalizations. But while there is always a risk in moralizing about significant yet necessarily partial social phenomena, "the history of women" recently seems to manifest a more or less explicit desire to dissolve all humanistic approaches. In France, historical work on women has a (sometimes disguised) tendency to belong to the current of thought best represented by Michel Foucault.[8]

The study of political formations, on the other hand, has tended to rely on a more limited and more homogeneous palette of information, and seems hardly affected by the recent methodological deconstruction of the historical subject and the historian. The anthropomorphism that historians attribute to the political party, which tends to appear as a person with opinions and the capacity to make coherent decisions, leaves little room for a Foucauldian discourse on history. So women's participation in political parties has often proved a source of confusion and conflict. These black spots, in the view of all too few historians, reveal crucially significant things about the functioning of the political groups under study. Charles Sowerwine's book on women and socialism has ventured to take a more sophisticated perspective.[9] Historian Madeleine Rébérioux, who wrote the preface to the book's French edition, mistakenly conceives of Sowerwine's work as fitting into a saga of socialist feminism. What is really at stake in this book is an analysis of the anomalies and variations that women introduced at the heart of socialist ideology and institutions. How was it that once in power, the Socialist party, after having campaigned for women's suffrage for a quarter century, repudiated its earlier stand and sought refuge in the Senate's refusal? By 1936 the Socialists, supported by a Left majority, were in a position to overcome the Senate's opposition to women's vote (an opposition that had prevailed since 1922). How could there be enough politicking voices among the ranks of socialist women to break the commitment made fifty years earlier during the immortal Third Workers' Congress at Marseilles, in 1879, where socialists and feminists had joined in unanimity?[10] The evasive and whining remarks of the "Forum of Socialist Women" [Tribune des femmes socialistes] took refuge behind the fatality of the parliamentary game. The great majority of the Socialist party had their doubts concerning the political competence of the female masses—in spite of numerous proposals they made in favor of equal political rights. These doubts nevertheless had their positive side. Party leaders developed a guilty conscience because women had not obtained the right to vote, long hoped for from the Popular Front government. So three individual women were appointed to high public office, as if women's access to political institutions required a symbolic apprenticeship. In 1913, one of them, "Suzon," condemned, in the name of the class struggle, the principle of women's solidarity which feminists were defending.[11] Similarly, the socialist activist Louise Saumoneau, known for her faithfulness (to the point of absurdity) to the struggles of her youth,[12] perceived in feminism a danger for working-class women.[13] It was a paradoxical approach indeed for those women who pursued the "woman question" within their party, but whose allegiance to their socialist education prevented them from approving any kind of action extraneous to the interests of organized labor.

In the first half of the twentieth century, the ideological range of political groups espousing socialism and feminism varied. After 1913, when the women's division of the Section Française de l'Internationale Ouvrière (SFIO) was created,[14] socialist women, under the leadership of Louise Saumoneau, maintained a distinctly antifeminist stance. The Couriau affair, which took on the dimensions of a national debate, became the occasion for this group to adopt an unequivocally antifeminist line. On the feminist side, the borders were less clear; many activists adhered to socialist objectives during a phase of their political career. To cite only the most famous: Hubertine Auclert (1848–1914), architect of a real—though short-lived—alliance between feminism and socialism during the Marseilles Workers' Congress in 1879; Hélène Brion (1882–1962), union activist and militant socialist who was first and foremost a feminist; Madeleine Pelletier (1874–1939), involved in the SFIO from 1906 on; the lawyer Maria Verone (1874–1938); and even Nelly Roussel, who collaborated on the paper *La Voix des femmes*, a veritable breeding-ground for communist sympathizers.

Fourier had conceived of women's emancipation as the mainspring of all social transformations, but his thought on this point did not gain much currency in the history of French socialism. Still, we should look at what he and his followers envisioned. The Saint-Simonism of the 1830s, under the impetus of Prosper Enfantin, had placed the enfranchisement of women at the center of its preoccupations. The importance of Saint-Simonian women's groups in the history of the feminist movement must not go unrecognized. Another Saint-Simonian woman, Eugénie Potonie-Pierre (1844–98), was responsible for numerous attempts to give a social dimension to feminism.[15] The International Women's Rights Congress, which took place in 1900 at the initiative of Marguerite Durand (1864–1936, who also founded the first feminist daily paper *La Fronde*), caused the definitive demise of this socially concerned feminism by pitting feminists against socialist women. Indeed, the efforts of these feminists were not enough to affect one of the most deeply rooted notions of French socialism, which considered women's return to the home to be one of the results of the much-desired Revolution. Proudhon, via his infamous motto "Harlot or housewife, no other choice," had put his stamp on this misogynist tendency in the French workers' movement. His follower Auguste Keufer carried on his attitude in the Fédération du Livre[16] (Proudhon himself had been a printer and proofreader): the union expressed a particularly virulent hostility toward women; the Couriau affair bears witness to this. The struggle of women socialists for women's causes was severely jeopardized in 1905, the year of the unification of the movement, when the SFIO refused to accept as a constituent organization the socialist-feminist group founded by Elisabeth Renaud and Louise Saumoneau. In 1913, under the obstinate leadership of these same two women, the socialist women's group was formed, but meanwhile the break between socialism and feminism had occurred once and for all.

A comparison between the extreme fragility and repeated lack of success of the socialist women's position within their own party, and the remarkable expansion of women's organizations in the Social Democratic party in Germany, reveals some prejudices inherent in the doctrines of the French socialists, and in the history of the workers' movement after the Paris Commune. The Popular Front socialists' perception of women's suffrage can be largely attributed to these antecedents: in their eyes, women's suffrage threatened secular republican France because women remained in large part tied to religion and conservative values. The parliamentary Left's great fear in this respect paralyzed every effort toward reform. Lest we forget, it was De Gaulle, not Blum, who would grant Frenchwomen the right to vote—the primordial act of public life in a democracy!

Women gained the right to vote in Germany in 1919 and, apparently, went on to take part in the electoral process in greater numbers than their men.[17] That they should have won this right so much earlier in Germany than in France reflects the profound differences in the cultural evolution of the two nations, especially when it comes to the changes taking place in the two peoples' religious convictions and in their social mores. However, as we review the history of socialism in the two countries, we see that the Left in both places shared a similar position on the importance of promoting suffrage for women, first in Germany, then in France, with the former influencing the latter. The tactics used by the German Social Democrats for over forty years subsequently became the model for the French Communists, a fact marked symbolically in 1920 by the participation of Clara Zetkin at a meeting of the party in Tours.

In its earliest days, the French Communist party,[18] deferring to nagging demands by the Third International,[19] launched a policy on behalf of women. In order to do so, the party drew on the ideological arsenal which Germany's Social Democratic Party had stocked at its very outset. August Bebel's book headed the list. After a notable socialist career, *Woman under Socialism* became the Communist party's panacea on the woman question and remained so almost to the present day. First published in 1879, and after many revisions, the appearance of its fiftieth edition in 1910 indicates the unprecedented success and unquestionable persuasive power of this work. According to Bebel, the domination which men exert over women was closely modeled on the social and economic organization of contemporary society. The abolition of private property and the institution of a socialist society should bring about a revolution in morals: women will become complete individuals in themselves; their lives will be no less desirable than those of their masculine counterparts. Bebel's almost utopian insistence on the way socialism would resolve and harmonize the disparities between the two sexes took on a tactical importance in the general economy of socialist discourse: in Engels's *Origin of the Family, Private Property, and the State*, published five years after Bebel's book, we read: "the first class opposition that appears in history coincides with the development of the antagonism between man and woman in monogamous marriage, and the first class oppression coincides with that of the female sex by the male."[20] This assertion rests on its author's "genealogical" notion of classifying social forms according to their presumed order of appearance, and results from an analogic form of reasoning between bourgeoisie and proletariat, men and women, to the benefit (to be sure) of the first oppositional pair. The female sex's subservience in contemporary society destined women, like workers, to the struggle against capitalism. Without threatening its internal integrity, socialist doctrine could not juxtapose two entities that are equivalent in their potential for social transformation: a weakening of the economic, social, and political contradiction between bourgeoisie and proletariat would have inevitably resulted. Hence the necessity for theoreticians of fundamental socialism to appeal to women to join the ranks of proletarian organizations without however becoming fully involved in the antagonism between the sexes. Imagine if the logic of the social and political overthrow of the bourgeoisie by the proletariat were also applied to this other relationship of men's domination of women! This possibility was conceptually inadmissible for the socialists. Economic, social, and political discrimination against women could only give rise to a subsidiary revolutionary force for the proletariat's action.

The century's closing years, characterized by a demographic decline that reflected profound transformations in society, found the socialists fighting against the Malthusian theses. For Malthus's followers, there was one sole remedy for poverty—birth control. Socialist leaders, convinced instead that poverty and war were nourished by the vices of social structure, felt compelled to struggle more actively against the ascendancy of Malthusian theory, favored by women's movements, by developing their theses on women's roles in the revolutionary project. Not only did Bebel apply the major themes of Marxist analysis to women; he added a previously unpublished essay on what social change would mean in moral terms. At a time when traditional female ethics were losing ground due to the waning of religion, it was important to sketch the broad lines of moral regeneration for a momentarily disoriented public. Within the indicated limits, *Woman under Socialism* boiled down the essence of socialist thought on the status of women and women's roles in the revolutionary struggle, and remains without doubt the most highly developed expression of this doctrine.

For understanding the further development of French socialism and communism, it is of unquestionable importance to refer to the Russian Revolution. In its first stages, the political figure of Alexandra Kollontai embodied the desire to change the condition of Russian women. The drama of this elegant, courageous, ambitious woman who managed to transform her political exile into a diplomatic office is full of episodes that were decisive for the future of women.[21] Her career, brief as it was, became the focus of international attention for socialist and feminist organizations. When (before her exile) she became the People's Commissar for Social Affairs, Kollontai's first concern was to develop a family code which would relieve women of the burdens that had hitherto been their fate: it established easy divorces and free and available abortions. But did such enlightened legislation necessarily signify a real transformation, in moral terms, of women's situation in the new state? The first reports from French women journalists traveling in Soviet Russia who were sensitive to women's issues—e.g., Louise Weiss[22] and Madeleine Pelletier[23]—paint a picture of an almost feudal social order, whose inertia the Bolshevik innovations were having great difficulty overcoming. How could it have been otherwise for a society so recently liberated from serfdom? Mass displacements of people during wartime had weakened the patriarchal aspects of society somewhat, but the impulse to preserve the family unit was deeply rooted nevertheless. For this reason the Bolsheviks' activity was taking on a paramilitary turn, which was amply criticized in the biting account of a trip to Russia written by Madeleine Pelletier. The new society was renewing the same prejudices and discrimination that women had endured before the revolution. Deprived of all personal initiatives, women were now witnessing models for their aspirations being imposed on them from without. The right to sexual freedom for women was the hidden agenda of only a minority of the Soviet intelligentsia. This right, which Alexandra Kollontai defended all her life, was already, by the first years of the revolution, the butt of attacks by the Bolshevik party, and was subsequently condemned as "antisocial" heresy. All that women's emancipation meant for the young Soviet state was the mobilization of a new labor force, freed from its domestic confinement, and still largely underutilized in the labor market.

In the history of relations between socialism, communism, and feminism, the spirit of reform in a state still stammering in its infancy held a primary place. This spirit nourished all the hopes that had been raised by the German Social Democrats (despite their limitations), and which the formation of a new International was gearing up to instill in its national sections. Under Stalin, the despotic evolution of the Soviet leadership obliterated even the slightest hints of change in the condition of women. The legislative revisions which the new family codes brought to the liberal measures that Alexandra Kollontai had passed seemed to signal a return to (patriarchal) family values.[24] In the Soviet Union, motherhood became women's only claim to fame, even though equal rights for women were guaranteed in the nation's constitution.

Following the Soviet model, French communism glorified the family and the devotion of mothers, and continued to oppose Malthusianism. In fact, birth control was still being condemned as late as 1956. Upon the publication of Dr. Derogy's book *Des Enfants malgré vous* [Children despite you], Maurice Thorez wrote, "Let us bear in mind that the road to women's liberation passes through social reforms, through social revolution, and not through abortion clinics."[25] This refusal to envisage any improvement in women's lives through birth control presented a considerable barrier to popularizing the major theses of feminism. The weakening of French communism, as it grappled with serious ideological difficulties arising not only from the international situation (Soviet invasions of Hungary and Czechoslovakia) but also within the country—the explosion of antiestablishment leftism in May 1968—allowed for a revival of the political debate concerning the status of women and its potential for change. In the early 1970s, the women's liberation movement, with a diversity of goals and initiatives, took as its primary objective the widest possible distribution of contraceptives and the legalization of abortion. Since 1960, the organization *Le Planning Familial* had prepared this political wave by establishing women's centers. But it took ten years and an unprecedented mobilization of French-women—an exemplary political unanimity—for this collective desire to materialize into a new law. The socialist and communist movements, in their various forms from unions to political groups, hardly advanced the cause of women. With very few exceptions, these movements refused to act on women's issues that went beyond the context of the family and its preservation. And if, under external pressures, socialists came out in favor of renewing the social and political status of women, they often shied away from taking a real stand when actually put to the test.

Bourgeois Feminism, Liberal Feminism?

The anathema "bourgeois feminists" appears too often in socialist writing for such extreme language to be ignored. No one disputes that there has existed a revolutionary feminism strongly linked to the socialist movement. Like Flora Tristan before her, Hubertine Auclert, founder of the organization "Le Droit des femmes" [Women's right] in 1876, did not separate women's causes from those of the working class. Marguerite Durand, founder and director of the feminist daily *La Fronde*, took a similar stand by creating a women's union, with headquarters in the Paris Bourse du Travail [Trade union center]. In choosing to create new institutions intended to redress the balance of social and political power between men and women, the projects of these feminists belong to a *liberal* conception of social change. The system of capitalist production and its harmful effects on women were not in fact called explicitly into question; the repeated affirmation of women's rights that were denied legal ratification found suitable means for this struggle in the creation of a new press, and in the arts of speechmaking and lecturing.[26] The feminists' characteristic emphasis on oral and written forms of political confrontation favored a recruitment of intellectual women, if not altogether bourgeois women. It is in fact very important to distinguish between the question of class origin and the question of a more complete social identity, which would take into account particular aspects of class origin as well as individual status on the professional and family levels, which can be just as significant. A close examination of the demarcation line drawn by socialists between bourgeois feminism and proletarian feminism shows that only rarely did feminist leaders—or socialist leaders—come from the working class.

Who were the women whose names punctuate the history of this movement?

Maria Deraismes (1828–94),[27] reared in a rich business family, refused to marry. She devoted her gifts as a journalist and orator to the cause of women. Having for that time an exceptionally good education, she insisted that gaining access to schooling was essential to women's emancipation. Julie Daubié (1824–74) fought misogyny within the university, where women were excluded from all instruction, by signing up for the baccalaureate and graduate examinations.[28] Although not many followed quickly in her footsteps, access to education and to professional careers traditionally closed to women became an issue for feminism, which thus reacted against the state of intellectual inferiority in which women were kept. Brilliant and gifted personalities, these women often embraced the liberal professions: lawyers like Jeanne Chauvin, Maria Verone, the doctor Madeleine Pelletier.

The large number of schoolteachers among the feminist ranks has often been noted.[29] Schoolteaching was after all the meeting point of two social axes: it was a step up for women of the lower orders, and a fallback for bourgeois women who had no other financial support. The teaching career offered them a very cohesive frame of reference. The republican ideal, which conferred on the people the means of exercising with heightened awareness the political sovereignty it had won, gave an almost apostolic meaning to this profession. Since women did not yet exercise political rights, teaching embodied their hopes for greater equality between the sexes; it would allow them recognition for their recently acquired skills and their intellectual and moral abilities. Their professional "success," sometimes touted as a symbol of feminist struggle, gave these women exceptional independence for their time. They were often nonconformists on the level of family relations as well: they refused to marry, and chose to remain widowed[30] or divorced,[31] often raising their children alone.[32] Some found in marriage an association advantageous to their ongoing work. This was the case, for example, for Eugénie Potonie-Pierre, whose husband admirably backed her militant activity.

The feminist movement's experimentation with new kinds of social action in its attempt to achieve a new identity on the political and social level issues from a liberal concept of change, in spite of the reductive critique which socialism attached to liberalism. The latter's two central theses, liberty and equality, emerge from a political philosophy based on the recognition of the individual's human rights. This "equal opportunity" feminism was not without its contradictions, however. Individuals did not always enjoy as complete an independence vis-à-vis the social group as might be desired; there were sometimes sociological impediments to their freedom of behavior. How, for example, could the feminist Hubertine Auclert contribute with good conscience to Edouard Drumont's racist and antisemitic daily paper La Libre Parole? The tone

Drumont adopted to present their collaboration was a mixture of populism, as righting of wrongs, and of social nationalism—seasoned with a generous helping of vicious antisemitism.[33] Auclert's weekly column "Le Droit des femmes" could not just spin out its analyses with impunity, in defiance of such virulent intolerance. The short duration of her association with the paper is proof enough of that. But it nevertheless shows a feminist voice taking part in a dominant social institution. Since France belonged to the French,[34] the feminist struggle addressed itself to Frenchwomen. Feminism was not just a secular republican movement or a pacifist one; it was also patriotic and religious. It found spokesmen at the heart of the bourgeoisie and even the aristocracy. Sometimes it directly plugged into the social interests of these groups. And contrary to what we might expect, a certain Christian feminism developed as well.[35]

Although feminist political groups proliferated in the nineteenth and twentieth centuries,[36] the emergence of these collective structures was not a new phenomenon. During the French Revolution, women had also assembled in "circles" and clubs. But the Civil Code of 1804 legislated women back into their former subordination, condemning them to hopeless legal non-status. Under the reign of Louis-Philippe, Saint-Simonism revived the political debate by putting the idea of women's emancipation at the center of its religious and metaphysical principles. Chronologically speaking, the social and political history of feminist movements contemporaneous with workers' movements is known because of work undertaken by historians of the last dozen years. The history of real advances for women during these same years remains murkier, since propagandas and ideologies screen us from clearly viewing the concrete results, whose slow progress is not likely to arouse enthusiasm.

Social reforms are rarely achieved at a single stroke; a series of precedents most often prepares the way. Legislators, in order to establish their point of view, have proceeded in various ways, which would be difficult to synthesize. It would be wrong to draw hasty parallels between the evolution of women's civil status in private law and the evolution of their political status in public law. The recognition of women's right to vote does not find its equivalent in the recognition of the equality of husband and wife; women's broad access to managerial positions and the professions can coexist perfectly well with a condition of civil incapacity and political inequality. Though the Second World War marks a decisive moment in the evolution of mores and institutions, it did little to alter the legal status quo.

Women in France before World War II did not enjoy a single political right.[37] It should be remembered that the Chamber of Deputies voted favorably on several occasions on bills according women eligibility to vote,[38] and that the Senate repeatedly rejected these bills.

The status of women in occupations has been the focus of numerous sociological and historical studies. How should we interpret the modern period's redistribution of women's work in society during the last hundred and fifty years?[39] Legally speaking, the massive transformation of women's work into paid occupations necessarily led to the establishment of an entire system of protective laws and regulations.[40] This legislation is abundant and aims particularly at protecting maternity.[41] Access to jobs in the public sector, in principle open to both married and unmarried women, was in fact subjected to rules that confined women to positions of little or no responsibility. Certain careers, like diplomacy and the judiciary, remained closed to women. Although an unmarried woman was as entitled as a man to choose her own occupation, a married woman[42] could only take a noncommercial job if her husband was not opposed;[43] and she had to request her husband's formal consent to go into business.[44] As for the enjoyment and exercise of civil rights: single women twenty-one or over, as well as widows and divorcees, had full civil capacity on a par with men. But in marriage, the woman was deprived of rights and had to request her husband's authorization in certain circumstances.

After the freeze that the Civil Code of 1804 placed on the legal status of women, legislation nevertheless began to reverse the situation of married women's legal incapacity, passing various acts of uneven import,[45] particularly concerning employment rights. These laws set a legislative precedent that culminated in the law of 2 February 1938, which granted married women civil capacity, and shielded them from the husband's marital rights by abolishing the Napoleonic Code's "duty of obedience" of wife to husband. However, the husband remained legal head of the family, and the wife's exercise of civil rights could be limited by the existing marriage settlement or by any other legal clause, for that matter. The 1938 law set in place the modern tendency for increasingly greater equality between spouses, but by no means did it eliminate the hierarchical relationship between them. Hardly was it voted in under the Popular Front government than the Vichy authorities revised it,[46] with an eye to clarifying the "effects of marriage regarding the rights and duties of the spouses," as its own title indicates. Enacted during the war, it gave married women the role imposed by events of the time (mobilization, husband's captivity, etc.). This law made it possible for the wife to assume the husband's position as head of the family, in a spirit very much in keeping with the Pétainist ideal of motherhood.[47]

The history of divorce in France[48] clearly shows that in matters of family law, the freedom of individuals has taken a back seat to the perpetuation of the family. The point of the law was not so much to sanction a salutary breakup as to regulate the conditions of remarriage. While women's status was equal to men's regarding formalities involved in marriage or annulment, the previously mentioned "effects of marriage" upon women's rights swayed the balance to the man's advantage regarding personal and financial relations between the spouses. Parental rights never belonged to the mother during marriage; only the father could exercise them, and many years would pass before this power was felt to be an injustice and it yielded to a new definition of spouses' roles in running the family.[49]

Women's status in the natural family was profoundly modified by legislation in 1912 that made paternity suits possible.[50] The drafting of this law had occasioned much contradictory debate in 1900 during the fifth feminist convention, the International Congress on Women's Condition and Rights.[51] Among the congress participants was the socialist deputy for Paris, René Viviani, who undertook to sponsor in Parliament the laws proposed at the women's congress. Many feminists rejected the law in the name of women's dignity, even though the congress as a whole declared itself in favor of paternity suits. After the vote, the debate continued more heatedly. Feminist Hélène Brion, for example, argued in 1916: "The paternity suit is a false principle which we feminists of the avant-garde strongly oppose. It tends to perpetuate the mistaken age-old idea that the family is based on the man, whereas its natural basis is the woman, and her alone."[52]

The inventory of legislation for the betterment of women's social status (whose positive nature was sometimes denied by feminists themselves as being counterproductive to the cause) cannot remove from the record the repressive laws concerning abortion and birth control practices whose consequences weighed so heavily on women's lives. In fact, it is remarkable that in the comparative law volume that I cited earlier [see n. 37], these laws are not mentioned, as if contraception and abortion came under the exclusive jurisdiction of the state, without any effect on women's lives. The story of these repressive laws[53] tells of one of Western society's most brutal aspects—the appropriation of women's bodies by interests external to their own experience.

During the evolution of industrial society a certain number of gender inequities have been eradicated. Even so, on the eve of World War II, the family unit in France remained under the husband's authority, and the nation's republican institutions, based primarily on the delegation of power and the right to vote, remained inaccessible to women. The contradiction between women's second-class citizenship and the characterization of these institutions as "democratic" has often been noted. However, it was in the legal status of women that the effort to do away with this system of inequality moved most sluggishly.

General de Gaulle took a decisive step in the history of political rights. The ordinance of 21 April 1944 granted Frenchwomen the right to vote, fulfilling the commitments that the Popular Front government had been unable to honor. Then the creation of a Secretary of State for the Status of Women in July 1974 came as an important event in the history of women's political and institutional representation, despite the small budget assigned to it.

Of course, women's participation in elections and in government is only one aspect of the improvement of their condition. A series of new laws passed 11 July 1974 gave additional rights to married women. These took effect on 1 January 1976, abrogating the laws which had defined in such an inegalitarian way the duties incumbent on husband and wife. The law of 13 July 1965, though retaining the husband's title as head of the family, granted women the right to employment without their husband's consent, and also the right to administer their property as they saw fit. The law of 4 June 1970 (mentioned above) adopted the principle of shared spousal responsibility in the family.

Despite this juridical equalization of women's condition, there still remained the problem of repression in the matters of abortion and contraception. To eliminate the effects of discrimination against women, the law needed to take measures to guarantee women's right to *choose* to bear children. During the sixties, the fight against clandestine abortions and the need to establish legal guidelines for female contraception took on such urgency that François Mitterrand proposed repealing the 1920 law during his 1965 electoral campaign. At Lucien Neuwirth's instigation, the law of 28 December 1967 authorized contraception within heavy constraints. A new law (4 December 1974), also sponsored by Neuwirth, simplified the controls on distribution of contraceptives.

The legislative battle to liberalize abortion took somewhat longer, and debates on abortion continued throughout the decade. Despite the vigorous political pressure of feminist groups and of public opinion, the battle had to be waged in two stages. The law of 17 January 1975, covering voluntary pregnancy termination, suspended for five years the "enforcement of the first four paragraphs of Article 317 of the Penal Code in cases where the pregnancy has been terminated before the end of the tenth week by a physician in a public or private hospital."[54] The law of 31 December 1979 effectively retained those parts of the 1974 law which declared abortion legal under certain conditions; however, several new clauses in the 1979 law made enforcement easier.

In a political system such as France's, it is difficult to attribute authorship of and responsibility for the laws solely to the government in power. Indeed, concerning the abortion law, while the majority took the initiative (in this case, the Simone Weil bill in 1975), the dynamics in Parliament between majority and opposition should be noted: 284 votes to 189. Of the yes votes, only 99 were cast by the 291 majority representatives; 77 majority representatives would refer the matter to the Constitutional Council, trying in vain to get the bill declared unconstitutional. Yvette Roudy commented on this alliance:

> In these 284 votes were included all the votes of the Left, without which the bill never would have passed. The communists and socialists tried throughout the debate to manage it so that delays in surgical procedure could be extended until the twelfth week . . . , that public education on contraception would be organized, and most important, that abortions would be paid for by Social Security. It didn't work: modern conservatives consider money to be an effective brake against the abuses which liberalizing the law threatens to cause.[55]

Mitterrand's Socialist government was duty-bound in 1982 not to forget these contemptuous remarks concerning Social Security reimbursement for abortions!

According to Georges Burdeau,[56] the term "liberalism" first appeared in 1893, but the philosophical and political current it designates goes much further back, just as feminism itself predates both Fourier's writings and the Congress of Feminist Organizations of 1892. The history of feminism's coexistence with liberalism does more than simply pose a problem of chronology: it challenges the hegemony of a "spirit of socialism" which reigned over the analysis of social transformations from Condorcet to Léon Blum, as a socialist pamphlet on women's emancipation complacently affirms.[57] If we study the progress in society of notions of equality and the individual, we can ultimately uncover the unknown landscape of women's individual and collective struggle, by examining the concrete conditions of their historical existence. In France this means not starting out with the Revolution, as is commonly done, but in the sixteenth century, when the idea of the nation emerges. Women's political participation in the general mobilization of society that we know as the French Revolution has meaning only in the perspective of the philosophical, religious, and political "revolutions" that preceded it.

I

CHRISTINE DE PIZAN AND THE PARADOX OF AN ORIGIN

Historians have approached the political origins of feminism with varying de-grees of success.[1] Though France has long had, in one form or another, an intellectual movement decrying the injustices endured by women, the secondary status to which this movement has been traditionally relegated within the his-tory of ideas obscures what it has to offer the modern world. The political and philosophical history of feminism so far remains unwritten since historians have limited themselves to a cursory descriptive study of women's presence in the country's cultural life. This relative neglect seemed justified by the historical scarcity of women authors, of established political doctrines, and perfected philosophical systems. The historian's task consisted only of unearthing facts that "speak for themselves," provided these facts had been properly established according to the rules of the discipline. This history of feminism has thus far been content to define itself within the conventional boundaries of major in-tellectual currents, thereby corroborating the view that women had little in-tellectual impact on formulating the ideas of their time. Whatever the historians' gender, this history thus perpetuated the inferior status of women in society, along with the idea that the field of political philosophy was an activity some-how separate from the totality of social practices. If, however, we analyze the philosophical implications of those texts that affirm the natural and legal equal-ity between the sexes within the context of the major documents of a given period, we will expose the deficiencies of a merely factual understanding of intellectual history, and reveal a solid logic determining the production of these values. Such a project constitutes one of the priorities of the present work.

The birth certificate of French feminism is most often accorded to the works of Christine de Pizan. But did this emblematic literary figure really give birth to contemporary feminist values, as the historians of French feminism unan-imously proclaim?[2] The importance they attribute to her works requires us to examine her published texts more closely.

In light of recent scholarship, this volume uses the original spelling, "Pizan."

No other vernacular literary work was more popular throughout the Middle Ages than the immense poem, *Le Roman de la Rose*, by Guillaume de Lorris and Jean de Meun. Though evidence shows that this work remained popular well into the sixteenth century,[3] it aroused particular interest near the end of the fourteenth. In this tormented period of the Hundred Years' War, Jean de Meun's poem fueled a veritable battle of letters and treatises in which the poet Christine de Pizan played a determining role. What was the feud about, and who made up the opposing factions?

A detailed chronology in the latest critical edition of the debate over the *Roman de la Rose*[4] gives us the background for the epistolary exchange between Jean de Montreuil, Provost of Lille, along with the Col brothers[5] on the one hand, and Christine de Pizan, aided by Jean Gerson, chancellor of the University of Paris, on the other. A few private discussions had already suggested Jean de Montreuil's disagreement with Christine de Pizan and an anonymous "subtle cleric"; Jean de Montreuil then put his contribution into written form for the first time. In May of 1401 he composed a treatise (no longer extant) on the merits of the *Roman de la Rose*. He submitted this to the judgment of a few prelates and sent a copy to Christine. The latter's response to Montreuil summarily condemned the sexual license advocated by Jean de Meun: "With all due respect to your grace, permit me to tell you that this is only an encouragement to vice, a justification for dissolute living, a doctrine full of deception—if not damnation! . . . the cause of suspicion and heresy . . . the shame of many people, which may lead to perdition."[6]

Her tone here is consonant with statements she made previously advocating the "honor and praise of women."[7] "L'épître au Dieu d'Amours" [Epistle to the God of Love] is in the form of a ladies' petition, carried by the God of Love to the assembly of the gods in order to plead for an end to the outrages women suffer on earth.[8]

The importance that Christine attributed to courtly values permeates all her prose and poetry. Courtly ideals served as her shield against a moral tradition that strongly condemned women and marriage in the name of natural rights. This longstanding tradition, already firmly anchored among churchmen, informs the larger part of Jean de Meun's work.

We must wonder, however, whether the power behind Christine's critique stems, as she claims in the *Avision*, from a personal identification with the cause of women, after having borne the brunt of a condition that made her critical of "irksome" commentary, "foolish looks," and the "amusements of men full of wine and ease."[9]

The original debate between Jean de Montreuil and Christine broadened when, on 25 August 1401, Jean Gerson preached a sermon in Latin before the faculty and students of the College of Navarre, challenging those on Jean de Meun's side. An unlikely ally from the clerical world of which Christine was so critical, Gerson would give a distinctively theological dimension to this literary argument. Perhaps the enlistment of such a prestigious name as Jean Gerson's led Gontier Col, an intimate friend of Jean de Montreuil and secretary to the king, to initiate a brief exchange of letters with Christine (on 13 and 15 September 1401):

> Woman of high and well-bred understanding, worthy of honor and great praise: I have heard talk from the mouths of many notable clerics . . . that you have lately written some kind of an invective against my master, teacher, and friend, the late Jean de Meun—who was a true Catholic, venerable master and scholar of his time in holy theology, and a profound philosopher.[10]

The debate was rekindled on 1 February 1402 when Christine sent a collection of letters to both Queen Isabeau and Guillaume de Tignonville, Provost of Paris.[11] Her initiative moved the debate over the *Roman de la Rose* from the level of a private dispute between "belle-lettristes" to the public arena, calling in the court and the town as witnesses. In fact, by removing the debate from the clerical world of Montreuil and Gontier Col, this far from innocent act offered a strategic advantage to Christine,[12] who was a favorite of Louis d'Orléans and a friend of Queen Isabeau.[13]

On 18 May 1402, Gerson published a condemnation of the *Roman de la Rose* in the form of a "vision," expressing the opinion that the work should be burned. In a dream, the writer is carried off to the "Court of Christianity" where he attends a debate on the *Roman de la Rose* and its author. About the time of this publication, Pierre Col, Gontier's brother and Canon of Notre-Dame, wrote a long treatise to Christine in an attempt to refute her and Gerson's arguments. Replying to Col on 1 January 1403, Christine also presented a copy of her response to the Queen and to the Provost of Paris. By that time Jean Gerson had already given a series of "Poenitemini" sermons (on 17, 24, and 31 December 1402), rebuking those "foolish lovers" who dared defend luxury. Then, in the winter of 1402–3, Gerson sent Pierre Col a Latin epistle, "Talia de me," in which he emphasized how serious he thought this controversy was.

The quarrel, rich in reverberations, engaged some of the most important figures of the realm, and Christine's strong convictions and persistent arguments elevated her to the rank of her opponents. A vast body of commentary has since noted the exceptional nature of this situation for a woman of that time. It would be reductive, however, to interpret Christine's line of conduct throughout this affair as due solely to her brilliant personality; the judgments in her writing refer implicitly to a philosophical position and a moral critique that has divided the history of medieval philosophy ever since Jean de Meun's time. The close relationship between the arguments of Christine de Pizan and Jean Gerson is undeniable, and even though we have no positive evidence concerning the actual circumstances of this "ideological complicity,"[14] we can still discern, across the tissue of references and complex exchanges that run throughout the quarrel, a more fundamental political struggle between two camps, the stakes of which were known to all the players. Christine de Pizan was writing within an aristocratic tradition which linked Prince and Poet in a privileged relationship, and it is possible to interpret her part in the quarrel as a reaffirmation of the courtly ideal. As Daniel Poirion writes, "At the time when naturalism was beginning to attract the first humanists such as Pierre Col and Jean de Montreuil, she was denouncing as dubious a certain superficial courtliness, which attempted to cover up its licentiousness."[15] But perhaps this moral critique also had roots in more fundamental philosophical and political issues of the period.

Some commentators[16] have pointed out the similarities between the positions taken by several of de Meun's characters (including the old woman, Genius, and the god of Love), and certain Averroist theses,[17] which had been condemned in 1270 and 1277, precisely the outside dates of the romance's composition. But should this be interpreted as the author's direct endorsement, or does it simply suggest the influence of questions that were stirring the intellectual world of his period?

Interpretations based on Jean de Meun's personality and intentions are various and contradictory. In his *Naissance de l'esprit laïque au déclin du Moyen Age* [Birth of the secular mind in the late Middle Ages], Georges de Lagarde reads the *Roman de la Rose* as the "testimony of an academic Averroism, the dishonest and impertinent affirmations of which had justly shocked the authorities."[18] More recently, Jacques Le Goff has characterized the second part of the *Roman de la Rose* as "a hymn to the inexhaustible fecundity of nature, an impassioned invitation to obey her laws without reserve, a call to unbridled sexuality."[19] For the British historian Norman Cohn,[20] Jean de Meun belongs to a revolutionary millennialist strain of thought.

Even today the enlistment of de Meun in the Averroist camp—the camp of naturalists and free-thinkers—fuels continued speculation. It is not within the scope of the present study to choose from among these readings of the *Roman de la Rose*. However, our interpretive range expands considerably, thanks to Roland Hissette's recent exegesis[21] of 219 "reputedly Averroist" articles in an ecclesiastical condemnation by means of which the Bishop of Paris, Etienne Tempier, proclaimed the imminent defeat of the doctrinal peril that lurked within the faculty of arts at Paris. Hissette's commentary on the articles provides us with both the explicit and implicit reasons for the condemnation, thus expanding our understanding of its relation to this "intellectual crisis," which originated in a desire to free philosophy from the grip of theology. Hissette points out the hybrid character of the "heretical" articles, which were condemned on moral as well as doctrinal grounds. Certain of the incriminated articles provided a secular framework for sexual mores,[22] thus directly threatening patristic teachings, whose influence extended into the universities.

At the end of the thirteenth century, the doctrinal landscape was divided into three sectors. In one group stood the commentators upon Aristotle: the most famous Latin Averroists, Siger de Brabant and Boëce de Dacie, argued for an autonomous philosophy. Their philosophy differed from Christianity in many ways, including the unity of active reason [*intellectus agens*], the denial of free will, astrological determinism, the eternity of the world, the mortality of the soul, and denial of the rule of divine providence over individuals or human actions.[23] This doctrine had already been the object of a condemnation on 11 December 1270 (*de erroribus philosophorum*). Opposed to these radical Aristotelians, according to Hissette, were two other key groups:

> on one side were the moderate Aristotelians, such as Thomas Aquinas, concerned with bringing their philosophy in line with the requirements of Christian thought;[24] and on the other side were the conservative theologians who, in order better to repel the attacks of pagan philosophy, rallied themselves around the banner of Saint Augustine. The condemnation of 7 March 1277 is the work of these neo-Augustinians.[25]

Nearly a century later, the debate over Jean de Meun's *Roman de la Rose* partially reactivated the intellectual confrontation that had so profoundly marked the end of the thirteenth century. The opposing forces arranged themselves along corresponding lines of demarcation: the Augustinians versus the partisans of "natural philosophy." Once transported onto literary terrain, however, the battle was perhaps less dangerous for its protagonists than during the preceding century. "Located at the origins of modern times," Eric Hicks writes, "in a period no longer the Middle Ages but not yet the Renaissance,"[26] the dispute over the *Roman de la Rose* inaugurated a model of literary expression that was to enjoy a long life in the quarrel-filled history of French literature.

Christine de Pizan is known as the first woman author to take an active role in literary life. Jean de Montreuil, the first of the French humanists, was famous for having cited only Terence[27] in a letter to the Pope on the evils of the Church, thus exposing his education as a secular one, steeped in the writings of other classical authors such as Cicero and Virgil. With the Col brothers he shared the intellectual optimism stemming from this revival of classical paganism. Jean Gerson's austere speculative theology, on the other hand, embodied religious authority, while it incorporated a mystical contemplation nourished by such Augustinian authorities as the Franciscan Bonaventure,[28] a principal in the condemnation of the thirteen theses of Arabic philosophy in 1270. In the "vision" he wrote in response to the *Roman de la Rose*, Gerson defined the moral responsibility of the writer. He cast his argument in the form of a trial, charging Jean de Meun with eight principal transgressions, including apologies for debauchery and immodesty, defamation of Dame Reason, of marriage, and so on. The central crime in Gerson's accusation, committed by de Meun through the intermediary of *Fol Amour* or "Foolish Love," was the systematic denigration of feminine virtues. This was a crime, because it was contrary to the cult of the saints and the Virgin. Gerson writes:

> Why didn't he make an exception for all the glorious virgin saints and the countless others who kept chastity in the temple of their heart even at the price of suffering severe tortures and cruel death? Why didn't he keep this reverence for the most holy of holy women? But no. He was mad with love, with no remedy;

he did not want to make an exception for any of them in order more brazenly to incite all women to abandon themselves.[29]

The moral frailty of human beings, Gerson claims, requires writers to be especially scrupulous and circumspect in what they write:

> And in order that no one believes or complains that I accuse anything but vices and not people, I make this kind of appeal and conclusion in the name of Chastity and Conscience against any painting or writing or saying that encourages people to Lust. Indeed, our frailty is all but too inclined by itself in this direction. There is no need to inflame it more and have it fall into the depths of vice, far from virtues and God, who is our glory, our love, our salvation, joy and happiness.[30]

If Jean Gerson revived the spirit of Saint Bonaventure[31] nearly a century later, it is because he, too, wished to rid Christian theology of its trappings of pagan philosophy in order to ground it more firmly in the tradition and words of the Church Fathers. Several months after the publication of his treatise, he gave a series of "Poenitemini" sermons in which he assailed the manifestations of "luxury," along with its hidden evils, and then addressed himself to those "foolish lovers" who took up its defense. The thesis under attack, according to which simple fornication was not a sin,[32] has been attributed to the "Gentiles" at the end of the thirteenth century, and does not appear to have come out of radical Aristotelianism. Rather, it expressed the prevailing atmosphere at the faculty of arts during this period, and attested to the influence of André Le Chapelain's overtly libertine work of indulgence, *De amore*. In the fourteenth century, Jean de Montreuil and the Col brothers may have been under the influence of this profane sensationalism. Thus they sought to defend Jean de Meun as a satirical poet whose art obeyed its own laws, not those of theology. Pierre Col writes: "I answer Lady Eloquence and you at one and the same time, and I say that sir Jean de Meun introduced in his book characters who speak according to their appropriate attributes: so that the Jealous Man acts jealous, the Old Woman acts like an old woman, and so on with the others."[33]

Jean Gerson's epistle, "Talia de me," to Pierre Col, put an emphatic end to the debate: Jean de Meun's poem, he states, is heretical, and the arguments of those who defend it can also be thus branded. The epistle's tone is firm and to the point; and because Gerson is writing to a Canon, he casts his argument in a theological mold. At the core of the debate over the *Roman de la Rose* is a particular conception of human nature, defined by Saint Augustine during the Pelagian controversy. According to Augustine's anti-Pelagian view, human nature is irretrievably corrupted by original sin, the legacy of which has been handed down as concupiscence.[34] This tarnished nature may be restored somewhat by baptism, but never to its original state of perfection. Death, suffering, evil lust, and ignorance are therefore inevitable.[35] Jean Gerson writes:

You say that a child of two or three years is in a state of innocence. That is Pelagian heresy, and whoever supports it should be treated as an obstinate heretic. Besides, all the arguments that you have brandished in the hopes of refuting the irrefutable merely have the effect of entangling you all the more in the knots of this heresy. . . . you thought, I suppose—and you were wrong—that the child would find itself in a state of innocence either because it is ignorant or because it has not yet sinned by action. But you should have kept in mind the original sin of unhealthy concupiscence, because that is what drags you into evil as it does all of us.[36]

Gerson advises his adversaries to read Bonaventure's work, "the itinerary of the soul toward God," from which they will learn that fallen man's intellect must laboriously reclimb the ladder of beings.[37] This religious tradition, based on a hierarchical structuring of the ideas at the center of its spiritual adventure—ideas about God, the angels, the Church, man, and individual responsibility—obviously found itself opposed to partisans of natural, secular philosophy!

If Christine de Pizan's effort to support Lady Philosophy[38] in the debate of the *Roman de la Rose* looks to us like a labored use of her talent, her conception of humanity suffering from sin and the moral imperative she places on the writer, are remarkably similar to those proposed by Gerson. In fact, her references to the Church Fathers and to the Augustinian tradition are identical to his.[39] She writes to Jean de Montreuil:

I cannot convince you with a better argument than human nature, which by itself is inclined toward evil; there is no need for anyone to remind us of the foot which makes it limp and walk crookedly. And as for all the good things that one can find in the aforementioned book [*Roman de la Rose*]: indeed, many more virtuous things better said, more authentic and profitable, for both political and moral life, can be found in many other volumes written by philosophers and Doctors in our faith, such as Aristotle, Seneca, Saint Paul, Saint Augustine, and others.[40]

She repeats this position in another letter, this time to Pierre Col:

Truly I believe that he would have a stronger appetite for the aforementioned things and that he would remember them better than the prohibition against indulging in them. This only serves to illustrate statements I have already made, and which you have repeated, that one should not direct human nature's attention to the foot which makes it limp.[41]

Christine demonstrates her distaste for explicit references to sexual passion in her attacks on Ovid, which were strongly criticized by adversaries who venerated antiquity. She can find no words strong enough to denounce Ovid's depictions which, more often than not, denied female honor and reduced women to the level of animals:

> A poor name for this book: *The Art of Love*! There is nothing here about love! The art of false and malicious industry in deceiving women might be a better title! What a doctrine! And what does one gain by deceiving women so well? Who are women? Who are they? Are they serpents, wolves, lions, dragons, griffins, or ravenous devouring beasts, enemies to human nature, that one should make an art of deceiving and capturing them?[42]

In these turbulent years of the late fourteenth century, Christine de Pizan struggled against a misogynistic clergy whose attacks echoed earlier cries of religious and philosophical heresies. The dialogue of Augustinian introspection[43] took on a distinct sense of dignity with Christine, which lies at the heart of the modern notion of individuality.[44] It is true that we can trace this idea as it develops from self-knowledge to self-affirmation, but it would be inappropriate and anachronistic to interpret this progression as the springboard for a transformation of the world itself by the individual will. "Faith, humility, and God"—these are signs belonging to a well-determined religious universe: that of Augustinian Christianity.[45]

The political and religious "conservatism" of Christine de Pizan, as it is revealed through her alliance with Chancellor Gerson in a moral critique, belongs to the contemplative tradition of Augustinian illuminism. In contrast, and despite its undeniable misogyny, Jean de Montreuil's irreverent humanism presents a more progressive expression of the desire for social change. The secularism of the Latin Averroists and the naturalism of the first humanists, both perfectly urbane phenomena, are correctly considered as the elements of a new rationality, wherein humanity began to move away from religious guardianship.[46] It is in this perspective that one might best view Christine's "Augustinian feminism." I have tried to reconstruct her intervention in this literary quarrel in order to reveal the behavior of a woman firmly situated at the center of intellectual life in her time, a position that is essentially at odds with any progressive definition of feminism. Christine's ability to call in turn on the humanists, the court, and the Church in order to form alliances, offers evidence of a woman who has mastered her environment. It is in the name of this independence that Christine de Pizan, as she emerges through the debate over the *Roman de la Rose*, contributed to the public life of her time.

II

THE SIXTEENTH CENTURY
SEXUAL EQUALITY AND
THE MODERN STATE

Jacob Burckhardt, in his notion of the cultural, intellectual, and aesthetic revival represented by the Italian Renaissance, did not overlook women's place: "To understand the higher forms of social discourse at this period, we must keep in mind the fact that women stood on a footing of perfect equality with men."[1] His project of illuminating this remarkably prolific period in the history of art by exploring the lives of its individuals led him to investigate the condition of women.

> For, with education, the individuality of women in the upper classes was developed in the same way as that of men. . . . The genteel woman, no less than the man, strove naturally after a characteristic and complete individuality. The same intellectual and emotional development that perfected the man, was demanded for the perfection of the woman.[2]

In Burckhardt's eyes, sexual equality was a mark of the supremacy of Italian civilization. This conception of the Renaissance has spawned the few historical studies we have that are devoted to Renaissance women. René de Maulde la Clavière saw in the moral power of Renaissance women the expression of a "peaceful and quiet revolution," characteristic of the Latin spirit.[3] Published contemporaneously with the women's suffrage movement, his study of manners offered an alternative to the suffragettes' noisy agitation. Emmanuel Rodocanachi followed Burckhardt's way of thinking, proposing Italian women as responsible at once for inspiring and for creating Renaissance values.[4] As long as Burckhardt's view remained the prototype for historians, the Renaissance in the transalpine countries remained little more than a vague concept, a mere zone of influence. Reflecting this subordination, a political analysis of changes in the female condition in France during this period of newly acquired savoir-faire and savoir-vivre was neglected in favor of a kind of poetic Italianism, which dominated all thinking about the Renaissance.

Wallace K. Ferguson's epistemological work helped to clarify the philosophical and political agenda of Renaissance historiography. His pathbreaking study of historians of the Renaissance stands out in the history of European ideas. Defining the spirit of "renaissancism" Burckhardt had characterized so well, he wrote:

> The closely associated currents of liberalism, new humanism, and German ide- alism in nineteenth-century thought had combined to establish as essential at- tributes of modern progress the growth of individual freedom of thought and expression, the full development of self-conscious personality, and the evolution of moral autonomy founded upon a high conception of the dignity of man.[5]

What precisely were the constitutive elements of this modernity in France?

In his history of France, Michelet did justice to the reign of François I, and to the innovative spirit of the sixteenth century.[6] But although he was extremely sensitive to women and their historical condition, Michelet seems not to have considered any aspect of Renaissance women's condition particularly worthy of attention. The importance of the classical age in French cultural represen- tation had, in the rationalist tradition of the eighteenth century, eclipsed the concept of the Renaissance. D'Alembert, for example, in the introduction to the *Encyclopédie*, named Bacon[7] and Descartes, rather than Rabelais or even Erasmus, as precursors of the modern era. Critics such as Lanson and Faguet took issue with Burckhardt's Italian-centered model in their refusal to attribute any unifying and creative functions to the Renaissance; for them, the Renais- sance did not represent the birth of thought, a liminal period. Thus, their investigations of the sixteenth century sought little more than the preliminary signs of seventeenth-century classicism. Their understanding of French hu- manism was submerged by the man-centered morality that the age of classicism brought to full development. In order for this rather unfocused notion to be- come a working concept, historians needed to explore the conflict "between a view of the world in which man as such was autonomous, and anxiety, born of sin, which could only be stilled by *sola fides* [the one true faith]."[8] Accord- ingly, Henri Hauser (1866–1946) distinguished for the first time in 1897

> two related and contradictory ways of conceiving the necessity of [the] com- bination and conflict [of Humanism and Reform], united as they were in the same effort of emancipation, in the common work of the same intellectual and moral revolt, and divided by the need men of the time had for doctrinal cer- tainties.[9]

Determining an intellectual and moral "space" specific to sixteenth-century France seems crucial for investigating the conditions under which the idea of equality between the sexes was produced.

Historians of feminism found themselves faced with an abundance of sources, but failed to distinguish the boundaries between the European character of the

Renaissance and its specifically French manifestations. This problem arose from a scholarly method that classified the period's texts based solely on whether or not they were "pro-woman." In his essay on the history of feminist ideas in France, Georges Ascoli subscribed to a traditional notion of the Renaissance: "The Gallic French spirit was tempered by the civilizing influence of the 'discovery of Italy,' and behind that, of Antiquity—in a word, of 'humanism.' "[10] The taste for compilation superceded the question of women's merits; controversies over the nature and value of matrimony surfaced. Although Ascoli was writing manifestly from a rationalist perspective with little sympathy for the inconsistent world of alchemists, he nonetheless accorded to the works of Heinrich Cornelius Agrippa von Nettesheim a paramount importance in the history of feminism. But he also thought that Erasmian humanism was better suited for explaining the conceptual framework of later generations.

Maïté Albistur and Daniel Armogathe's more recent work, *L'Histoire du féminisme français* (1977), further problematizes the sixteenth-century marriage question by introducing the issue of sexuality. Be that as it may, opening up new subjects of investigation does not necessarily contribute to a clearer understanding of social change. Henri Hauser's distinction lay in avoiding the historiographical trend toward classifying and compiling, in favor of delineating a contradictory and complementary historical "space" and studying its economic and social foundations. For him, the sixteenth century's modernity was defined by four revolutions: intellectual, moral, political, and economic. He was the first to focus on the specific national articulations of these upheavals.[11] In order to study the concept of equality between the sexes as it emerges in the sixteenth century, researchers need to delimit their field explicitly within national boundaries. The topic of women's status, including the views expressed by the cultivated elite who placed great store in international relations, was intimately bound up with the country's vital political issues. The debate over the Salic law—the question of women's succession to the throne—is a prime example; the political stakes of the debate were more important than its cultural dimension.

Certain researchers tried to open up the territory of investigation by reconstructing a new doctrine for women on a European scale. The American Ruth Kelso, in particular,[12] collated all manner of societal features that belonged to the period's four great powers. Her project assumed that the universalism of the Renaissance was somehow an extension of the universalism of the Middle Ages, through the movement of an elite group that drew the period's new ideas from the common fund of Greco-Roman thought, and spread them across Europe. But this conception of the period's intellectual revolution fails to take into account either the specific material implementation of the new ideas, or the institutional structures whereby a handful of secular and religious men, in spite of doctrinal oppositions, gave impetus to these ideas.

With all due respect to Burckhardt, equality in formal education between men and women existed neither in France nor in Italy in the sixteenth century.

The *collèges* did play a decisive part in creating an intellectual renewal—but enrollment was restricted to men. Jean Delumeau demonstrated this in his volume on Renaissance civilization, where he set out to show the symbolic development of upper-class women's place: Alcala de Henares (Spain), we are informed, was the first European town to have a school for girls since the beginning of the sixteenth century. This development was far ahead of its time, Delumeau continues, "since it was not until 1574 that the Ursulines founded a girls' school in Avignon—the first in a French town. Only in the seventeenth century would girls' education outside the home become a phenomenon of considerable social importance, thanks primarily to the Ursulines and the Visitandines." Schools and universities, the sanctuaries of the new thinking, were closed to women. But even though they could not frequent these halls of learning, there were still more cultivated women in the sixteenth century than in any preceding period, due to the close relationship between royalty and culture that developed during the reign of François I.[13]

The history of François I's rule and the importance of the Italian wars are now so well known that we hardly need to review the sources of French humanism. François's desire to educate his subjects, particularly the nobility, led to the creation of the printing houses and of the Collège Royal, whose function was to teach Hebrew, Greek, and Latin, and to restore integrity and influence to classical culture. This was the humanists' civilizing mission. Embodiment of the exemplary scholar, the philologist Guillaume Budé issued from a bourgeoisie that had long tied its fortunes to that of royalty. Persuaded that the kings' renown depended on the favor the crown bestowed upon literature, he wrote for François I *L'Institution du Prince*,[14] a compendium of sayings on that subject by great men of antiquity. A tireless translator, Budé not only disseminated Greek and Latin texts, but he also adapted them to France's specific needs. Several passages from his *Annotations*[15] reveal his interest in French history.

Extant correspondence from Budé to Erasmus of Rotterdam makes no specific mention of the education of women.[16] But in his correspondence on the cultural community, initiated by Thomas More, Erasmus's own references suggest nevertheless that Budé was interested in women's education. More, the author of the famed *Utopia*, had in fact organized his family life according to a new model, by including his wife and daughters in his moral and literary pursuits. He submitted the happy results that he had obtained to the approval of Erasmus, who thereafter maintained a friendly relationship with More's daughter Margaret Roper. In a letter to Budé, Erasmus notes:

> It is not solely because, being very learned himself, he encourages scholars with all his heart, that he lends such brilliance to learning, but also that he has his entire family participate in literary pursuits. This is certainly something new, but which, if I'm not mistaken, will be much imitated before long—so well has it succeeded. . . . A year ago More dared to show me what progress they had all made in literature. Believe me, Budé, never had I felt so much admiration.

... The heavenly little choir, including man and wife, all live under his roof. There you will never see an idle girl, nor ever a girl attached to feminine foolishness.[17]

The concern for pedagogy, so central to the humanist project, found a new field of application in the education of women. We must take care not to idealize Erasmus's views on this question, however: although he was convinced of the principle of women's education, we find him declaring that "women and especially children are best adorned by silence."[18]

Even though sixteenth-century women had no access to educational institutions, and though their abilities in art and learning still received only tenuous recognition, it appears nevertheless that in the context of family trades, some women developed exceptional taste and knowledge in letters. One such case was Nicole Estienne (later to become Madame Liebaudt), granddaughter of the famous printer Henri Estienne and author of the *Misères de la femme mariée*; another was Pierrette Bade, a printer's daughter, a "good Latinist who also helped her husband in correcting proofs."

Alongside a scholarly humanism enamored of glory and power as well as solitude, the development of French court life under François I had a considerable influence in spreading the idea of equality between the sexes. Marguerite d'Angoulême, the king's sister and queen of Navarre, was an enlightened protector of arts and letters. At her court of Nérac she sheltered a wide range of intellectuals persecuted for the audacity of their ideas and for their sympathies with the Reformation. In so doing, she supported the fledgling idea that a woman could become learned.[19] Women had maintained a presence in the court since Anne de Bretagne;[20] but just as in Italy, it was Marsilio Ficino's neo-Platonism that supplied the conceptual framework for recognizing women's abilities. Not that Ficino had really focused on this topic,[21] but his doctrine of love, as elaborated in his commentary on Plato's *Symposium*, gave to Diotima, the learned prophetess from Mantinea who instructs Socrates, the function of initiator into the creation mystery. Where Plato's Diotima invited us to move from physical beauty to moral beauty, from moral beauty to wisdom, and finally to "the beautiful in itself," Ficino translated, "Diotima takes Socrates from the lowest level to the highest. She leads him back from the body to the soul, from the soul to the Angel, and from the Angel to God."[22] Raymond Marcel comments, "Diotima's message reveals to us an asceticism which carries us from beauty to God; in God are blended all the sublime values that attract us and give us life."[23] This metaphysical doctrine was extremely successful in sixteenth-century France. Marguerite d'Angoulême became one of its most ardent promoters, seeing in this trajectory of pure love a means of establishing woman's superiority; she was called "protectress of Dolet and Ramuz who revealed Plato, of Bonaventure des Périers who translated the *Lysis*, of J. de la Haye, translator of the commentary on the *Symposium*, of Saint Marthe and of Heroët, Platonist poets."[24] To this revival of the Platonists we must add Castiglione, Ficino's disciple who, at François I's request, wrote *The Courtier*. Virtually as well received in France as in Italy,[25] this nobleman's work, a manual of perfect courtly behavior in the form of a Platonic dialogue, seemed to offer a deliberate rehabilitation of women, who were so suspect in the eyes of theologians. His list of the qualities required of "la donna di palazzo" gave rise to a literary combat. Among those who took part in the debate were Charles Fontaine, who penned "La Contr'Amye de court" (1541), Antoine Heroët, with "La Parfaite Amye" (1542), and Maurice Scève, with his "Délie, objet de plus haute vertu" (1544).

Neo-Platonism had the effect of proliferating "either/or" dualities, such as sensationalism vs. conceptualism, which lent themselves well to the artistic expression of the era's moral conflicts and anxieties. Panofsky writes,

> We can easily see how Ficino's philosophy was bound to stimulate the imagination of all those who, in a period of growing psychological tensions, longed for new forms of expression for the frightening yet fruitful conflicts of the age: conflicts between freedom and coercion, faith and thought, illimited desires and finite consummations. At the same time, however, the praise of a sublime love divorced from "base impulses," yet allowing of an intense delight in visible and tangible beauty, was bound to appeal to the taste of a refined, or would-be refined, society.[26]

We can sense this ambivalence in the work of Marguerite d'Angoulême, between her "Miroir de la pécheresse" [Mirror of the sinner's soul, an orison to Christ] and the latent sensuality of the *Heptameron*. Although her neo-Platonism has been the subject of countless theses, can it not be said that this predominance of ethics, this attention paid to nature and its order—the mark of new individualistic inclinations—was an extension of Stoic philosophy, whose traces are also to be found in Castiglione's *Courtier*?[27] Through the first tentative articulations of new rules of behavior, these social debates revealed the rudiments of a feminine individualism, taking the form of varied responses to the submission forced on their sex. Whatever their differences regarding the love relationship, the Amye de Cour, the Contr'Amye and the Parfaite Amye all agree in condemning "men's bestiality," "the venality of matrimony"; and they wish to destroy "the savage customs man has fashioned to his advantage!" At the time her first poetic works were published, Louise Labé, "La Belle Cordière" of Lyon (1520–1566), became a self-appointed spokeswoman for her sex by proclaiming loud and clear women's right to express themselves: "The time having come . . . when men's severe laws no longer prevent women from applying themselves to learning and knowledge, it seems to me that women who have the means must use this honorable freedom which we have so strongly desired . . . in order to learn these things."[28]

But there was a more austere side to the question than the new well-being available to cultivated women. The sixteenth century witnessed passionate debates about the value of marriage and women's place in it. While we still find

voices like that of the jurist André Tiraqueau[29]—a friend of Rabelais, who like
the clerics of his time appears by his frenzied misogyny to be the inheritor of
medieval debates—the marriage question was the object of a new scrutiny that
tended to restore feminine dignity. What religious and political context enabled
this reevaluation of an institution that had so often been denigrated?

Humanism saw itself as criticizing the evils of the time. Political evangelism
actively participated in forming the "new man" in several ways—by demanding
respect for the individual and his liberty, and by promoting pedagogical and
cultural renewal. Debates at the beginning of the century regarding priestly
celibacy and monastic vows spawned a reexamination of the institution of marriage. Criticism of certain religious laws brought about a movement in favor
of a secular state. Historian Emile Telle has pointed out the extent of this preoccupation in the minds of sixteenth-century men and women:

> Marriage was the locus of moral, social, economic, physiological, and mystical
> preoccupations of society. . . . I do not mean that marriage was the one and only
> question that preoccupied men in 1520. Of course not, but it was the one that
> allowed them at that time to understand better all the other problems besieging
> them. . . . This question was relevant to all; it intensely interested the learned
> and the unlettered alike, so much so that it is difficult for us today to take seriously
> what was so serious about it in 1520. Other than the excitement aroused by the
> egalitarian doctrines at the dawn of the Revolution, I see nothing comparable
> in all of modern history.[30]

The extraordinary proliferation of polemical and didactic literature on marriage supports Telle's argument. Telle had been sensitized to the marriage issue
by the insistence with which the Protestants, who opposed the sharp distinction
between clergy and laity, would harp on it.

The tragic affair of the Chevalier de Berquin shows us the height of the
political stakes raised by the defense of marriage. Counselor to François I, Berquin was condemned as a heretic for his translations of Luther and Erasmus.
Even though he had royal protectors, he was burned at the stake in 1529 following his French translation of Erasmus's text, the *Encomium Matrimonii* [in
laud and praise of matrimony],[31] published in France under the title "La Déclamation des louanges de mariage" in 1525. This work had gone through numerous translations and was well known throughout Europe.[32] Erasmus's
praise of marriage arrived in France at a time when the guarantors of Christian
orthodoxy in doctrinal matters were already on guard against the advances of
Lutheranism.[33] The theological import of Erasmus's antiascetic and antimonastic pronouncements did not escape the doctrinal censors, especially since the
author of the *Adages* and of the *Praise of Folly* was also the publisher of the first
Greek New Testament and the complete works of St. Jerome. Between Erasmus's evangelism, out of favor with the Sorbonne authorities in 1524, and Luther's offensives, the fervently religious and biblical personality of Berquin
seemed to meet all the criteria for condemnation. Historians have noted this

Flemish gentleman's obstinacy in turning his adversaries' accusations of heresy back on them instead of putting the matter to rest.[34] His obstinacy proved fatal.

But accounting for this religious context should not allow us to forget the book that touched off the whole affair. For Erasmus, the *Praise of Matrimony* carried with it a corollary: women's moral equality. To the notion of perfection gained from asceticism, he counterposed the idea of a natural morality embodied in the harmonious life of the married couple. Women seemed to be the first to benefit from such a change in the status of marriage. The argument ran something like this: "You, future husband, have the responsibility to choose a good woman worthy of love and esteem. If she turns out badly, you have only yourself to blame." Erasmus offered a list of names of women famed for their noble sensibilities and exemplary lives; this list was further developed by Berquin, so important did the latter deem it to keep the reader informed on this point. The eight lines of Erasmus's Latin text, which cite Cornelia, Alcestis, Julia, Portia, Arthemisia, Hypsicratea, Tortia, Aemilia, Turia, Lucretia, Lentula, and Arria, turn into eight pages in Berquin's text, borrowing the rest from the author Valerius Maximus.[35]

This was certainly a humanist strategy, to think that recalling these illustrious historical examples would establish a precedent for change. The author's reference to antiquity was a reminder that his proposition, in spite of its boldness, already existed in the realm of possibility. Just as education molds a child into what one wishes him to become, so understanding marriage as the ancients had sometimes succeeded in practicing it could make women virtuous and loving.

For these humanists, the idea of a pedagogical relationship between man and woman allowed them to think that conflicts between the sexes, generally attributed to women's "bad nature," could be overcome. Using the example from antiquity offered the possibility of fighting against the prejudices of the day by relativizing them. The ascetic rituals that ruled monastic life during the entire medieval period had proved nonproductive and even pernicious as far as spiritual elevation was concerned. Minus its angelic and divine function, the question of virginity became everyone's concern. Why deprive monks and priests of the advantages of marriage? Erasmus's apologetic, taken up also by Berquin, did not hesitate to proclaim matrimony as a sacrament of the first order. Although marriage had been confirmed as a sacrament at the Council of Florence a century earlier, it was still a delicate matter in 1525 to grant it "primary" sacramental authority.[36] This lack of historical and religious rigor was not uncommon in Erasmus; in fact, it was part of his polemical style. His little book on marriage posed a new set of questions for the period, placing man into a new orbit of humanity and naturalness. Erasmus also made it his goal to deliver women from the evil spells that hung on them, by restoring to them a capacity for secular heroism. Wasn't the Chevalier de Berquin, by illustrating his translation of the *Praise of Matrimony* with more examples than Erasmus had thought of in 1518, expressing the desire to secure a wider female audience? With the publication of the colloquies on matrimony (August 1523), Erasmian evangelism in the 1520s popularized a matrimonial and antimonastic

Paulinism among women and worker populations.[37] On 5 February 1526, the Paris Parlement forbade not only the printing or possession of Luther's books, but also any translations of St. Paul into French.

The historian of ideas cannot hope to understand the modernity of the six-teenth century without studying the formation of the Protestant ethic. History has in fact emphasized the importance of the Protestant ethic in accounts of the economic dynamics of Western societies; Max Weber's work offers the best-known example.[38] France under François I had found its glory in the breadth of the humanists' emancipatory dream: how could it possibly encompass the religious reformation without imperiling the crown, when church and mon-archy were tied so closely together? Was Protestantism, which so quickly became a force of opposition, if not resistance, in France, the crucible of new values wherein the man-woman relationship would be transformed?

John Calvin's *Institutes of the Christian Religion* (1536)[39] is addressed to Fran-çois I[40] in whom the Protestants still placed their hopes—even though the king seemed resolved to come to the assistance of the Roman church in its attacks on the Reformation.[41] Calvin wished to show that the purpose of evangelical doctrine was not to disturb the established order, and that the vicious perse-cution of it amounted to defamation. For at the heart of Calvinist society lies discipline. "What is discipline? a social constitution, a set of rules for organizing a society. And these rules say everything and set in place everything a society needs: the government, the manner of election, and the obligations of all, par-ticularly the practical and social obligations, those of the deaconate."[42]

Even in the period of severest repression, Calvin preached fidelity to the sovereign, and unequivocally condemned the spirit of revolt. Up until the St. Bartholomew's Day massacre in 1572, this loyalty was a distinguishing char-acteristic of French Calvinism. Only after the massacre did the pamphleteers finally sound the call to revolt.

In Geneva, the church city, Calvin managed to put into practice the new principles of social organization based on his religious precepts. A true states-man, he strove to translate the major themes of his doctrine into the com-munity's fabric of life. Some of these themes were consonant with the evangelical humanism of the beginning of the century, and with Lutheranism. His strong antimonasticism challenged the privileged forms of medieval reli-gious life; he also launched repeated attacks against vows of chastity and pov-erty. Nuns in particular, and women who were religious bigots, filled him with genuine repulsion:

> these little bigots who wish to eat the crucifix (as they say) . . . Saint Paul calls them "femmelettes"[43]—he does not say "femmes," but rather he says "femme-lettes." . . . They pretend to be next to God, they will have their little baubles and make little shows of this and that, in order to say then that they are more pious than others. However they never do or can come to the knowledge of truth: for they only go in circles, and do not keep to the straight path.[44]

[These women] have questions, I know not which, to say, "Well, Master or Father, what ought I to do when it is the day before such-and-such saint's day? How ought I to distinguish between the Virgin Mary and Saint Agatha or Saint Gertrude?" and then, "how do people behave in paradise? and when I get there, will I be put in with the martyrs or with the confessors?"[45]

Founded as it was on parasitic religious rituals, this representation of feminine piety lay, for Calvin, in direct opposition to the role women should assume in married life. The *Praise of Matrimony*, for which Calvin made himself the spokesman, restored feminine dignity that had been sorely damaged by medieval prejudices and the Roman church's structure. If gender roles were distributed equally, he maintained that there would ensue a "union of spouses in love and faith into one complete being."[46] At the same time, however, Calvin saw these roles as clearly differentiated. The woman must devote herself to her obligations as mother of the family, no matter how humble and painful her duties were as such. God has so prescribed it:

> whatever hypocrites or wise men of the world may think, God is better pleased with a woman who considers the condition God has assigned to her as a calling and submits to it, not refusing to bear the distaste of food, the illness, the difficulty, or rather the fearful anguish associated with childbirth, or anything else that is her duty—God is better pleased with her than if she were to make some great display of heroic virtues and refuse to accept the vocation given her by God.[47]

André Bieler, in his book, 'L'Homme et la femme dans la morale calviniste," noted these salient features of Reformed anthropology: "The human unit is not the individual man or woman, but the couple. . . . Therefore, through the unit of the couple which is his primary mode of existence, man sees himself as first and foremost a social creature, or as Calvin says, *une créature de compagnie*."[48]

This complementarity rests, of course, on the woman's subordination. There is no doubt as to the importance of Pauline thought in this regard, as is exemplified by Calvin's commentaries on the Epistle to the Ephesians: "Wives, submit yourselves unto your own husbands, just as unto the Lord." He continues:

> besides the universal bond of subjection, some are more closely bound to each other, according to their respective callings. Domestic society consists of three kinds of ties between persons in which there is a mutual obligation of parties. The first tie is the marriage between husband and wife; the second tie binds fathers and mothers to their children; the third connects masters and servants. So in domestic society there are six different classes, for each of which Paul lays down its peculiar duties. He begins with wives, whom he enjoins to be subject

to their husbands, in the same way as to Christ. Not that the authority is equal,
but wives cannot obey Christ unless they yield obedience to their husbands.[49]

Must this hierarchical representation of the family necessarily be attributed
to historical conditions of the period?[50] It is generally accepted that Calvinist
religion laid the historical ground for liberal individualism; what, then, were
the underlying tenets of Calvin's moral philosophy regarding women?

For Calvin, faith is more than simple intellectual consent to God's word;
God's word must resonate in the deepest part of one's being, and thus be felt,
consented to by the whole subject. Woman, then, must accept the duties and
burdens of marriage and motherhood in her deepest self. She binds herself to
the divine plan not by expressing an individual will (necessarily marred by inherent human weakness), but by spontaneously consenting to serve through a
"natural instinct of things." While eighteenth-century philosophers tended to
define nature in terms of the opposition between the registers of heart and
mind, Calvin does not oppose the two terms in his conception. "In the eyes
of God, man and woman are one in the totality of their being."[51] Thus Calvin
in no way views the sexual aspect of conjugal life as a sign of the fall of humanity.

Despite the dignity he accords to sex in marriage, we ought not to forget
Calvin's categorical condemnations of free love (which the spiritual libertines
had elevated to the status of a theological doctrine) and of adultery and prostitution. The religious framework of Calvinism as it defines itself appears unified, by dissolving any opposition between earthly love (natural knowledge)
and supernatural life (revealed religion). The anthropological subjectivism of
Calvinist theology allowed for the inclusion of human activities in the religious
sphere,[52] and thus these activities were integrated into the doctrine. However,
as Calvin had an almost Platonic conception of marriage,[53] at once male and
female, we are not authorized to consider his thought as the starting point for
a new mentality, contrary to what the liberal Protestant feminism of the nineteenth century, when writings on the relationships between Protestantism and
liberalism would be in vogue, would have us believe. The Calvinist ethic added
absolutely nothing new to women's social status, and in fact echoed the ambivalence of St. Paul's thinking. While woman was man's absolute equal with
respect to the fundamental principles of Christianity in matters such as redemption and holiness, "many passages of the Pauline writings leave no doubt
that in the apostle's eyes, man enjoys superiority over woman as a matter of
fact."[54] St. Paul's authority cleared a path that would be trodden later by those
Church Fathers who did consider the situation of women.

We have seen that Calvin followed Pauline convictions very closely. Doumergue's monumental study of Calvin recounts a story that further illustrates
the Calvinists' position on women's participation in the affairs of church and
state. Renée de France, duchess of Ferrara (1510–75), became Calvin's catechu-
men. Having taken refuge in the French court when widowed in 1559, she retired
to her domain of Montargis where François Morel became her pastor. The

duchess wished to be present at the meetings of the consistory, and on 6 December 1563, Morel hastened to warn Calvin of her request:

> If Saint Paul deems it dishonorable for a woman to speak in the assembly, more shameful still would it be for her to make decisions and issue orders. Few will attend our church if they know that all the matters which they are called upon to discuss will be examined before such a great personage! And how ridiculous our consistories, governed by women, will look to papists and anabaptists.[55]

In the letter he sent via Budé to the Duchess of Ferrara, Calvin insisted that no one and nothing should hinder the democratic workings of the consistory. To which Renée answered on 21 March 1564, that she had submitted to Morel's demands. "Since he told me that women should not be present and that I should not be there, and as I knew that the Queen of Navarre, Madame l'admiral, and the King's wife were in their houses, and that he was going there from my own house, I did not insist on going."[56]

This epistolary exchange allows us to gauge the idea of "sexual equality" as Calvinism understood it at the time. To men, it was inconceivable for a woman to take part in the work of an organ that made decisions on the community's moral and religious matters, even though the group had representation from both pastors and laity. We must add, also, that Calvin sought to establish a government that would in principle be free of the nobility's power. No doubt, Renée de France reacted as a woman greatly vexed by her exclusion, but also as a noblewoman prone to approve every idea that would reinforce her social privileges. Her brand of "courtly feminism" had among its goals to domesticate the manners of the feudal aristocracy (which tended to hold women in brutal contempt) and to produce models of behavior appropriate to the developing life at court, in accordance with the demands of an absolute monarch whose idea of ruling did not include sharing power or asking advice. Noblewomen and even queens were the first to benefit from this new way of thinking, whose dignity each promoted at the level of her own social rank.

The confrontation between Calvin and Renée de France reveals much about the place assigned to women in his political philosophy. If we go on to examine the conditions of his founding of the religious office of deaconess, we discover an ambivalence about women in this important act that continues to pervade modern thinking even today. We have seen what importance Calvin accorded to marriage; he did not wish under any pretext to excuse the woman from this primordial obligation. However, his contempt for the papist Church's nuns— diabolical, perverse creatures of unwholesome chastity—led him to institute a female religious office which would answer to the needs of the new reformed faith. To his thinking, bringing back the primitive church's ecclesiastical post of deaconess would provide an additional opportunity for women to participate in the community's religious life. In order not to conflict with the sacerdotal vocation of marriage, deaconesses (appointed for one year by the members of the presbytery)[57] had to be widows at least sixty years old. "In short these widows were as different from the nuns as the prophetess Anna from Claudia the Vestal Virgin."[58]

The qualifications for this apostolic post were not always respected, and sometimes the appointed deaconesses were married. By the beginning of the seventeenth century, however, this office was done away with, and only in the nineteenth century did it return, under considerably different conditions. There is no doubt as to its importance in Calvin's mind; the management of public monies needed by society, as well as aid to the needy and the sick, fell on the deaconesses. He wrote in a sermon, "This calling [is] honorable, just as in the house of God all callings are sacred. And just as people say serving the poor is as praiseworthy as many sweet-smelling sacrifices to God, so this calling [is] noble before God and his angels."[59]

Was the rapid disappearance of the deaconesses a consequence of the stringent restrictions Calvin put on the office? Was it so difficult to recruit women with all the prerequisites? Or did their demise have something to do with the male-dominated bureaucracy, which might not have wanted to yield to women the control of funds for the poor?[60]

Our rapid survey of the place of women in Calvin's thought permits us now to evaluate what Protestantism brought to the question of sexual equality. In France, those rare thinkers sensitive to the problems of women's condition (i.e., those who perceived the need for change, or who argued rationally for the maintenance of existing power relations) were for the most part Calvinists or Calvinist sympathizers. Poullain de la Barre, exiled to Geneva after the repeal of the Edict of Nantes in 1685, authored treatises on women's equality. Condorcet, from a Protestant family that returned to Catholicism in the eighteenth century, had a determining influence on the elaboration of liberal thinking in France by bringing in Anglo-Saxon currents; he raised the analysis of women's condition in France to an unprecedented level of political importance. On the other hand, Jean-Jacques Rousseau used Calvinist doctrine to argue against the political empowerment of women. The ideologues of the Jacobin revolution stridently followed in Rousseau's footsteps by eliminating the claims to equality which women had voiced during the days of the Revolution.

It would be exaggerating to attribute to Calvin exclusive paternity of this contradiction-riddled area of religious and political history. But Calvinism did clearly give it a specific inflection, particularly regarding the definition of "natural rights." A running debate on women's religious, moral, and political emancipation developed, between the French Huguenots as they resisted persecution on their home territory, and the dominant pole represented by Geneva, the church city. Alliances formed through the centuries, based on elements already present in the renascent humanism of evangelical and reformed philosophy. These alliances evolved very slowly, for the question of women's emancipation remained prey to the sluggish progress of society, and would not easily be conquered by small groups of advocates. Even so, intellectual life in the seventeenth and eighteenth centuries was irrigated by these pro-woman developments.

Let us return to sixteenth-century France, and to the *Institutes of the Christian Religion* (1536; French translation, 1541), following which the Reformation's doctrinal lines hardened. The final years of François I's reign had been darkened by more intense persecution, executions, and retaliations.[61] The reign of Henri II was no more lenient—the Edict of Compiègne (24 July 1557) ordered death to all heretics. But ironically the edict only reinforced the Protestants' religious organization and increased their numbers. The Reformation won over the high nobility, and Parliament became divided over religious matters. The councilor Anne de Bourg paid with his life for defending the Protestants. Any reconciliation of doctrines became impossible. The growth of Calvinism, and its adherents' persistence in the face of the Christian humanism inspired by Erasmus, brought about a shift in priorities; henceforth the Reformation counted princes of royal blood among its ranks, and would have to be contended with as an important political faction. Catherine de Medici's policy of appeasement in the early period of her regency (after the death of François II in 1560), a policy supported by her chancellor Michel de l'Hospital, proved to be a failure.

In all the attempts to restore balance in the exercise of royal power, there was no attention paid to changing the condition of women. Indeed, the affirmation of the family and the state as *natural* associations, distinctly separate from ecclesiastical society, only reinforced women's submission to the demands of family and state.[62] Michel de l'Hospital so characterized these institutions on 3 January 1562, in a speech opening the assembly whose project was to preserve the unity of the kingdom. Reformed religion may have restored some honor to the female condition by restoring value to the institution of marriage, and by its tendency to secularize the marital sphere. But if we bear in mind the concurrent political impulse toward the civil liberties of the individual, there was no echo of this call to be heard regarding the relations between the sexes.[63]

Under the pressure of historical events, the Reformation period in France witnessed a flowering of political theories which, if not what we would call democratic, were at least more liberal.[64] Following the St. Bartholomew's Day massacre of 1572, texts written in a frankly republican spirit appeared. Etienne de la Boétie's "Discours de la servitude volontaire" was first published anonymously in an incomplete edition in 1574, in a collection called *Le Réveille-matin des Français* [The Frenchmen's wakeup call]. It would probably be mistaken, however, to classify its author among Calvinist thinkers.[65] The mentality embodied in the "Discourse" actually extends across the entire range of parties involved in the era's conflicts—the royalists, the Calvinists, and also the militant Catholics of the League.[66]

The "Discourse" takes up a moral and political enigma: why do men not revolt, why do they give up their freedom by accepting the terror that a single person can exert over the many? More often than not, the tyrant's power is all the more incomprehensible by virtue of his mediocrity; the terror and tyranny come not "from a Hercules nor from a Samson, but from a single little man. Too frequently this same little man is the most cowardly and effeminate in the nation."[67] Furthermore, among the despot's exactions, the debauching of women seems to be ranked right alongside other breaches of propriety. But at no point does the idea cross La Boétie's mind to establish a relationship between, on one hand, humanity subjugated by the habit of serving, and on the other, the social and political destiny of women—a group afflicted with every incapacity. On the contrary, being female seems to carry a negative value by nature.

La Boétie's "Discourse," clearly influenced by classical thought, inherits a misogynistic tone from Greco-Roman prejudices against women. This blind spot about women also marred the Athenian democratic tradition, on which La Boétie drew for examples to illustrate the struggle between liberty and domination. In her study of citizenship and the division of the sexes in Athens, the classicist Nicole Loraux writes,

> There is no first Athenian woman citizen, there was never an Athenian woman citizen. Political life did not recognize female citizens; the language has no name for the woman of Athens. There is even a myth that establishes a causal connection between the exclusion of women and the invention of the word "Athenian."[68]

Be this as it may, we must be careful not to overestimate the "pure" classical humanist in La Boétie. Humanists were, all the same, sixteenth-century men, and their perception of antiquity was filtered through sixteenth-century values, not least in respect to their attitudes toward women.

Montaigne's texts on friendship are so well known that we hardly need to mention them here. And it is quite evident that La Boétie shared his friend Montaigne's idealization of the kind of friendship that is based on the mutual acknowledgment of individuals equal in rank and intelligence. Note that this excludes the possibility of friendship between members of opposite sex.[69] Friendship or alliance appears then as a political principle of self-definition, and has little to do with personal lyricism in the Romantic style. The "Discours de la servitude volontaire" offers evidence of this principle of self-definition, which permits man to escape the forced bonds of lineage and family; by self-definition, man can arrive at the full dignity of his existence.

For La Boétie, tyranny is defined as a principle of uncertainty. The tyrant can have no friends, for he can have no equals, and he perverts all personal relationships by dominating. The historian Louis Delaruelle comments,

> In order to show that favorites . . . are never sheltered from a tyrant's cruelty, La Boétie cites in succession Poppea, Agrippina, and Messalina, and he finally reminds us of the word of this tyrant "who, gazing at the throat of his wife . . . caressed her with this charming comment: 'This lovely throat would be cut at once if I but gave the order.' "[70]

From these examples, one can see the man-woman relationship as the very matrix of the relations of violence which debase humanity, and which are obviously incompatible with the kind of transparent certainty that unites two souls in friendship. And although La Boétie does not explicitly reject the possibility of an egalitarian relationship between persons of the opposite sex, his strong Stoic convictions lead him to think of friendship between men as the exclusive framework for a democratic society. We will see that Mademoiselle de Gournay, Montaigne's other friend, would take up this notion of friendship between individuals in a more egalitarian feminist spirit. By summoning its readers before the strange spectacle of tyranny, and thereby shaking the confidence of subjects in their government, the "Discourse" gave evidence of political, moral, and religious uncertainty, in spite of its "transhistorical" strategy of never mentioning the current events that inspired its writing.

Four years after the St. Bartholomew's Day massacre, political philosopher Jean Bodin's *Six livres de la République* [Six Books of the Republic, 1576] had an enormous success. This work described the variety of forms and practices of sovereignty. In his project of defining a coherent political framework in which to reconstruct a society destroyed by civil war, Bodin was also compelled to examine the place of women. Was it political and legal realism that led to his uncompromising position on women? In the introductory definition of the Republic, Bodin affirmed, "A Republic is a lawful government of many families, and of those things that are their common concern, with sovereign power."[71] What notion of "law" underlay this claim? What sort of political architecture did it imply?

Bodin writes, in commenting on Plato, that there are two kinds of Republic. The first, attributed to Socrates, "taketh away these words, Mine and Thine, as the source and fountain of all evil, and would have all goods, yea wives and children, to be common." The second, the Republic "of laws," does away with the commonality of goods and of women and children; for after his first Republic, "seeing every man to find fault [with Socrates' model], he quietly left it, as if he had so writ more for argument sake, than for that he so thought, or to have the same put into effect."[72] Thus did Bodin take up a widespread idea of the sixteenth century,[73] i.e., the unrealistic nature of Plato's philosophical project. He was more comfortable with a definition of laws as legislation: "either they should express reason . . . or they should replace reason as a rule of conduct, and must be obeyed."[74] This prescriptive definition of justice assumed the perfection of the individual, and held that "the good of the individual and the good of the Republic are one and the same, and to be a good man is also to be a good citizen."[75] However, in what may seem at first contradictory with the place accorded here to the individual, it is the family that is made the cornerstone of the Republic. For Bodin the family household is an institution mediating between the sovereign and the community. Since in terms of social organization it came first, it acts as a brake against possible encroachments by the governing power. In order to guarantee this counterweight function, the family unit must be perfectly homogeneous. Bodin advocates absolute paternal power; parents must be the severest and most rigorous overseers of children, and the relation of women to men is to be no less strictly enforced. Bodin

cannot find terms strong enough to characterize the wife's absolute dependence
on her husband. He sees in this subordination the very foundation of civil and
political society. "So we will leave moral discourse to the philosophers and
theologians, and we will take up what is relative to political life, and speak of
the husband's power over the wife, which is the source and origin of every
human society."[76]

The extensions of Bodin's ideas on the family come as no surprise. "Gynocracy" [*gynécocratie*] must go,

> gynocracy which originated when women were allowed to inherit fiefs, when
> the male heirs were dying out both in the direct and collateral lines . . . little by
> little permission was extended to dignities, counties, marquisats, duchies, prin-
> cipalities, and at last to kingdoms . . . but the Salic law cut the matter short, and
> expressly forbids women from succeeding by any means to any fiefs.[77]

The memory of the bloody St. Bartholomew's Day massacre, which had been
ordered by Catherine de Medici, the regent, was doubtless implicit in his condemnation of government by women. Invoking Salic law as the kingdom's
founding principle, established by an allegedly "national tradition," was in
keeping with arguments frequently used by legal theorists during a period when
the premature death of numerous kings presented serious questions regarding
succession to the throne. The Salic law argument was not new; Philippe le Long
(1294–1322) had already used it to his benefit. And in order to allow Henri de
Navarre to accede to the crown, the Parlement's Lemaitre Edict of 28 June 1593
consecrated its use.[78]

In Bodin's *Republic* we find constant allusion to the 1560 Estates of Orleans.[79]
A deputy for the Third Estate at the Estates of Blois (1576–77), Bodin had faith
in the Estates as a tempering influence on the royal will. In opposition to the
notion of seigneurial monarchy, wherein the prince was lord of property and
persons, the royal and legitimate monarchy left the ownership of property to
its subjects. Taxes were not to be levied without their consent. Henri III, who
asked for subsidies to carry out his wars against the Protestants, encountered
a refusal by the partisans of civil tolerance. Bodin convinced the Third Estate
to reject the king's financial requests, and publicly argued that subjects could
not be forced in religious matters.[80] Since he was a partisan of religious unity
as a principle for the maintenance of the state, the destructive schisms and rifts
in France under Henri III nevertheless inspired in him a realistic sense of moderation: "It may well be that the members of the sects are so powerful that it
would be impossible or at least very difficult to ruin them without endangering
the State itself." Elsewhere he added, "If a prince who is sure of the true religion
wishes to attract to it those of his subjects who belong to sects and factions,
in my opinion he should not employ force."[81]

Bodin was a liberal thinker not only because he was impressed by the flood
of currency that was inundating France,[82] but also because he conceived of law
in the form of preestablished rights of the individual. He enumerated the sub-

ject's rights which the prince could not violate: rights of property and of belief, both based in natural law.

The legal philosopher Michel Villey sees in this the advent of subjective rights.[83] Bodin writes:

> And we must not leave out Pope or Emperor; some flatterers say that these two may seize the property of their subjects without cause. But many Doctors and even canonists reject that opinion as contrary to God's law. . . . Seneca wrote: *ad reges potestas omnium pertinet, ad singulos proprietas*, and then: *omnia reximperio possidet, singuli domino.*[84]

How can this conception of individual rights in Bodin's work be reconciled with his strong adhesion to Roman law? and which Roman values were at stake?

The notions of women's exclusion from political life, and their submission to paternal and parental domination, are in the spirit of classical Roman law. The *pater familias* had exclusive control over his small agricultural domain, and enjoyed a power almost as complete over the members of his family—slaves, children, and women.[85] All the same, one must emphasize the transformations that this old system of rigorous laws underwent in the classical and postclassical Roman era. Michel Villey writes, "A new order emancipated the married woman, and offered her legal independence from her husband. This was in keeping with feminist values of the late Republic."[86] And Jean Gaudemet, writing on women in the Roman Empire: "By the beginning of the Empire, women acquired a freedom of movement and a legal status which contrasted strongly with the old Roman customs."[87]

It certainly seems that Bodin was unaware of this transformation in family law during the classical age. Was there a contradiction between his attachment to an "archaic" status of women (as in the older Roman law), and his liberal and individualistic aspirations?

Stoicism, as embodied in Cicero's moral works *De Officiis* and the *Tusculanae* (Cicero's stoicism was highly respected by Renaissance philosophers), included morality in its definition of justice, in outlining rules of conduct and appropriate behaviors. Roman law, as reflected in Gaius's *Institutes*, does not deal with the legal status of individuals. Michel Villey writes, "A [legal] action is not described as a sanction intervening for the protection of rights." He also states: "Each of the juridical realities, each of the objectively described entities, is an indication of the events that give them existence (birth, adoption, *conventio in manum, mancipatio*)."[88]

Villey contends that classical Roman law and subjective right, forerunners of modern categories, obey two kinds of logic that are mutually incompatible. Bodin took inspiration from Stoicism in order to give a philosophical foundation to his reform of legal philosophy:

> We may say that everything deriving from the sciences and from contemplation proceeds from nature or divine principles, but that the prudence which rules our

conduct owes its norms to nature, and the rest, to human institutions. . . . For
if it were true that right, insofar as it emerges from nature does not flow from
man, or (to use the Stoics' formula) that justice comes not from institutions but
from nature . . . [89]

He asserts women's legal and political incapacity by using the murky logic of
the humanistic tradition of jurisprudence based on natural rights. Jointly with
this development, we may also note the disappearance of canon law as a legal
source.

Bodin's intransigence regarding women, rightly emphasized by his commentators, calls for clarification. To our knowledge there is no study devoted
to the legal situation of women in the sixteenth century. However, the commentaries of Bodin's contemporary Etienne Pasquier on the *Institutes* of
Justinian[90]—commentaries considered to be the "manual of sixteenth-century
law"—give us several indications about the legal provisions then in force concerning women. The tone of this work is very different from Bodin's.

On several occasions, Etienne Pasquier mentions ways in which French common law[91] modified the original Roman rules concerning women. He depicts
these changes as progress due to Christian society. On paternal consent for
marriage, for instance, he writes:

> From the Law of the Romans, the fathers' consent was required for the marriage
> of their sons and daughters to be binding, but as for us in our Christian religion,
> all doctors in canon law are aware that the father's consent is required only as
> a matter of honor and not of necessity . . . this is why since, as time has passed,
> all nations having been emancipated from this paternal power of the Romans,
> our forbears have judged that for marriage between Christians, the father's con-
> sent and authority were no longer required.[92]

On one hand, Bodin's respect for marital authority leads him to regret the
removal of the death penalty for adulterous wives (he goes so far as to express
his indignation at the laxity of French morals on this point). On the other
hand, let us note what Pasquier wrote in his commentary on the grounds for
divorce.[93] After considering divorce in Rome, he examines the kinds of conditions that led to divorce in France, and he emphasizes the competence of
royal judges in these matters. For Pasquier, feminine nature itself is the cause
of women's unequal treatment in the case of adultery—their modesty prevents
them from punishing their husbands. By being relegated to the level of customs
rather than of principles, this glaring distortion of the idea of justice thereby
becomes simply a social fact, left to the discretion of members of society.

In *La Démonomanie des sorciers* [The demonomania of sorcerers, 1580], Bodin
sternly called for the repression of witchcraft, whose practitioners were endangering Christianity throughout Europe. Reaction to the growth of demonology in fifteenth-century France resulted in waves of persecution, beginning
in the latter sixteenth century, between 1560 and 1630.[94] The persecution was

directed primarily at women (roughly three or four women to every man). Historians have often questioned the meaning of the paradoxical coexistence of philosophical obscurantism as developed in the "Demonomania of Sorcerers," and ideas on religious pacification and tolerance, one of whose spokesmen was Bodin, the very author of the *Republic*. Examining Bodin's refutation of the opinions of Johann Wier, a Lutheran physician from the Rhineland, suggests that the cultural universe of the two men was ultimately more similar than one might think.[95] Through their opinions on witchcraft, we can see that both men were concerned with the general problem of working out "women's guilt," as it revealed itself in this particular social form.

   Johann Wier was the disciple of the alchemist philosopher Cornelius Agrippa von Nettesheim, author of a treatise entitled *The Nobility and Excellence of Womankind* (1529). Wier published *De praestigiis daemonum* in Basel in 1563. Even as he acknowledged the existence and the delusive power of "the deceiver" [Satan], he also attempted to discern the role of mental illness in sorcery cases. For Bodin, too, the world of sorcery seemed close to madness—as his title, "Demono-mania," indicates. All the same, with Johann Wier he embarks on a veritable battle of authorities, drawing on references from antiquity and refusing to take into account the clinical observation of sorcery cases. Bodin even turns to Galen's medical authority to dispute the melancholic nature of women.[96]

   The passion with which Bodin argues his case may be explained by the importance he attributed to the workings of justice: to give too much credence to mental illness among an uncultivated and unhappy people, and to the possibility that people had delusions of the imagination, meant risking the credibility of legal procedures based on testimony and confession. A man of politics and law above all else, Bodin could perhaps sense the institutional threat of abandoning this tool of social regulation to the medical community, whose influence was on the rise (e.g., starting in 1545, medicine was being taught at the Collège Royal). Yet establishing incontestable proof of sorcery required all of Bodin's juridical skill;[97] he was intent on analyzing the bizarre behavior of witches by means of systematic procedures that would leave no room for doubt. Here were ancient forms of social behavior, whose deepest forces seemed to reside in women,[98] being destroyed by the imposition of a new cultural model with a more rational interpretation of the world. Was royal justice, not yet widespread at the time,[99] aided in its project of unifying the realm by promoting this cultural change led by the country's elite? Although our knowledge of witchcraft trials is still far from complete, Robert Muchembled tells us that "the repression of witchcraft which reached its climax between 1580 and 1610 was essentially localized on the kingdom's periphery,"[100] in the provinces that were least strictly subject to the king, and only conquered later.

   The distinction between the attitude of someone like Johann Wier, a founder of clinical medicine, and the superstitious Jean Bodin, appears greatly overestimated. For example, the doctor Wier explained women's vulnerability to the devil's deeds in this way: "The devil, a clever, cunning, and crafty enemy, purposefully guides the female sex—which is unsteady (owing to its complexion

of fickle belief), spiteful, impatient, and melancholic—unable to control its affections."[101] However, it is undeniable that Bodin had a formidable institutional influence which Wier could not have, at a time when the practice of
medicine in connection with mental illness was at such a rudimentary stage.
Robert Mandrou is absolutely correct in writing that "Bodin was listened to
more than the Duke of Clèves's daring doctor. His vehement call for ruthless
repression was heard by magistrates, high officers of justice whose role it was
to curb those common offenses and crimes, which certainly included witchcraft."[102]

Bodin's work leads us straight to the heart of a major contradiction in sixteenth-century political thinking—a contradiction that lies at the origin of our
modern constitutional system. In the framework of the time-honored alliance
between France's men of law and its royal power, a political and philosophical
individualism took form, nourished by every occasion to define and limit the
crown's prerogatives. But also it drew sustenance by initiating vast projects,
undertaken in the king's name, to consolidate the monarch's power. The ambivalence of the secular ruling class's historical interests, which took advantage
of every benefit of the cultural renewal of the Renaissance, must be a focal
point of our inquiry, since these men were at the same time the architects of
women's exclusion from the political sphere.[103] The repression of witchcraft is
one of the most brutal forms of this exclusion, an extreme case of the domination of one sex by the other. While from time to time Renaissance humanism
may have allowed the development of philosophical arguments favoring
women, it remained incapable of firmly establishing a humanistic definition of
the social place of women as well as men. After all, Erasmus and Bodin were
humanists, and both belonged to this general movement of secular rationalism;
but events taking place in the political sphere at the century's close renewed
the basis for prejudice against women.

Humanism in the name of women's emancipation advanced in fits and starts.
It is at the dawn of the seventeenth century that the work of early sixteenth-
century ruling-class feminism resurfaced, with Anna Maria van Schurman
(1607–78) and Mademoiselle de Gournay (1566–1645). Although Mlle. de Gournay's *De l'égalité des hommes et des femmes* [The equality of men and women]
appeared in 1622, and *Grief des dames* [The ladies' grievance] in 1626, the cultural
archetype to which both works refer remains that of Renaissance humanism.

The longevity of Marie le Jars de Gournay,[104] adoptive daughter of Montaigne and of the Dutch Stoic Justus Lipsius, earned her the scorn of many of
her contemporaries, and also of later critics devoted to Montaigne.[105] Although
she was impossible to ignore, since she was responsible for several editions of
Montaigne's *Essays*,[106] virtually no one produced commentaries on her own
writings. The sole modern publisher of her writings felt compelled to recount
several denigrating anecdotes, ridiculing this learned woman at the expense of
a solid analysis of her work.[107]

Even though she translated Virgil, Ovid, Sallust, and Tacitus, Mlle. de Gournay did not limit herself to the humanist project of retransmitting classical texts. She participated fervently in a new form of social life called "amours d'alliance," which had spread among the aristocracy, thanks to François I's sister Marguerite d'Angoulême,[108] who cultivated the practice of "adoption" in a struggle against the brutishness of the times.

We know all the intensity Montaigne devoted to the cult of friendship. Here is what he wrote about Mlle. de Gournay in his *Essays*, in the chapter "On Presumption," modifying his previous judgment that women are incapable of friendship:[109]

> I have taken pleasure in making public in several places the hopes I have for Marie de Gournay le Jars, my covenant daughter. . . . She is the only person I still think about in the world. If youthful promise means anything, her soul will some day be capable of the finest things, among others of perfection in that most sacred kind of friendship which, so we read, her sex has not yet been able to attain. . . . The judgment she made of the first *Essays*, she a woman, and in this age, and so young, and alone in her district, and the remarkable eagerness with which she loved me and wanted my friendship for a long time . . . is a phenomenon very worthy of consideration.[110]

Marie learned of Montaigne's death indirectly, by a letter from Lipsius. She had asked for news of her adoptive father, not having heard from him for six months. The Dutch humanist answered her in a tone both serious and lyrical, demonstrating the emotional investment in this elective family tie during the period.[111] "I love you, my child, but in the way I love wisdom: chastely. Love me also thus, and since he whom you called your father is no longer of this world, look on me as your brother."[112]

Montaigne and Justus Lipsius had placed great hopes in Mlle. de Gournay's talent and merit. Her intellectual endeavors seemed by no means ridiculous to them, but on the contrary entirely in keeping with their standards for a philosopher and humanist. However, others have often judged her work as mediocre. Georges Ascoli judges the impetuous young woman rather severely on her unimaginative positions:

> Compiling—almost exclusively it is women and clerics who devote themselves to this kind of work. Both groups learnedly affirm woman's superiority; but the arguments they keep trotting out to support their thesis, are the very excellence of the name of the first woman, and the circumstances of her creation. . . . Their greatest recourse to illustrate this thesis lies in examples from secular and sacred history. In the tracts of Mlle. Gournay we find nothing more than this.[113]

Ascoli's long article makes an enormous contribution in presenting a chronological inventory of works on the "woman question," published between the late sixteenth century and the prerevolutionary period. However, his exclusively diachronic view of the history of ideas concerning women erases the distinctive features of this field; what he concludes is that the era's intellectual horizons were limited by conformity and lack of originality. But is Mlle. de Gournay's treatise on the equality of men and women,[114] dedicated to the queen, nothing but a pale rhetorical exercise on a subject which had already caused much ink to spill for a century? Does her treatise fit into an apologetic tradition?

In the very first lines, Mlle. de Gournay rejects this orientation. "Eschewing extreme statements, I am content to consider [women] the equals of men, as nature is opposed to superiority just as much as to inferiority on this matter."[115] In other words, using the strategy of making nature synonymous with equality, she takes up on the Stoic idea that peace and harmony are reserved to those who follow nature. The later feminist Léontine Zanta, whose 1914 doctoral thesis examined the revival of Stoicism in the sixteenth century, thus summarized the particular philosophical junction that took place between humanism and Stoicism: "At the beginning of the Renaissance, man newly took stock of his own strength, and above all the strength of his reason; henceforth it is to reason that he would appeal for practical rules of living, and to examine speculative truths."[116] The Stoics conceived of individual liberty not in terms of the rights of the individual, but rather on the level of morality. They rejected external comforts in order to cultivate virtue, which alone could assure happiness. In this light, and as far as the rather brief philosophical premises of Mlle. de Gournay's treatise allow us to see, we can discern the influence of Stoic morality in her definition of the harmony engendered by equality, but also we can recognize her adherence to a theory of natural rights. Her recognition of the individual's moral autonomy leads her not to accept subordination, but rather to sonorously denounce it: "For some men it is not enough to prefer the masculine sex over women; they also confine [women] to the distaff with an irrefutable and insistent mandate." How inequitable women's condition remained under humanism—the so-called reconquest of the meaning of Man, and the restoration of humanity to itself! To account for this inferior position Mlle. de Gournay points the finger at the malevolence of presumptuous men. Contrary to what Ascoli suggested, it is with stinging irony, articulated in ways that would serve contemporary feminism well, that she exposes men's presumption and deceit. "It is quite difficult to imagine a great woman calling herself a great man [*grand homme*]"; and "sometimes with a single word, [men] can undo half the world." The modernity of the adoptive daughter of Montaigne resides in having understood the significance of women's numbers in suggesting the reversibility of an oppressive situation at a time when a society established according to orders found any declaration in this direction unthinkable.

The civil wars had shaken the royal authority. The flowering of political theories justifying tyrannicide[117] abetted this weakening of the monarchy's legitimacy by submitting sovereignty to a contractual limitation of its power. Consequently, the value of the individual's judgment of his own conditions of existence took on a new political weight; there was an impulse toward the democratic ideals that had been inherited from the classical age. Mlle. de Gournay hoped that like herself, other women would be able to participate in the major movements of the time. Pierre Bayle, in his dictionary's article on Mlle. de Gournay, accuses her of straying into politics—a concern incompatible with women's state.[118]

The arguments she makes to justify this desire for recognition are borrowed from both religious and cultural authorities. Her method is that of classical humanism, taking stock of contemporary problems via knowledge of the classical world.[119] Her references to classical philosophers[120] permit her to open the chapter (deprecated by her colleagues) on women's equality in learning. However, Mlle. de Gournay, who revised her manuscripts ceaselessly,[121] concluded her inventory of scholarly and famous women of antiquity with praise for her contemporary, Anna Maria van Schurman,[122] "in eloquence the emulator of these illustrious ladies and also of their lyric poets, even in their own Latin language, and who possesses along with that language all the other classical and new tongues and all the liberal and noble arts."

Making reference to the ancients, and giving praise for moderns, did not amount to analyzing the state of cultural and social inferiority in which women were submerged. Marie de Gournay saw women's lack of education as one of the principal causes of their inability to affirm themselves as individuals.[123] In her analysis of the influences that determine individual destinies, she distinguishes city life from country life, and also points to the cultural and moral importance of national character.[124] Mario Schiff notes that Mlle. de Gournay had already developed similar remarks in her *Traité de l'éducation des enfans de France* (written on the occasion of Marie de Medici's first pregnancy).[125]

Her attention to the influences of specific national character on manners—which contradicts the claims of humanistic universalism—may well be one of the most original points of her political thought, and explains her literary penchant for the poetry of the Pléiade. Indeed, in her treatise *De l'égalité des hommes et des femmes*, she does not hesitate to take on the question of the Salic law's legitimacy, which in France deprived women of succession to the crown, even though her protector Henri IV was its principal beneficiary. In a partisan spirit she indirectly compliments the regent Marie de Medici: "It served the French well to invent the system of regents, as an equivalent to kings." Her ardent desire to find ways around the Salic law shows her frustration at seeing women excluded from succession to the throne. Such legalized injustice defied the laws of common sense and the laws of history: she interprets Joan of Arc as the sign of the divine will favoring women. The theological aspect of her argument is less interesting in that Mlle. de Gournay supports more common points of view: she takes an evangelical approach (which, incidentally, neglects an apology for marriage in order to underscore the importance of the other sacraments).

Starting from a simple idea, Mlle. de Gournay constructed a defense of women, which outlined the specific talents and merits of the female sex, and reconciled womanhood with humanity. "Nothing more resembles a tomcat on a windowsill than a female cat," she wrote with humor. Unquestionably, she thus managed to impress on her readers the need for a reform of customs and morality as it concerned women's condition. Her approach remains interesting because it presents an analysis of women's subordination which foreshadows the most contemporary feminist thought, and also because it offers the individual woman the capacity to change her own destiny. However, her essay is not truly pedagogical, in the sense that she does not advocate any particular course of action for women. Her main concern is to affirm the dignity of this "person" to whom her society refused most of life's joys. In *Grief des dames*, she rebelled angrily against the injustice of a society that deprives women of the most basic freedoms and constrains them to ignorance and servitude: "Happy are you, reader, if you are not of the sex that is forbidden all good things, forbidden freedom . . . so that the sovereign and only virtues of this sex are constituted as these: to remain ignorant, to play stupid, and to serve."[126] Equality and liberty are words that return time and again to her pen; she defended them with all the ammunition she could muster as a woman of letters. The image of an hourglass "which marks the hours and measures the day," matched with a poem, decorated the first edition of the treatise on equality. Should we see this only as evidence of a precious mannerism, or rather as the sign of a counting mentality, closely associated with her definition of equality?

III

FEMALE EDUCATION AND FEMINIST HUMANISM UNDER ABSOLUTE MONARCHY

Those who dominated literary criticism under the Third Republic—elitist intellectuals and academics for the most part—estimated the seventeenth century above the eighteenth and the Romantic period. Although a defense of the seventeenth century is already evident in Voltaire's writings, the literary critic Ferdinand Brunetière late in the nineteenth century articulated it with precision. Albert Thibaudet succinctly summarizes Brunetière: "The seventeenth century believed in genres and kept to distinct genres, within rationally defined bounds. The seventeenth century was Christian, and it was French."[1]

The above statement offers itself as a definition of French classicism; but what it actually reveals is a series of mental operations structured by a value system deeply implicated in academic rhetoric. In a book on French prose style published in 1929, for example, we read:

> The clarity of a thought, of a work, depends on many conditions: all elements of that thought or work must be clear in themselves, sufficiently distinct that one could not confuse them . . . these elements must then be selected, sorted out. . . . Finally, these distinct elements that have been clearly determined and carefully selected must be arranged in order to lead us conveniently from the beginning of the work to its end.[2]

At the close of the Second World War these academic values were revitalized for new reasons; the events of the war had underscored the importance of defining personal ethics in the face of general instability. French classicism was once again called on to resolve a crisis in humanism, engendered this time by the war's collective irrational behavior that had not only defied all logic, but threatened all humanity as well. The "morals" of French classicism thus became the springboard for intellectual "recovery" on a national scale. Paul Bénichou's book on the seventeenth century, titled *Man and Ethics* (1948), is part of this "impulse." He writes:

The interest we feel for the history of thought almost always springs from the
desire to make some new use of it, and this desire is the very expression of the
perfectibility of mankind. If today we still consider the classical centuries great,
it is because in those centuries a moral philosophy developed that gave humanity
a true sense of its own value.[3]

Bénichou was not about to enrich his reflections on this question by examining
either the reinforcement of monarchical control or the Gallicanism of the
church.

While this modern humanism was derived in part from classical antiquity as
well as from certain representations of the human during the Middle Ages, "a
new power emerged," Bénichou writes, "encouraged by general progress in life
and social relations."[4] The great religious and secular controversies that spanned
the century traced the contours of the moral issues involved. During this shifting of priorities, the "woman question" received ample exposure. It was a positive aspect of a humanist anthropology that brought to the foreground the
issue of women's equality. Bénichou writes: "there is no period in which the
image of womanhood, in all its clearly discernible power and attraction, held
a higher place than in the three great centuries during and following the Renaissance."[5]

In France at the end of the 1960s, however, a critique of the values of this
nationalistic humanism appeared, influenced by a rereading of Nietzsche. This
triggered a reappraisal of the classical period's canonical texts. In his book *Spinoza et le problème de l'expression*, Gilles Deleuze underlined the inadequacy of
Descartes's "clear and distinct" ideas when confronted with the Spinozist conception of adequate ideas: "The clear and distinct idea only forms real knowledge to the extent that it flows from an idea adequate in itself. . . . Descartes
has not advanced beyond the form of a psychological awareness of the idea."[6]

To pursue the philosophical debate among Descartes, Spinoza, and Leibniz
meant challenging the hegemony of Cartesianism, or at least the form of Cartesianism disseminated within the French university tradition. In his *Madness
and Civilization: A History of Insanity in the Age of Reason*, Michel Foucault
created a comparable interpretative upheaval within the field of institutional
discourse. The glorious century of Louis XIV becomes, in his reading, the
century of mass imprisonment. "It is common knowledge," he writes, "that
the seventeenth century created enormous houses of confinement; it is less commonly known that more than one out of every hundred inhabitants of the city
of Paris found themselves confined there, within several months."[7] We are further informed that these severe measures fell most readily on the less powerful
sectors of the population, ranging from the unemployed, the poor, and va-
gabonds to the heterogeneous world of the sexually diseased, the dissolute,
homosexuals, alchemists, and libertines. These repressive measures had the effect of repositioning the line between the so-called mentally normal and the
abnormal. From then on the classical city would no longer confront its "anoma-
lous" elements face to face. People who previously roamed freely in the open

were henceforth submitted to coercive regulations whose severe cruelty was comparable to that of any prison. In the name of reason, a wall was thrown up, and the so-called moral city (where the laws of the state effortlessly fused with those of the heart, or natural reason) was safely barricaded against the less harmonious world of various disorders, characterized by the inability to work or to be integrated into a group. Bénichou, however, is glaringly reticent on this topic. For him, it was the crisis of Jansenism that represented "the only form of bourgeois or modern mind that was not acceptable in the France of Louis XIV—that which asserted the rights of conscience against outward authority."[8] It is unfortunate that his study of seventeenth-century morality is so dependent on literary history; his analysis does not take into account the world of marginals and outcasts, who are even more abject than the imprisoned.

Trial records indicate that there was a real growth of devil worship in the sixteenth century. But this kind of personal relationship to the irrational became desacralized during the seventeenth century, due in large part to an incarcerating superstructure firmly anchored in a rational foundation. Thus the darker side of the much-analyzed cult of the *honnête homme* becomes apparent. And so we can no longer broach the question of women's emancipation, located at the crossroads of religious and scientific humanism, without taking into account the history of the state's control over society.

By the end of the confrontations between the last Valois kings and the Estates General in the sixteenth century, royal absolutism no longer tolerated political or financial constraints, or any other limitation of power that representation of its subjects would have entailed. When the Estates General of 1614 tried to reform the government and change some of its fundamental laws, the king responded by dissolving this annoying organization. The juridical and political voices of royal absolutism were unequivocally clear in their position toward women. Cardin le Bret, one of the principal theoreticians of absolutism, reaffirmed the Salic law's all-powerful authority to exclude women from the French throne. To reinforce the principle of masculinity, he invoked the inherent physiological weakness of women:

> As for the second maxim derived from the Salic law, which prohibits women from succeeding to the throne: it is in conformity with the law of nature which having created woman imperfect, weak, and incompetent, both in body and in mind, placed her under the power of man who has been endowed toward this end with sounder judgment and greater courage.[9]

Women's role in public affairs and in the government of the state appears to have been treated with equal contempt by both the partisans of royal absolutism and those, such as Jean Bodin, who advocated a more restricted monarchical power.[10] The neo-Stoical lessons of subjective rights, deriving rights from the individual nature of man, might have encouraged the legal philosophers to be more sympathetic toward the notion of sexual equality. On the contrary, however, this doctrine appears only to have favored a codification of women's inferior status, the liabilities of womanhood winning out over the positive aspects of individuality. Jean Portemer[11] has noted that the legal theorist Jean Domat, author of *Lois civiles dans leur ordre naturel* (1713), did not believe it necessary "to justify the inferiority of women's status, but merely treated it as self-evident, a primary truth that would be superfluous to prove." Domat himself wrote, "Men are capable of all kinds of activities and functions, except when excluded by a specific obstacle, while . . . women are incapable of most kinds of activities and functions by the unique reason of their sex."[12]

Although theories of royal absolutism offered little that was particularly original on this point, absolutism as it evolved, institutionally, deserves very close scrutiny because it entails the development of new attitudes toward women.

In the seventeenth century, the economy was for the most part subordinate to the state. By extending the model of the corporation to all occupations, the state sought to establish better control, and if possible, to reorganize production, which had been so devastated by the earlier religious wars. The development of corporation and guild structures has usually been studied from the standpoint of economic history; but such an approach has not taken into account the general legal context within which this development is rooted. To study the history of Parisian occupations under the *ancien régime* is to locate women's status within the social hierarchy of work; its importance is suggested by the very fact that royal privilege accorded guild masters of Paris the authority to exercise their trade throughout France.

The historian René de Lespinasse writes:

> The sixteenth century . . . (a period of progress and fiscal exigencies) invented certificates of mastery and offices, contrary both to the very principle of "métiers" as well as to the authority of the guild officials. With the edicts of 1581 and 1597, the regularly administered occupations were forced to have their regulations confirmed [by royal authority] under threat of forfeiting their privileges, and occupations that were not incorporated were required to submit regulations.[13]

With Colbert as his finance minister, Louis XIV perfected this standardization policy by renewing the previous edicts without trying to conceal his fiscal objectives.[14] Though most trades were open to women as well as men, the different statutes regulating these trades indicate that women were active only in those that were very new or very old; in some older occupations they held a monopoly. Lespinasse writes: "This is the case of linen, fabric, and canvas weavers . . . the linen trade began in Paris long ago through privileges granted to fabric and second-hand clothing vendors who were encamped in a corner of Les Halles near the church of Saints-Innocents."[15]

The expansion of the linen trade increased its importance considerably.[16] In silk production women were also very active. The ribbon manufacturers' statutes of 1404 give evidence of even-handed treatment; the linen-weavers and hemp-dressers received occupational statutes in 1581; Louis XIV's confirmation of these statutes in 1660 introduced no serious modifications.[17] Lespinasse writes: "Women masters, apprentices, and guild officials are constantly discussed, the occupation being for the most part filled by women who were content to sell their wares to manufacturers or directly to the town-dwellers."

In contrast to these older occupations were the women's guilds with a much more recent legal status, which therefore had a more flexible social structure. The statutes of the *grainiers* [seed merchants] showed an exemplary concern for sexual equality. A comparatively new occupation that did not really come into existence until the end of the sixteenth century,[18] the *grainier* profession promoted women and men equally to the status of master. The statutes consistently mention both men and women masters [*maîtres et maîtresses*], as well as men and women seed merchants [*grainiers et grainières*]. Out of four guild officials, two were men and two were women. The community of florists, hairdressers, and feather-stuffers had no written statutes before the seventeenth century. Their statutes consist of twenty-one articles.[19] Women and girls alone constituted this occupation in which no man would become a master. Four guild officials—two women and two girls—were in charge of administrative duties.[20] Seamstresses were finally accorded occupational status by patent letters of 30 March 1675, although they were only permitted to cut and sew *robes de chambre*, skirts, and jerkins. (The main parts and skirts of dresses were reserved for the tailors.) These strongly feminized occupations were nevertheless classified as "mediocre and small" within the guild hierarchy, which excluded women from master positions whenever possible. The parliamentary decree of 2 June 1589, ruling between male fruit-vending officials and several female fruit vendors exemplifies the volatile relations between the two sexes over the issue of female representation in a guild where women were already very numerous. The decree states:

> It is really quite a novelty to say that women should become masters in a trade, and there would need to be a very clear necessity to do so, because normally women want what men do not want; the court orders that the inspection of said butters and cheeses be made by the master fruit guild officials in the customary manner without women being involved in it.[21]

In all the occupations it appears that the wives of masters could accede to the master position upon the spouse's death, provided that the widows not remarry and that they obey the restrictions concerning the hiring and training of apprentices.

Did this new state control of occupations signify a regression in women's activity and influence? On the contrary, a brief historical survey of trades and occupations in Paris reveals that the standardization of certain guilds, sanctioned by letters from the king, opened up new possibilities for women. The provinces demonstrate the same tendency, despite some local variations; as historian Emile Coornaert points out, it was thanks to an edict by Louis XIV that seamstresses in Aix and Marseilles were permitted to make women's garments.[22] The struggles among the trades were bitter and difficult, and the competition between the female and male guilds was formidable: the linen-weavers fought against the encroachments of the haberdashers, the seamstresses felt the competition of the tailors, the flower-sellers that of the gardeners. The question of female representation in the guilds was not the result of systematic thought under the old law. Each occupation had its tradition and its privileges—the residual influences of an earlier social structure—and it had been difficult for a woman to carve out a place for herself. The February Edict of 1776 provisionally annulled the guild-regulating bodies in favor of creating a nonhierarchical system, wherein practitioners simply registered with the police and had no special privileges. The king's reforming finance minister Turgot openly opposed the multiple regulations and bans that hampered commerce and industry:

> Innumerable statutes dictated by monopolistic intentions to discourage industry, to concentrate commerce into the hands of a few by multiplying formalities and expenses, by subjecting guildsmen and tradesmen to ten-year apprenticeships for occupations that could be learned in ten days, by excluding those whose fathers are not masters and those born outside of certain specifications, by prohibiting the employment of women in the textile industry.[23]

The type of liberalism Turgot advocated was incompatible with a principle that would prevent half the population from engaging in productive labor, regardless of the economic developments. As with all other monopolies, the pushing-aside of women in the productive sectors constituted an attack on the freedom of commerce and industry. Can we detect here the ambiguous intimations of the role that cheaper, more docile women laborers would play in the capitalist economy during the nineteenth century?

The efforts toward unifying the kingdom in the economic sphere took place through a juridical plan that sought to end the autonomy of corporations and their regulating bodies. But despite the monarchy's concurrent effort to shape its subjects—for example, through founding the Saint-Cyr school for girls—the movement to unify the realm's education fell almost totally to the Catholic church. The theorists of Gallicanism at the end of the sixteenth and beginning of the seventeenth centuries subordinated the Church of France to the king, and partially relieved the Pope of his authority, which he now had to share with ecumenical councils. The major disciplinary measures formulated at the Council of Trent (1545–63) were translated into ordinances, institutionalizing the extension of the monarchy's authority into the spiritual realm. Thus the king was even authorized to regulate the administration of sacraments!

The ordinance of Blois, subsequently followed by the principal texts legislating marriage law,[24] assimilated a large number of the council's prescriptions, but slightly modified their orientation toward a more "Gallican theory of marriage." A major point of contention between the *parlements* and the Council of Trent concerned parental consent. Thus, in one ordinance we read:

> We must enjoin the priests, vicars, and others to inquire carefully about the station of those who would marry, and whether or not they are noble children, or under another's authority. We forbid them from proceeding with marriage ceremonies unless it is with their father's, mother's, or guardian's consent: transgressors will be prosecuted as rapists. . . . It is thus our intention that those found guilty of seducing minors under the age of 25, on the pretext of marriage . . . against the desires and express consent of the fathers, mothers, or guardians, be condemned to death without hope of mercy or pardon.[25]

Henri Rollet writes, "The Council had rejected the demands by several prelates, the French ones in particular, to establish the lack of parental consent as an insurmountable obstacle"[26] to marriage, while at the same time it adopted regulations that would render clandestine marriages impossible. The Church's exclusive jurisdiction over annulments was also affirmed:

> There must be no doubt that clandestine marriages contracted with the free and voluntary consent of the concerned parties are valid and real marriages, as long as the Church has not nullified them, and that in consequence, one must condemn, as the Holy Council condemns with anathema, those who deny the truth and validity of such marriages.[27]

The council thus refused to weaken the individual's own personal obligations and moral responsibility. Keeping in mind the Reformation arguments on marriage and the mutual obligations of spouses, the council fathers' intention was to promote respect for the marital institution, while at the same time they clearly valued the condition of celibacy over that of marriage.

The Counter-Reformation's restoration efforts, pursued under the king's authority, had a twofold impulse: the commitment to secular interests in the name of the nation's education; and on the other hand, the effort to create living models of saintliness in order to forestall further erosion of the religious vocation. Female education was shot through with these two contradictory desires. The enclosing of the secular communities or "institutes of simple vows" nevertheless quickly seemed to guarantee their teaching vocations. This situation resulted from the combined pressures exerted by both the episcopate "reluctant to see congregations of female teachers let loose in the world," and by families, "for whose daughters religious commitment was to be absolute so as to preclude any possibility of subsequent inheritance rights."[28] Encouraging women to belong to religious orders in solidly established institutes was a significant attempt to raise the French people out of its ignorance, while retransmitting a model of piety nurtured in the shadow of the cloister seemed the surest way to combat the gains of the Reformation. Thus Pope Paul V defined the Toulouse Ursulines' pedagogical obligations in this way:

> In order to lead her to the piety and virtue worthy of a Christian virgin, the convent nuns must fully devote themselves to teaching the young girl first, a summary of Christian doctrine (the way to examine her conscience, to confess

her sins, to take communion, to attend Mass, to pray to God) . . . and second, teaching her to read, in order to instill in her greater ardor for this institution and save her from heretical schools.[29]

The reconciliation of two such requirements within a single religious congregation explains the remarkable dynamism of the Ursulines, whose influence swept through France early in the seventeenth century.[30] It is also interesting to note a simultaneous, perhaps related growth in female contemplative orders. Mother Marie de Chantal Gueudré writes that "between 1604 and 1662, the Carmelites founded 60 Carmels in France; but not a single additional one would be established before the Revolution."[31] The Ursulines and the Carmelites were complementary projects responding to a profound religious, social, and political demand of the period. If in no other way, this is borne out by the account of their respective origins: the two orders were founded at about the same time by women related to one another. Madame de Sainte Beuve, with the Ursulines' assistance, instituted public education in France for young girls. Abbé Reneault describes her thus:

> Widowed after three years of marriage, she insisted on devoting her heart and fortune to charitable causes. Madame de Sainte Beuve's intentions were clear by the time her cousin, Madame Acarie, was establishing the Carmelites in Paris. After having chosen from among the future nuns gathered around her those who appeared most likely to follow the Carmel's austere rules, Madame Acarie entrusted the others with the education of girls.[32]

What did this education consist of? The various orders with educational missions (such as the Ursulines and Visitandines)[33] ordinarily distinguished between girls destined for convent life and those who would return to life in society once they had finished their education. The education of the boarders tended to follow the monastic model, while that of the day-students sought to produce "good Christians." This pattern is indicated in the Rouen Ursulines' constitutional charter, which was roughly equivalent to a pedagogical manual for the period. The Ursuline teachers, we read,

> will shape the girls' morals to standards of propriety and honesty, so they can become the wisest and most virtuous Christian women of their time, taking care not to intermingle that which is specific to religious life, either in conversation or in action . . . because the Ursuline nuns are responsible for instructing not only the girls in residence, but also the young day-students in matters dealing with Christian doctrine and piety. . . . The girls will learn reading, writing, and even to do certain tasks according to their abilities.[34]

Moral and religious training, sewing, reading, and writing: such was the educational program of these orders which were more concerned with transforming their young charges into accomplished homemakers and respectful spouses than into educated women.[35] The influence of Saint Jerome's letter to Laeta can be felt here: the two main lines of his educational advice were the fear of "damaging" the girls with too much education, and the desire to develop the modesty appropriate to their sex. He recommends: "Let them follow praying with reading and reading with praying; time spent in this manner will appear short to them; the time that the others spend in adorning themselves . . . would be better spent in enriching their souls with maxims from the Bible."[36]

We should refrain, however, from attributing these anti-intellectual programs for girls in this period wholly to a chronic and unchanging distrust of women by the Catholic Church. A recommendation for basic education is not lacking in patristic literature. In the seventeenth century, the importance that the Church attributed to girls' education was linked to an emphasis on women's spirituality that was specific to France at the time. In a 1964 article about women and spiritual life in the seventeenth century, Mother Marie de Chantal Gueudré went to great lengths to demonstrate the many facets of this blossoming feminine spirituality:

> The French Ursulines seemed to be supported more by the French spirituality of the period than by the heritage of their founder, Angèle Merici . . . Saint Theresa's writings had a key influence in the seventeenth century, and the Spanish Carmelites established an obvious connection between Mother Theresa and her "Filles de France." Much ink has been spilt over the question . . . Berullian Carmels or Theresian Carmels.[37]

Without being so bold as to decide among these theological controversies, we should underscore that in spite of Christian universalism, even in the rarefied atmosphere of trends, a new attitude was cutting through the related orders and their texts. One pattern clearly emerges: childhood, as symbolic of the humility of the human condition, was becoming an object of veneration. The Ursuline C. Ranquet writes:

> I believe that God in the infinite lowliness and littleness of its state has destined my poor soul, weak as a newborn child, to carry the foolishness of the cradle to the place of the eternal Word . . . the foolishness of the cradle reassures me because everything that is rare and precious is concealed in the stuttering gibberish of childhood.

A Carmelite, Mother Catherine of Jesus Nicolas, declared: "The spirit of childhood helps the nuns to achieve a child-like state in order to honor Jesus . . . this requires total self-abnegation and self-annihilation."[38]

A contemplation of the manger as a lesson in simplicity developed in the cloisters, paralleling the emerging lay cult of the child-king. "The prayer manuals were filled with litanies for the Infant Jesus," Mother Gueudré wrote. Is this symbolization of childhood, so prevalent in the spiritual life of the early seventeenth century, a sign of women's accession to the spiritual realm of asceticism? Mother Gueudré apparently thinks so, as she suggests a hidden correspondence between womanhood and the development of this religion of the heart.

The idea of the cloister was pushed to its extreme limits in the convents where girls got their earliest years of schooling,[39] thereby associating the child's intellectual formation with her physical separation from the society. This state of affairs suggests some suspicion of children in general and a distrust of young girls in particular; both spring from the common well of the Catholic tradition. But during the reigns of Henri IV and Louis XIII, the Counter-Reformation drew on Augustinian pessimism for help in its struggles against the Stoicism of the humanists.[40] This philosophy of redemption influenced the pedagogical organization of girls' education in convents. The watchful discipline[41] for which Jansenist pedagogy (which was otherwise very respectable) was so much criticized drew its coherence directly from Augustinian thought.

Jacqueline Pascal, sister of Blaise Pascal (author of the *Pensées*) was responsible for girls' education at Port-Royal. She wrote a book summarizing the constituent principles of an education based on austere isolation, as well as on an acute psychological understanding of the adult/child relationship. What notions of childhood do we find in this educational "charter"? The three- or four-year-old girl should receive help for the "infirmities" associated with her tender age. The young girl's instructor, by constantly monitoring her own reactions, should keep in check the emotional excesses attendant upon a prolonged familiarity. The child is dependent on her environment, on the social milieu into which she is born. The Port-Royal pedagogues' moral instruction consisted less in providing young girls with edifying maxims than in introducing, on the physical level, a discipline of personal hygiene which set them apart from the practices of their social milieu. Jacqueline Pascal wrote in 1665: "The girls are exhorted to comb their hair and get dressed as quickly as possible in order to accustom themselves to spending the least amount of time in adorning a body destined to be consumed by worms, and in order to counteract the futility with which worldly women dress and style their hair."[42]

Throughout these guidelines the female child is portrayed as a fragile being, threatened by the weight of her impending womanhood. The vain and futile preoccupations of contemporary noble and bourgeois women reinforced this theological agenda. Port-Royal's educational concerns for young girls were mainly centered around the regulation of emotion—a privileged terrain made instrumental by a philosophy of history according to which, as Antoine Adam has noted, "the history of humanity is the history of a long decline, and although Christ could indeed save a small number of the elect, he could not save everyone."[43] From this perspective, then, we can discern a double suspicion: that of an overly precocious religious devotion (e.g., young girls should not go to confession); and that of too much intellectual progress. Jansenism prolonged the early seventeenth-century Augustinian current of the Catholic revival, by safeguarding this "affection for the savior Christ and his grace."[44]

Women's exceptional role in early seventeenth-century spiritualism, which elaborated educational programs for girls, corresponded to a worldwide Christianization movement. The establishment of these new female religious orders answered a pressing need to contain the progress of the Reformation by introducing an increasingly larger population to the "cultural" benefits of Catholicism. By opening small schools and by taking in nonpaying students, the Ursuline order broadened the social scope of the convent. This admirable effort permitted parents of the less privileged classes to send their children to school,[45] and opportunities for primary education multiplied through the establishment of parish schools.[46] A whole network of congregations aimed outward into the countryside proliferated in the second half of the century, between 1660 and 1730,[47] as the Catholic reform movement extended its reach. Nor did this messianic zeal stop at France's borders: from the very beginning of the century, it extended into some of the colonies.[48]

This remarkable expansion of education for girls was somewhat tempered by clerical prejudices concerning coeducational schools. A letter dated 15 December 1640, from Louis XIII to the Bishop of Poitiers, called for "the suppression of coeducational education."[49] As a consequence, girls from communities with insufficient funds to support two schools were deprived of any education. By allowing the clergy to maintain its grip over the schools, the monarchy indicated its concern to eradicate heresy through the education of the realm's children. Toward this end, teachers were required to profess the Catholic faith and to give religious instruction to those children whose families had been affected by the Reformation:

> Art. IX: It is our wish that male and female teachers be placed, whenever possible, in all parishes where there have been no teachers, in order to instruct all children, especially those whose mothers and fathers have professed the RPR,[50] in catechism and in the prayers necessary to bring them to mass on working days, as well as to give them instruction on this subject.[51]

Without exaggerating the significance of the Collège de Saint-Cyr at Saint-Louis by reading it as a political act of royal will, the opening of this first secondary school for girls, headed by Madame de Maintenon, a lay woman, was an important event. It presented a distillation of the period's ideas on the education of girls. The school was founded in 1686, one year before the publication of Fénelon's *Traité de l'éducation des filles* [Treatise on the education of girls]. Its pedagogical orientation reaffirmed that woman's importance in society derived from her role within the family: as mother she is her children's first teacher, and as virtuous wife, she can exercise a good influence on her husband and his associates. Just such a program is unequivocally announced in the Saint-Louis school's charter: to prepare lay women for the functions they

will need to fulfill, for the greater glory of the Catholic religion.[52] In its first years, the Saint-Louis school had a liberal tendency. But this relative secularism did not last long, as Roger Chartier has noted:

> the Ladies of Saint-Louis, founded in 1686 as a community of simple vows, transformed itself six years later into a regular monastery of the Order of Saint-Augustine, with solemn vows, strict cloistering and, in 1707, religious dress. Louis XIV's reservations notwithstanding, the evolution that had occurred with the Ursulines and the Visitandines early in the seventeenth century was repeated here.[53]

For both Fénelon and the Saint-Louis teachers, education was not meant to train intellectuals or *précieuses*, but to turn out women of good sense, capable of assuming their future roles. A domestic, moral, and religious education was thus conducted toward this end; but because of the social rank and distinction of the students, it was supplemented with history and geography. With productions of Racine's *Esther* and *Athalie*[54] by her students, Mme. de Maintenon achieved such a level of success that her methods of active pedagogy soon came under attack from Church authorities. From the beginning, Hébert, the parish priest at Versailles, had refused to attend these productions. "Amusement," he said, "should be prohibited from any good education. All convents are watching Saint-Cyr, they will follow your example, and instead of training novices, they will produce actresses."[55]

The school's reform, announced shortly after the *Athalie* production, returned the royal institution to a path more in keeping with the Church's views on educating girls. This education already shied away from offering sustained intellectual activity, a tendency that was reinforced with the institution's reform directed by Mme. de Maintenon. She warns, "They write too much at Saint-Cyr, and our girls cannot be sufficiently discouraged from it. It would be better for them not to write so well, than to give them the taste for writing, which is dangerous for girls."[56] Fénelon's treatise, strongly influenced by Saint Jerome's advice, also forbade women access to any knowledge other than what could be gleaned from sanctioned Church texts. Moral instruction alone could save them from the natural state of inconstancy that threatened their faith.

Support for these educational principles was not unanimous, and many attacks came from the elite sectors of the enlightened nobility. Mme. de Sévigné for example, advised her daughter:

> Ah, my daughter! Keep your child with you. Do not believe that a convent can provide an adequate education either on religious subjects, which the sisters hardly know anything about, or on other things. You will do much better at Grignan when you have the time to apply yourself. You will have her read good books . . . and discuss them with you . . . I firmly believe that this is better than a convent.[57]

It is now well known that there existed circles of educated women from prestigious families who had contact with the period's men of learning. As Gustave Reynier has written: "Few educations were as solid as that of Mme. de La Fayette. At one time she was Ménage's pet student, and throughout her life she remained in close contact with him."[58] Gilles Ménage had once written in Latin a history of women philosophers which is closer to the apologist tradition than to any critical reflection on women's abilities to skillfully develop philosophical arguments.[59] Dedicated to the distinguished Greek and Latin scholar Mme. Dacier,[60] this book did, however, give evidence of a classical precedent for the contemporary desire by a few women for scientific knowledge. But it would be a mistake to see these circles of sparkling personalities as typical.

With the rise of absolute monarchy, institutional control came to bear more directly on women. This control was not limited to excluding women from the internal functioning of the state apparatus, but also developed in different sectors of social life, which until then had been regulated in other ways. The existence of a movement favoring woman's equality requires the historian to examine the more elusive networks constituting the country's intellectual life, where both ideological and "institutional" values are elaborated.

Théophraste Renaudot's work to promote public hygiene was a part of the monarchy's effort to eradicate any pockets of resistance that might thwart its power in any way. In proposing the state's use of the able-bodied poor to clean the streets of Paris, Renaudot hoped to solve the threatening problems of both indigency and idleness, problems which the "great confinement" would later take care of in its own way.

The strongly philanthropic intent of this proposal was also brought out in articles delineating the project: it was to facilitate contact with members of the most disadvantaged classes and thus give new cohesiveness to these neglected, unemployed Parisians.[61] In any event, the goal of this enterprise proved to be very different from the goals of the bureaus of assistance and other charitable initiatives that flourished at that time. On a restricted scale, Renaudot's group set out to attack commercial transactions as they occurred within the constraining guild mechanisms. The compilation of a catalogue offering all types of services hinted at an intensification of supply and demand, creating the rules for a new internal market. In contrast to the existing collectivities, this new strategy accorded an important place to the individual. It is significant, therefore, that Théophraste Renaudot called his catalogue the "address inventory of the resource bureau where everyone can give and receive advice concerning all the necessities and comforts of life and human society."

This marketplace egalitarianism proclaimed every man's right to aspire, without reservation, to a better life. Such liberal individualism, which became more general throughout the eighteenth century, nonetheless had a darker side. How did it affect women's right to work and their right to a better life? Given this definition of social life, could one reasonably exclude a large portion of the population from this new economy? In Article V of the Address Bureau's summary we read: "because of the corruption of the times, its suspicion and malicious gossip, ladies and virtuous demoiselles will excuse the bureau for permitting entry to men only." A somewhat mollifying sixth article was added, however, to say that

> it did not appear right that these women and women who are in need be denied this convenience which ought to be public; for this reason, and in accordance with the power invested in us by his Majesty, we give the order that those who come to the bureau on their behalf be directed to the oldest women who provide the best examples of modesty both in life and in morals, the most exemplary of whom will be the model, to have them meet the said conditions.[62]

The Address Bureau's goal was to reach those sectors of the population least apt to engage in business trade, even though it must be noted that the services offered ranged from humble nursemaids to apostolic notaries. The path Renaudot followed, beginning with the idea of aid to the poor, then persons who needed assistance, and arriving ultimately at the idea of "public" utility, was dictated in part by the need to concede to morality and prevailing religious customs some restrictions to the principle of universal free trade. Because of the religious and social anathema weighing on them, women had to first pass through this moral filter as an ostensible precaution before being integrated into the process.

The indefatigable Renaudot wanted the Address Bureau to assume a greater cultural role, rather than limiting itself solely to economic exchange. From a reading of the bureau's collected minutes, it appears that the question of women's equality was broached at the "Conférence XLVI du Caprice des femmes" [Forty-sixth lecture, on the whims of women]. Under this traditional though confusing title, an argument in favor of women was developed. The order in which woman was created indicated her perfection: "He created man as the master of all things and finally woman as a masterpiece of nature and model of perfection, master over man, and stronger than him."[63] From this superiority in the order of creation there followed exceptional moral virtues: "Altogether, women's actions are more virtuous than men's." In addition to this, women's intellectual aptitudes were highly praised. "In conclusion," we read, "there has never been a single science or art without women being involved: the damsels Desroches, de Gournay, and the Viscountess d'Auchi" conclude a list of famous women stretching back to antiquity.

This apologetic argument, already frequent in the writings of defenders of women and certain sixteenth-century humanists, was actually quite banal by this period. But here the argument took an unexpected turn. From a conference report we read:

> This is why those who look for the cause of the nobility or virility of men or women in their sex, are looking in the wrong place. It is not being a man or a

woman which makes one noble or ignoble, but rather being an excellent man or an excellent woman. If there are faults, they come from the individual and should no more be attributed to a sex than to a species.[64]

Thus the individual is given responsibility for his or her destiny; gender was no longer considered a determining cause of either elevated morality or degeneracy. The modernity of these views was incompatible, of course, with the ban on women's direct access to the Address Bureau. Renaudot believed in the moralizing value of these lectures which allowed debate across a wide range of interests.[65] It is important to realize that the very presence of an argument in favor of women situated the question of sexual equality among contemporary issues. It is also important to recognize the political significance of the Address Bureau; otherwise the significance of its prioritizing this issue would make little sense. The bureau's meetings were a kind of laboratory of ideas enlisted in the service of the crown. Historian Howard Solomon argues that the fundamental questions of the realm were discussed there, and there may even have been a reciprocal interaction between Cardinal de Richelieu's economic program and the principles developed at the Address Bureau.[66] Yet, despite its noticeable repositioning within the hierarchy of values, the issue of sexual inequality did not yet pose a serious threat to French economic development!

The legal incapacities and restraints plaguing women were legion. The logic of monarchical institutions had certified women's exclusion from public affairs, even as it encouraged the creation of new women's guilds for financial reasons, and promoted the expansion of religious communities[67] dedicated to educating girls for reasons of religious stability. Concurrent with these measures was a literary and social movement of profound feminist significance: named *Préciosité*, this movement became widely influential at mid-century by cultivating society life and opening *salons* where high society could gather. Already in the sixteenth century, the development of court life had favored women's cultural ascendancy. The spread of poetical and philosophical debates on love, inspired by Italian neo-Platonism, had revealed women's new influence in the refinement of manners. As for men, there was no shortage of apologists for women, who would develop their (often laborious) arguments based on history and myth.[68]

While Marie de Gournay's egalitarianism, influenced by philosophical skepticism, contained the seeds of an individualism directed toward women, "*préciosité*, on the contrary, developed the desire to restore on the plane of language the most characteristic qualities of woman, qualities of both sensibility and intelligence."[69] From social circles presided over by the great female personalities of the period, the most disparate voices expressed a common preoccupation with language, as a sign of protest. Awakened to the need for action by the Fronde revolt,[70] the women of this worldly aristocratic society, who valued both heart and imagination, meant to equip themselves with a linguistic instrument commensurate with their vision of the world. Antoine Baudeau de Somaize, one of their detractors, writes: "These women still strongly believe that a thought is not worth anything if it is understood by everyone, and it is with this in mind that they direct all their efforts to destroying the old language, and that they have made another, one which is not only new, but which is theirs alone."[71]

The unbridled inventiveness of the *Précieuses*, with their pronounced taste for metaphor and hyperbole, was often scoffed at. Somaize collected for his amusement some of the expressions making up this new language; and it is thanks to him that we can appreciate the extent of this lexicographic treasure to which modern French is more indebted than is generally recognized. The *Précieuses* also wanted to reform spelling, "in order that women could write as correctly and with as much assurance as men." The question of whether words should be spelled as they are pronounced, or instead follow traditional orthography, was also asked at Renaudot's Address Bureau. The concern to restore to French its flexibility, liveliness, and expressiveness stemmed from the group's twofold desire both to understand one another and to create a medium of communication that could be truly for everyone, free from the ponderous weight of scholarly history. Imagination and sensibility were annexed through intelligence (defined as a state of mental tension always on alert), which was applied "to finding the right words and unusual expressions."

To devote oneself to such an ephemeral art as conversation might seem excessive; but in doing so they showed their refusal to acknowledge a history that had always come to the aid of male impudence with its pronouncements against women. The abbot Michel de Pure's satirical novel, *La Précieuse*, refers to this: in this work the rejection of history appears in the form of an obscurantist culture that is ignorant of modern women's freedoms.[72]

Préciosité attributed a great deal of importance to the *visible* aspect of the female sex's power; the woman's body was groomed, adorned, and presented within a complimentary space: the *ruelle*.[73] The desire to surprise the imagination, to stir it into action, was an abiding concern in the *Précieuses'* doctrine. Thus, by enlisting themselves in the fight against the hardened arteries of knowledge, they took as their own the idea that "enabled the seventeenth century to define *honnêteté*, and showed how knowledge clutters the mind and constrains the imagination."[74] "Women," Michel de Pure writes, "are capable of more inventiveness than men by very reason of their ignorance."[75]

That women were ignorant was a notion widely held by much of seventeenth-century high society, despite some spectacular popular educational programs on their behalf. Generally speaking, the opposition to knowledge, seen as impeding the ability to express feelings and the nuances of the heart, was widespread, but understood in a very different sense than that of the *Précieuses*, or that of Madame de Maintenon[76] and Fénelon, the main Catholic proponents of women's education. This prejudice could also be found in the writings of the educated, those whose mission was to fight against women's ignorance. Following the success of Renaudot's lectures, Louis de Lesclache, professor at the *Palais précieux*, called together intellectuals of both sexes for a similar lecture program. He justified initiating women into philosophy with the following words: "I would like women to have a clear understanding of what we call capital vices in order to guide their conduct through life."[77] Too much ignorance was perceived as dangerous to feminine morality and to a woman's ability to manage her household!

Was it a logical consequence of the *Précieux* movement wholeheartedly to endorse[78] the social division of knowledge along gender lines? Was it because of their culturally hermetic isolation in an elite group that they were accustomed to rule without being required to show their credentials for doing so?

But the social message of the *Précieuses* is unequivocal in its critique of the marriage institution (of "permitted love," to borrow an expression from Somaize's dictionary!). They refused to submit to the common woman's fate of the time, rejecting the constraints imposed by marriage, with its multiple and debilitating pregnancies.

Parental guardianship usually meant that the family's perceived self-interest canceled out the freedom of girls (who were too young to fight parental decisions). The horror stories of gross mismatches resulting from arranged marriages are all too well known. The married woman's legal status during this period delivered her up, as the legal historian Jean Portemer notes, bound hands and feet, to her husband's pleasure: "The woman, whatever type of matrimonial contract she had, was subordinate to the husband's authority. Her situation had worsened markedly, when compared to previous centuries where only the communal property, and not the woman herself, were given to the husband as lord and master."[79]

With even less access to legal protection than underage females, married women who committed adultery brought upon themselves the severest of punishments. Portemer writes: "In any event, at the end of the seventeenth century, French jurisprudence relaxed its rigor against the adulterous woman. The recluse was permitted to regain her freedom after the death of her husband by remarrying."[80] It is against this background that we can best understand initiatives of the *Précieuses*. The contracts for a substitute for marriage, envisioned by the heroines of Michel de Pure's narrative, can thus be seen as Malthusian precursors. Though French morals of the period were reputed to be quite liberal, social and religious constraints still permitted only discourses on love (presuming that the *Précieuses* might have wished for a less ethereal form of amorous activity!). Illicit desires would appear to have scarcely disturbed the hegemony of spiritualized and mysticized love. Concerning marriage, Somaize writes: "Elsewhere one sighs, here one writes, and the ecstatic transports and languid looks that serve as lovers' interpreters are reduced here to little notes and verses, and no one languishes except on paper; the general custom is to unite only in mind, not in body."[81]

By way of compensation, the *Précieuses* in their struggle against marriage had invested love with moral dignity, making it incompatible with physical union. Ninon de Lenclos (no doubt during her meetings with Queen Christina of Sweden), had baptized them "the Jansenists of love":

> Like the Jansenists, they refused any compromise in favor of the absolute. It is
> in this sense that Mlle. de Scudéry, who is rightly considered the theoretician
> of *préciosité*, could write to Mme. Deshoulières that her love novels [*romans d'a-
> mour*] were written against love. Herein lies the paradox of *préciosité*.[82]

Amid all the disadvantages plaguing women's condition, the *Précieux* movement sought to define a "feminine specificity," via rhetorical means. In this way
it embodied a kind of revolt against the inferior status imposed on women by
men. Does this then justify drafting the *Précieux* movement into a larger "feminist upsurge,"[83] indiscriminately grouping together Mlle. de Gournay, Poullain
de la Barre, and Fénelon's educational precepts for girls? So many diverse meanings and inflections to the century's omnipresent woman question! New social
demands made an issue of women's relation to knowledge; still, there was a
conflict between the *Précieuses'* celebration of femininity (and its attendant
graces), and the conception of education (understood as the acquisition of
knowledge) as the key that would allow women open access to social opportunities. Up to that time, female education had not been able to separate itself
from the prejudices concerning women that permeated patristic literature. The
Counter-Reformation only accentuated this tendency in its passion to follow
the saintly models that had served as the Church's spiritual and temporal en-
ergizing force: accordingly, the seventeenth century was the century of saints.

Poullain de la Barre[84] was a partisan of both the Reformation and of Cartesian philosophy. Perhaps it was due to this dual membership in two of the
period's minorities that he was able to inject an original argument into well-
worn themes. Like Mlle. de Gournay, he addressed "the equality of the sexes,"
rather than indulging in another apologetic exercise on behalf of women. We
will return to discuss the title of his last work, *On the Excellence of Men*.

If one insists on comparing Poullain's work with that of Descartes,[85] one
discovers beneath the defender of women only a mediocre metaphysician and
a fair physiologist; the interest of his political philosophy resides more in the
originality of his project than in the rhetorical qualities of his arguments. This
project consisted in bringing the domination of men over women out into the
open, in order to confront it head on, by reconstructing the narrative of its
supposed development as it had been determined and punctuated by the history
of political institutions. A plan for education for "ladies" would create the
concrete conditions favorable to change.

Poullain was not satisfied with a merely historical approach. He also compared the customs and morals of his country with those of other places in the
world (e.g., the East, China). By way of these moves through time and space,
he attempted to find some logic or system that would help him defuse the violent
nature of gender conflicts. Indeed, the question of women's social and political
status—caught in the crossfire between Catholics and Protestants—was the
nerve center of the period's social equilibrium. Poullain found many reasons
to act as the interpreter of the "turbulence" of his era.

Little is known of Poullain de la Barre's personality. We do know that he suffered personal hardship in the climate of persecution that surrounded the reformed religion during the Counter-Reformation, and that he often lived in hiding.[86] He was born in 1647 in Paris, and died in May 1725 in Geneva. A doctor in theology, he was a practicing priest for seven years, first at La Flamengrie (in a parish of 278 homes), and then at Versigny (in a much smaller parish of 98 homes). This drastic change in parish size strongly suggests that disciplinary action had been taken against him. In 1688, three years after the revocation of the Edict of Nantes, he moved permanently to Geneva. To a degree that is difficult to determine, his adherence to Cartesian ideas contributed to the insecurity that surrounded his life in France. At the time, Cartesianism represented an intellectual current open to attacks from religious authorities. As Bernard Magné writes in his doctoral thesis on Poullain's feminism:

> The University had placed Descartes on the Index in 1663. In 1669 candidates for the philosophy chair at the Collège Royal had to defend anti-Cartesian theses. In August of 1671, the Archbishop of Paris made known his desire to the theological, medical, and law schools that the teaching of any doctrine other than that expressly supported by university statutes be prohibited. Sanctions were levied against partisans of Cartesianism.[87]

Drawing from his own experience of these attacks on freedom of conscience, Poullain sought an end to such repressive violence by introducing an analysis that would unravel society's age-old power relations. The search for their origins, analyzed countless times by social contract philosophies, was still novel as discussed by Poullain—so much so that the question of his possible influence on Rousseau[88] has been raised. What in fact were the elements of this "historical conjecture?"

According to Poullain, the physical disparity between the sexes might have given the male a slight advantage over the female, but this made little difference at the "beginning of the world." Men and women then enjoyed relative equality: "Men and women, at that time simple and innocent, were equally involved in cultivating the earth or in hunting, as savages are still. The man went his way, the woman went hers, and the one who brought in the most was the most respected."[89] The affirmation of a presocietal equality between the sexes provided the basis for searching for an equality that could be recovered.

In opposition to such legal theorists[90] as Domat and Lamoignon, for whom social inequality between the sexes followed logically from inequality in nature, Poullain explained women's dependent state in relation to the evolution of social institutions, most specifically the family. The tyranny of fathers and husbands, as well as the practice of primogeniture, provided models of domination which mothers and daughters had then internalized. Thus a division in functions and social space was instituted. Poullain writes: "It is easy to imagine . . . that women who were forced to remain at home and raise children took care of what was inside, and that men, being more free . . . took responsibility for the outside."[91]

Women's condition was aggravated by the advent of political control over family organization, by some malcontents who to this day force most families to practice exogamy. This historical approach to institutions, depicted as a series of violent power struggles between groups, attracted little respect. The division of sex roles in the emerging kingdom was explained by the author in this way: the functions of government fall to those who had taken part in defending the frontiers; men recognized as qualified to contribute to the preservation of the realm "won the day over women." Within this narrative on the origins of inequalities, Poullain found the state apparatus particularly culpable because of its inherent tendency to divide the population. The author was little inclined, it appears, to perform reverential acts before royal authority. Perhaps it was Poullain's Reformatist convictions that led him to be suspicious of a power that demanded only "external submission."

Because scientific work is so intimately bound to the social and political space provided for it, Poullain could explain women's lack of scientific expertise largely by the fact that they were excluded from the state's political machinery. He writes, "Academies have been established that do not admit women; they are in this way excluded from the sciences as they are from everything else."[92] Poullain was profoundly pessimistic about the state's ability to benefit all its citizens. "In fact," he writes, "chance, necessity, or self-interest" governs each person's destiny. To try to justify the existing state of affairs seemed dishonest to him: women's condition was the result of one group's power over another, and in order to maintain its dominance this power claimed that women were naturally weak. And although it was the injustices done to women that crystallized Poullain's indignation, he was also acutely concerned for the peasants, whose impoverished condition condemned them "to the void of ignorance."[93] This breath of democracy gave a politically radical orientation to the question of gender inequality, which presaged that of the revolutionary period.

Before the inequalities between the sexes were established by society, there existed a minimum unit of association: the couple. Using the image of embryonic development, postulating a state of innocence or pure nature made it easier to judge the conventions of civil society. The search for what "is according to nature"[94] led back to what the author, as a man, could attest to with his own eyes, and to what all men could join him in attesting: women possessed the same aptitude for judgment as men.

To support this argument and thereby persuade his reader, Poullain directly interviewed women themselves. His broad sampling allowed him to claim a certain exhaustiveness. "It has been my pleasure," he wrote, "to talk with women from all walks of life, from both the city and country, in order to discover their strengths and weaknesses."[95] Poullain held learned discourse especially accountable for popular prejudices against women because it actively reinforced misconceptions. Poullain took courage from the sixteenth-century humanists who had already demonstrated the potential of the human mind. But does this mean his thought should be assimilated, as it has often been, to a scientific rationalism akin to that of Descartes? Paul Hoffmann has written:

> selfhood that is constitutive of being . . . is alien to organic phenomena and establishes the dignity of both men and women equally, regardless of their historical destinies. It is this aspect of Cartesian thought that appealed to idealist and Christian philosophers; in particular the feminist authors of the late seventeenth century would invoke the superiority of the soul, so highly touted by Descartes, in order to justify their theory of female equality in all social functions.[96]

Descartes, however, never seemed overly concerned about the equality question per se; his interest in questions of sexual difference was limited to formulating a few hypotheses concerning the morphological differentiation of the fetus.[97] The difference between the sexes carried no ontological value in his eyes, and he classified it under modes of diversification[98] for corporeal or extended substance. Poullain, on the other hand, directly addressed the effects of social differentiation between the sexes in order to affirm women's personal liberty. He refused to bring physiological determinism into his egalitarian argument. In this regard, Poullain differed from all those who tried to attribute a specific nature to women, whether to deprecate them (as the legal theorists had done), or to celebrate them (as the *Précieuses* had attempted).[99]

Several philosophical influences seem to be at work in Poullain's analysis of sexual difference. The weight he accorded to opinion, especially the diverse and discordant opinions of the philosophers, reveals his debt to skepticism, which had experienced a revival since the sixteenth century. His faith in the ability of human reason to correct sexual inequities indicates an orthodox Cartesian bias, according to which methodical doubt was the indispensible preamble to truth. However, this loudly proclaimed adherence to Cartesian principles made it difficult at times for him to remain consistent. Accordingly, he showed very little interest in the search of the new physics for scientific objectivity, whose operational laws, based on Descartes's mechanical principles, did not question the latter's fundamental distinction between "a thinking substance and a corporeal substance."[100]

Poullain's understanding of the body and its attributes did not take up this distinction. By defining the body as a language,[101] as an instrument of communication which provided social cohesion within the human community, as well as between man and nature, Poullain postulated an animism of matter that Descartes had expressly condemned.[102] For Descartes, no path led from the body alone to the soul alone. It is precisely in this perpetual opposition of the intelligible to the lived and of the lived to the intelligible that, as Ferdinand Alquié has suggested, "the freedom of the Cartesian being is achieved. . . . The path of the meditations is therefore always ontological; it does not lead from confusion to clarity, or from the sensible to the intelligible, but only from existence to existence."[103] From the allusive exchanges among his various and evocatively named characters (e.g., Sophie the Wise, Timandre the Honest, Stasimaque the Peaceful, etc.), we could hardly impute a specific philosophic program to Poullain. Rather, we should be suspicious of any interpretation that would posit his femininism as a direct descendant of the Cartesian theory of liberty. Poullain's philosophical eclecticism does not follow so straight a path.

Pierre Bayle,[104] the indefatigable chronicler of his period's intellectual life, informs us that Poullain's thought took shape within a context of free thinking, and that because of his talents, he helped edit a book titled *La Foi dévoilée par la raison* [Faith unmasked by Reason].[105] Published by Jean Patrocle Parisot in 1681, this work drew on the natural theology of Raymond Sebond, as presented by Raimond Lulle. In this book, Parisot attempted to reconcile an explanation of the universe according to religious faith with a scientific understanding capable of establishing a stable body of knowledge. Though his synthesis was condemned as soon as it appeared, it was not based on a "principle of faithlessness"; instead, the author sought to establish both sacred texts and the natural world as legitimate objects of modern knowledge. In this framework, both "poles" were equally expressive of divinity.[106]

Poullain's work reverberates with numerous echoes of Sebond's natural theology, which Montaigne had earlier translated into French. Montaigne defined this natural theology as follows:

> This doctrine teaches all men to see, without trouble or difficulty, and to the extent possible through natural reason, the truth that is necessary for a knowledge of God and of oneself, and of what is needed for one's salvation to achieve eternal life; it amply permits the access to knowledge of what is prescribed and commanded in the Holy Scriptures, and causes human understanding to be relieved of many doubts and to confidently agree with what Scriptures say concerning knowledge of God and oneself.[107]

This was a radical idea: a human doctrine founded on the knowledge of what constitutes one's own humanity as well as that of one's neighbor! Humanity thus had access to two books for this purpose: the universal order of things (the book of nature), and the Bible (the book of God). Any distinction between the initiated and the lay person was thereby ignored; this approach must surely have appealed to Poullain's religious evangelism. We can see and know for ourselves![108] This "self-knowledge" enabled one to recognize another person's humanity in accordance with the Holy Scriptures. Reading the phenomenal world by interpreting corporeal substance as a language was at the heart of this enterprise, and it is here that we should locate the origins of Poullain's universalist feminism.

In Poullain's third work, ambiguously titled *De l'excellence des hommes* [On the excellence of men], the author returned to textual analysis and to the critique of scriptural traditions,[109] abandoning the search for philosophically more rigorous arguments that had informed his work on the education of women. This courageous step by Poullain was characteristic of his philosophy of action. In this ingenious work, he employs subterfuge that borders on satire in order to critique the political and religious thought of his time. With an almost insolent aplomb, Poullain pushes his adversaries' own arguments to the absurd:

> Adam was created after the mud, he was made out of the mud and clay of the earth, and therefore earth and mud are more noble than he. And if I want to use conventional reasons, (that is, imaginary ones), I would have to say in turn that God created the first woman in a more remarkable place than He did Adam, and made her body out of a harder and stronger and even more noble material, since she was made of a man's rib, instead of being made of mud like Adam, all of which informs us that women are more excellent than men. How would those who tell us how to behave answer that?[110]

Pierre Bayle puts us on the scent in his historical dictionary. He writes,

> the other author is the one who published a work in 1673 in Paris with the title *De l'égalité des deux sexes, discours physique et moral* [On the equality of the two sexes: A physical and moral discourse], which emphasizes the need to rid ourselves of prejudices. The author believed he was threatened by other writers who were writing against him; but on seeing no refutations appear, he himself wrote against his own book, because in 1675 he published the treatise *De l'excellence des hommes contre l'égalité des sexes* [On the excellence of men against the equality of the sexes].
>
> On close examination of this later work by Poullain, however, we discover that he had no intention of refuting his previous statements, but rather that he intended to confirm them indirectly. In any event, both of these works were reprinted during 1679 in Paris. The author remained anonymous for a long while: the *République des Lettres* revealed in October of 1685 that the author was a man named Frelin, but shortly after that they revised their assertion and named Poullain. This is actually his real name, despite the fact that "de la Barre" appears on the third edition of 1691.[111]

The very difficult conditions under which Poullain developed his ideas on the equality of the sexes cannot be separated from the analysis of his works; surely these conditions must have influenced the somewhat elliptical path of his thought more than we can imagine today. It is therefore possible to interpret Poullain's proclaimed adherence to Cartesian theories as little more than an additional sign that he belonged to a persecuted religious minority, since Cartesian theories were certainly less threatening to a priest than an outlawed religion.

By portraying experience as "the immediate presence of thought to itself,"[112] Descartes's *cogito* permitted Poullain to develop a philosophic universalism suitable to his messianic evangelism. His interest in the woman question attempted to expose the arbitrary division which church and state had imposed, denying to half the civil population the benefits of civilization. Their exclusion of women stemmed from an obscurantism that was incompatible with the century's modernity. Poullain declared himself for the moderns, and because it had been traditionally treated with contempt, the woman question seemed to him to be the necessary point of departure for establishing a more equitably distributed justice throughout society. Related to Descartes's criteria of "clear and distinct" ideas (attributed to the embattled moderns), Poullain's concern for objectivity took on a Calvinist theme: the recovery of a lost interiority that had become encrusted with dogma. Women as well as men possessed the necessary qualities of mind and heart to take part fully in the kingdom's political and social life. Poullain had no trouble envisioning women in society's highest positions.[113] This equalization of men's and women's social functions with no hierarchical restrictions (unusual for the period, we must remember) was justified for Poullain through an intellectual and spiritual appropriation of this strictly personal sphere. The state could only exercise external controls over people. And though we will never find the word "individual" in this feminist's writings, it is to this internal exigency (reinforced by Poullain's experience of going into hiding) that we must connect the origins of modern political individualism, which can be defined as "liberal" in the sense that each person "shares equally in the totality of nature and reason and is therefore competitive with everyone else."[114]

Writing under the pseudonym of Aristophile, Gabrielle Suchon, a nun from Semur, published *Le Traité de la morale et de la politique* [Treatise on morals and politics] in 1693. With a perspective similar to Poullain's,[115] this book expressed women's desire to be recognized for their intellectual abilities and for the quality of their imagination. But in the hands of this unknown nun, the treatise suffers from the habitual restrictions imposed by the Counter-Reformation on Christian humanism. It reaffirms the role of the Catholic church as a regulating force in conflicts between the state and the individual; in accordance with the fundamental principles of Christianity, she invokes the egalitarian content of canon law; and it is in this highly improbable context, trailing in the wake of the Church Fathers, that Gabrielle Suchon's thought is anchored: "Even though this divine authority is more than sufficient to persuade one of the things most difficult to believe, I also call on the authority of a large number of Church Fathers who are reputed to be experts. . . . For example, saints Augustine, Jerome, Ambrose, Gregory, Chrysostom, Bernard, Thomas. . . . "[116]

The author appeared reticent, however, on the topic of marriage: although it was a sacrament, marriage seemed to offer an almost intolerably constraining condition. Given the two alternatives offered to young girls—marriage or the nunnery—Suchon denounces the mechanisms which in both cases placed the woman under someone else's control. Her claim to liberty is backed by Stoic philosophy, whose authority she often cites. From the Stoics comes her conviction that the sexes are equal on both moral and intellectual grounds.

Her claims, however, are of a political nature. Appropriating for her own purposes the Stoics' theory of natural right, she postulates a number of rights for women: in opposition to Salic law, women's right to govern; but also, and unexpectedly, their right to travel in the name of free enterprise:

> Of all the freedoms denied to women, the freedom to travel and see the world passes in most men's opinions as a crime to be abhorred. . . . Persons of the female sex have proved on innumerable occasions that they are capable of seeing the world and that their bodies are well equipped to withstand the vicissitudes of travel.[117]

The writings of this nun, whose ambivalence inherited from Christianity has already been mentioned, thus sketch out a political theory based on the exercise of liberty as it would be developed in the eighteenth century by the liberal constitutionalists. "The author of the Stoic sect," she wrote, "held that, generally speaking, all men should live in no way divided or separated from each other by laws, rights, and customs, but that all should universally consider themselves bourgeois[118] and citizens."[119]

By returning to classical texts, this woman's voice, directly anchored in the Christian humanist tradition, counterbalances the undue weight accorded to the influence of rationalism in advancing women's cause. In Suchon's treatise, reason is part of women's intellectual abilities, but it is given no special value or particular use with respect to women's emancipation.

Cartesian philosophy, whose synthetic force was to captivate the intellectual world for centuries, devoted no systematic attention to rethinking the feminine condition (despite a tradition that has accorded him feminist sentiments based on his exchange of letters with famous women such as Queen Christina of Sweden and Elizabeth of Bohemia). Indeed, Descartes's form of Stoicism[120] could certainly be employed to serve women's cause. For example, Descartes argued that we should not totally repress the passions as the Stoics recommend, but only learn how to put them to use. He thereby proposed a way to reconcile gratification of the senses with peace of the soul—a conflict that was perhaps more acutely experienced by women due to the social and moral constraints surrounding their condition.

But Descartes was addressing queens in particular. Were they subject to the same constraints as the general population of women? In his book *Descartes, Corneille, Christine de Suède*,[121] Ernst Cassirer seems to explain Queen Christina's support for Cartesian doctrine by her desire to resolve the internal conflicts that finally drove her to convert and to abdicate the throne, in an example of exercising one's own will in the face of religious and social predestination. Are we therefore justified in interpreting Cartesian philosophy as demonstrating a general propensity for sexual equality? Though such an argument has often been suggested—as far back as the seventeenth century and even in Poullain's own writings—it nonetheless appears suspiciously simplistic and opportunistic.

It is more likely that the humanist tradition, highly sensitive to the religious conflicts of its time, anchored the idea of an egalitarian feminism which was to flower in the eighteenth century under the revolutionary impulse. The principle of a single, unified religion as guarantor of an indivisible power had been fractured by the Reformation. The Counter-Reformation sought to patch up the cracks in the Church, and at the same time to reinforce the state's power. The question of the individual's (and by extension, women's) place in social and political life thereby took on a topicality it had never previously had. Thus we find hovering on the periphery of the seventeenth century's religious thought, whatever side it might come down on, the most radical and daring of political proposals: equality of the sexes.

IV

LIBERAL INDIVIDUALISM, NATURAL RIGHT, AND SEXUAL EQUALITY IN THE POLITICAL PHILOSOPHY OF MONTESQUIEU, ROUSSEAU, AND CONDORCET

I.

Montesquieu is generally considered to be one of the founders of modern liberal thought, as his *Spirit of the Laws* lays out the first theory of the separation of powers. This view has had exceptional credit among American political scientists, as is evidenced by the recent work of Thomas Pangle on Montesquieu's liberal philosophy.[1] In France, however, Montesquieu's constitutional thought has recently received scathing criticism. Charles Eisenmann, in particular, has worked to correct modern constitutional science's misinterpretations of Montesquieu's text. "In the sense of a separation, which is at once functional, personal, and material, of state governing bodies: . . . Montesquieu neither advocates nor accomplishes this. He does not separate parliament and administration."[2]

To what extent does the questioning of Montesquieu's idea of separation of powers (the cornerstone of political liberalism) affect the impact of his work?

In book II, chapters 2–3 of *The Spirit of the Laws*, Montesquieu defined liberty as observance of the law—as "a right of doing whatever the laws permit."[3] Liberty, then, is a product or result of law, and its nature legally determined. It is thus distinct from a notion of subjective right,[4] based on man's natural dignity. Accordingly Montesquieu says nothing about the rights that might ultimately be derived from such liberty, for this kind of liberty cannot be claimed for itself. A people's power is not to be confused with a people's liberty. In his view, monarchy is the type of government that best brings together the institutional conditions for liberty.

This definition of political liberty leaves little room for feminism as a political principle of sexual equality. Nonetheless, in *The Persian Letters* Montesquieu protests in a playful tone against the superiority presumptuously claimed by men. To the question whether "natural law submits women to men," a gentleman philosopher in the *Persian Letters* utters a categorical no. If we are to believe Jeannette Geffriaud Rosso, the philosopher in question stood for Poullain de la Barre (and not Fontenelle)[5]—which would imply that Montesquieu himself was sympathetic to the plea of his pro-woman character.

However, in the *Spirit of the Laws'* famous chapter on the English constitution, the author seems barely interested in pursuing the issue. He makes no mention of women as potential voters for legislators, stating merely that "all the citizens in the several districts ought to have a right of voting at the election of a representative, except those who are in so mean a situation as to be deemed to have no will of their own."[6]

For Montesquieu the passage from natural independence to civil society was accomplished by the convergence of individual wills. "The strength of individuals cannot be united without a conjunction of all their wills. 'The conjunction of those wills,' as Gravina . . . very justly observes, 'is what we call the civil state.' "[7] This statement is reminiscent of the arguments promoted by the Levellers during the English Civil War,[8] who advocated masculine suffrage for all except servants and indigents, and who can be called forerunners of liberal democracy. But Montesquieu's description of the system for electing the legislative body painted an idealized picture of the English situation, of whose abuses he surely was aware—that there existed, for example, electoral constituencies which, based on tradition and privilege, sent representatives in the total absence of any voters! Could women, despite their numerous legal disabilities, make any claim to citizenship status with the right to vote for legislators? While this question remained unanswered in the chapter on the English constitution, it is nevertheless clear that for Montesquieu women's liberty was tied to the values of monarchy.[9] Is this liberty political? Does a study of the French monarchy introduce new factors for consideration?

In his own analysis of the French monarchy (whose implications would later be developed by Tocqueville), Montesquieu focused attention on all the institutional curbs to the royal will—particularly the fundamental laws of the realm, which by virtue of their independence could check temporary abuses of the monarch's power. Among the fundamental laws that kept the monarchy from evolving into despotism was the Salic law, which denied women access to the crown, and to which Montesquieu devoted an in-depth genealogical study. Originally a civil law among Germanic peoples, it took on the force of a political law at the time of the successions to the French crown. We cannot fail to notice with Rosso the curious paradox in Montesquieu's approach, concerned as he is to interpret the Salic law as a purely economic measure, thereby excluding the idea that it privileges males over females.[10] His effort to substantiate his thesis via such a painstakingly detailed sociohistorical analysis conveys his uneasiness about the discriminatory, "unjust" nature of this fundamental law—and perhaps even a desire to obscure its injustice. Once we are aware of Montesquieu's immense legal erudition, including his knowledge of the sixteenth-century legal theorists (particularly Bodin, who so extensively justified the application of the Salic law), we begin to see that he has implicitly yielded in favor of women's political liberty and access to government. He makes this concession, however, with some defensive irony regarding the abilities of females to conduct affairs of state.

> It is contrary to reason and nature that women should reign in families, as was customary among the Egyptians; but not that they should govern an empire. In the former case the state of their natural weakness does not permit them to have the preeminence; in the latter their very weakness generally gives them more lenity and moderation, qualifications fitter for a good administration than roughness and severity.[11]

Moderation, here promoted to the rank of politics, is necessary to preserve a balance between the fundamental laws, the power of intermediate bodies, and the monarch. Failure to maintain this equilibrium leads to despotism, wherein "a single person directs everything by his own will and caprice."[12] The danger of despotism returns constantly to Montesquieu's thought. His emphasis on the way the English constitution guarantees the citizen's "safety" through a cosovereignty of powers indicates his objections to the vesting of power in a single person.[13] The peril he saw in despotism is evident in his critique of Louis XIV's policies: "Heaven, that knows our true interests, favored him more by preventing the success of his arms than it could have done by crowning him with victories. Instead of raising him to be the only sovereign in Europe, it made him happier by rendering him the most powerful."[14] That republics are not exempt from political monolithism is shown in his example of the Venetian republic: the Venetians neglected to diversify the functions of government when they called solely on the body of magistrates.[15] Montesquieu's model of despotic government derives from the Orient: "From the nature of despotic power it follows that the single person, invested with this power, commits the execution of it also to a single person. . . . The creation of a vizier is a fundamental law of this government."[16]

The despot's power, unchecked by any institutional limits, was directly responsible for the equally unlimited practice of enjoying women. The seraglio makes its appearance in his text as the symbol of this tyranny. Yet we ought not reduce Montesquieu's reflections on despotism solely to a concern with a licentious orientalism. The effects of this form of government on its subjects' mores are universally applicable. Despotism characteristically is contemptuous of others and of the collectivity. Montesquieu proposes the metaphor of the savage who cuts a tree down at the roots in order to obtain its fruit,[17] to illustrate a single person's desire for immediate gratification, with utter disregard for any economic or social future.

Polygamy, a form of women's servitude to which Montesquieu often returns (and which might appear as an indulgence by the author of the *Persian Letters*, fascinated by that sequestered world), is depicted in the framework of an

economy of waste similar to the metaphor of the savage. The causal network
that Montesquieu painstakingly establishes among diverse phenomena such as
climate, politics, and manners and customs suggests the following explanation
to him: in tropical climates, women's beauty deteriorates too rapidly; men consequently grow weary of them and desire a change. Nevertheless, more for
reasons of "utility" than morals, he is quick to issue a condemnation of polygamy. He cannot sanction it, since it has pernicious effects on family equilibrium and deprives the child of the father's love:

> With regard to polygamy in general, independently of the circumstances which
> may render it tolerable, it is not of the least service to mankind, nor to either
> of the two sexes, whether it be that which abuses or that which is abused. Neither
> is it of service to the children; for one of its greatest inconveniences is, that the
> father and mother cannot have the same affection for their offspring; a father
> cannot love twenty children with the same tenderness as a mother can love two.[18]

In *The Spirit of the Laws* Montesquieu refused to separate political laws from
civil laws. On this issue he wished to remain at a theoretical level capable of
articulating ensembles or "totalities"—by which I mean the sum of relations
which "the laws may bear to different objects."[19] Such a theory of knowledge
in search of geopolitical determinations of societies gives his study of political
and civil institutions a capacity to synthesize the spirit of a people. Despotism
means women's servitude, and monarchy, women's liberty! In the constant see-
sawing of history, the private space of the family appears intimately bound up
with the preeminence of men, as if domestic tyranny by women could somehow
give rise to political despotism. Thus the transmission of political values from
generation to generation was guaranteed by fathers.[20] This is crucial, considering the importance Montesquieu attributed to the political virtues that are
supposed to characterize each type of government. His patriarchal conception
of the family, supported by frequent references to the Roman authors, leads
to the conclusion that fathers have natural supremacy over mothers; marriage
has as its foundation the father's obligation to provide for his children.

In the case of adultery, unequal punishment in the man's favor seems legitimate to Montesquieu. He rejects the egalitarian aspirations of canon law and
instead extols the principles of Roman civil law:

> As the husband may demand a separation by reason of the infidelity of his wife,
> the wife might formerly demand it, on account of the infidelity of the husband.
> This custom, contrary to a regulation made in the Roman laws, was introduced
> into the ecclesiastic court, where nothing was regarded but the maxims of canon
> law. . . . But the political and civil laws of almost all nations have, with reason,
> made a distinction between them. They have required from the women a degree
> of reserve and continency, which they have not exacted from the men; because
> in women, a violation of chastity supposes a renunciation of all virtue; because
> women, by violating the laws of marriage, quit the state of their natural de-
> pendence.[21]

In the *Persian Letters*, Montesquieu had acknowledged the social power of women,[22] and had admitted some principles in favor of improving their status. But in *The Spirit of the Laws* he adopted the most retrograde points of view on the question of woman's subordination in the family, where all authority is accorded to the father. Montesquieu rejects religious explanations of the nature of civil institutions, and affirms the independence of law from theology. His ambivalence on the question of women's "natural dependence" is very similar to that of John Locke; we see here an indication that women's legal position in this period, although growing more flexible, did not undergo any radical change. The "reign of women," as it has often been described, was actually little more than a "rhetoric in arts and letters,"[23] leaving society's deepest foundations intact.

Doubt persisted among these partisans of natural law who sought a method other than revealed religion to explain institutions. In fact, they clearly perceived that part of their caution with regard to women was theological in origin. For Bodin this did not pose much of a problem. Women's subordination was necessary to the familial and patriarchal order, and monarchy found "its foundation and its model in the paternal empire." Locke and Montesquieu were more hesitant. As much as he criticized the false principles of Sir Robert Filmer, advocate of the doctrine of the divine right of kings, Locke proclaimed the equality of the two parents with regard to their children:

> [Paternal power] seems to place the power of parents over their children wholly in the father, as if the mother had no share in it; whereas if we consult reason or revelation, we shall find she has an equal title, which may give one reason to ask whether this might not be more properly called parental power.[24]

and later:

> [T]his power so little belongs to the father by any peculiar right of Nature, but only as he is guardian of his children.[25]

Logically, his own premises should have led Locke to establish the equality of rights between the sexes. Nonetheless, his arguments ultimately fall back on the thesis of women's natural dependency:

> But the husband and wife, though they have but one common concern, yet having different understandings, will unavoidably have different wills too. It therefore being necessary that the last determination (i.e., the rule) should be placed somewhere, it naturally falls to the man's share as the abler and the stronger.[26]

Montesquieu's logic bears strong resemblance to Locke's. He refuses to found his monarchy on the power of fathers, as does Bossuet. On the other hand, he does not hesitate to invoke women's natural subordination in marriage as a hierarchy which should not be transgressed.

We see some of the same hesitancy in Montesquieu and Locke when it came to imagining concretely what women can do to rise out of their position of inferiority. We know what importance Locke placed in individual upbringing and training as a means for achieving a happier society.

> I have [spoken of boys] here, because the principal aim of my discourse is, how a young gentleman should be brought up from his infancy, which in all things will not so perfectly suit the education of daughters; though where the difference of sex requires different treatment, 'twill be no hard matter to distinguish.[27]

The author simply called on tradition regarding the education of girls, and readers are left to correct in their own minds what in Locke's text does not apply to the weaker sex. At the same time, he condemned women's sequestered education, calling it unhealthy. As we have seen, Montesquieu also felt the need to acknowledge that education played a role in society's discrimination against women, but he proposed no remedies.

In France during the first half of the eighteenth century, tyrannical monarchy was being challenged, and religious plurality was being recognized (for Montesquieu, the latter translated into an actual apology for Protestantism—which he saw as Europe's religion of the future, supplanting the sterile social models promoted by Catholicism). These critical movements left no room as yet for attacking that other process that impeded social unification, namely, patriarchal authority.

The moral freedom that was fashionable in French high society at the time made women the supporters of luxury and arbiters of taste. On this account, woman became central to a debate on happiness. Let us examine Montesquieu's reasoning when he states that feminine vanity lies at the origin of luxury in monarchies. "Each courtier avails himself of [women's] charms and their passions, in order to advance his fortune: and as their weakness admits not of pride, but of vanity, luxury constantly attends them."[28] But contrary to the theological tradition that habitually denounced the pointless and trivial morals of courtiers, human vanity became for Montesquieu a positive value capable of having a beneficial impact on civilization. "Vanity is as advantageous to a government as pride is dangerous. To be convinced of this we need only represent, on the one hand, the numberless benefits which result from vanity, as industry, the arts, fashions, politeness, and taste."[29] These urban values, fostered by the concentration of riches in the cities (especially Paris), are based on the inequality of fortunes and the growth of commerce between private individuals. The sumptuary laws imposed on women in antiquity and especially during the Roman Republic are for the most part seen as incompatible with the monarchical form of government, which, on the level of institutions as well as that of individual persons, valued liberty over equality. Thus in Montesquieu's eyes, luxury appeared in monarchies as "the use of what liberty one has";[30] government aims to increase it by means of the security that it brings to society. Could this notion of luxury be a basis for a political theory of appropriation? In any event, the woman who promised pleasure became the symbol of a social life in which seduction held an increasingly important place and in which artists were "chosen by a new public" to be the depositories of "a valued liberty"[31] which began taking over the personal sphere. The editors of the *Encyclopédie* added to Voltaire's article on taste some posthumous fragments by Montesquieu, the "Essay on Taste in Things of Nature and Art." To account for the pleasure we experience from certain perceptions, Montesquieu distinguishes two sorts of taste, natural and acquired. The two were not really at odds; they differed according to the level of awareness and mastery of these emotions permitted by sensibility (this personal zone that had so long been undervalued). The idea of "acquired taste," insofar as it demonstrated that there exist universal reponses to certain aspects of our civilization, formed the crux of this project of rehabilitating sensibility. It embodied a glorification of the century and of its material and artistic productions. Natural taste represented a preexisting capacity for emotion which the individual does not owe to society. Through these two states of Man arise invariables:

> The law of the two sexes established, among the civilized and savage nations, that men would ask and women would but accept: from this it follows that the graces are more characteristically found in women . . . and such is the wisdom of nature that what would be nothing without the law governing modesty takes on an infinite price because of this felicitous law, which consolidates the happiness of the universe.[32]

The attribution of socialized behaviors to sexual difference is raised to the status of a universal principle, as if the attraction of one sex for the other sums up all the happiness of existence.

> Our connections with the fair sex are founded on the pleasure of the senses; on the charm of loving and being loved; and likewise on the ambition of pleasing the ladies. . . . This general desire of pleasing produces gallantry which is not identical with love itself, but the delicate, volatile, perpetual simulation of love.[33]

Identified with the pleasure she arouses (in men), woman appears as a motivating force of this society in which amusements and "the surplus of consumption beyond what was necessary to survival"[34] were becoming a factor in economic and social development. Do we see here the emergence of a bourgeois ideal of happiness? Robert Mauzi cautions us not to "give too much weight to the social content" of this philosophy of life,[35] whose inspiration was Stoic philosophy, reinterpreted by a culture that perceived itself as frivolous.

Montesquieu's analysis of the limits of the state in relation to individuals effectively subordinated his thinking about the question of women's status. He was ultimately more interested in the political and social principles of regulation under different governments. For "the liberty of women," a subject found at some points under the rubric of manners and at other moments promoted to the idea of a principle of political economy, he does not have any concrete modality. On the contrary, a patriarchal conception of the family, assigning subsidiary functions to women without batting an eye, belies the seeming open-mindedness of his philosophical liberalism. Even as he based his study of governmental treaties on a hypothesis of presocial man's natural equality, Montesquieu contented himself with the assessment of natural forces (especially climate) that could affect the existing political structures. The recognition of a rationally established and universally acknowledged order overshadows the question of society's origin, and consequently the question of the individual's natural rights. On this point it is illuminating to compare Montesquieu with Rousseau.

II.

We could choose to contrast Montesquieu's enlightened monarchist convictions with Rousseau's intransigent republicanism. But the two philosophers' overall political choices only superficially affect their interpretation of sexual difference. The ways in which the two authors deal with notions of nature, reason, and the individual result in varying degrees of freedom and equality for women. Rousseau is so haunted by the loss of equality between individuals—despite the mediating role of the family between the state of nature and political society—that in the course of his writing one can see a progressive exacerbation of the opposition between a past nature (a nature he hoped to restore in the future) and a convention-bound, unnatural present. In Montesquieu's case, as we have seen, his interest is fixed on the institutional present and on positive laws. Rousseau clearly perceives the difference between his project and that of Montesquieu, for whom he professes the greatest admiration. In *Emile* he writes,

> In modern times the only man who could have created this vast and useless science was the illustrious Montesquieu. But he was not concerned with the principles of political law; he was content to deal with the positive laws of established governments, and nothing could be more different than these two branches of study.[36]

Rousseau's insistence on the distinction between the state of nature and civil society indicates to us his confidence in man and in man's capacity to forge his own political destiny. Montesquieu entirely neglected to differentiate the state of nature along gender lines—much as we would expect, given his relative indifference to natural law and his institutional conception of liberty. He hardly even mentioned, among the laws of nature, that of the "natural inclination" between the sexes![37] The question of sexual difference takes on an unprecedented philosophical dimension with the theoreticians of natural law, of whom Rousseau is one the most prominent.

Barbeyrac's French translation of *The Law of Nature and Nations* by Samuel, freiherr von Pufendorf, the German theoretician of natural law, assured the latter a wide readership in eighteenth-century France. In Pufendorf, sexual difference is defined as part of the state of nature, since it does not result from any human institution. But women are also an integral part of civil society: "For although variation in sex and age is not due to imposition, still such things involve some moral distinction among men in common life, since different things are recognized as becoming to persons of different sex, and it is proper to treat them differently."[38] The rise of anthropology renewed the question of the "natural" and "conventional" differences between the sexes. Pufendorf envisaged (rather reticently) the presocial state of women. Since the state of nature was defined in relation to the order of Creation, the fallen couple Adam and Eve figured in an unfortunate way in this urge to distinguish the natural from the conventional. For Pufendorf

> the natural state of man is when men order their lives on nothing but a simple universal kinship resulting from the similarity of their physical nature, before any human act or covenant has arisen which has rendered one man beholden to another. In this sense those who have no common master, who are not subject to another, and who are unknown to each other by way of either benefit or injury, are said to live in a mutual state of nature.[39]

Philosophy of natural law required other scenarios than those imposed by the Christian tradition: the doctrine of original sin, with Adam and Eve, was disturbing the innocence of the presocial humanity it posited.

The episode of the wild girl (*puella campanica*), captured in September 1731, revealed a female being, a savage who could be perfected through the acquisition of language, table manners, and city manners, hence, accessible through reason. Voltaire, who believed in human nature and innate reason, commented on this capture:

> The savage girl found near Chalons admitted that in anger, she had struck her unfortunate companion who then died in her arms. As soon as she saw her companion's blood flow, she was sorry, she wept, she staunched the wound, she placed herbs on it. . . . Call reason and remorse what you like, they exist, and they are the foundations of natural law.[40]

In Voltaire's eyes, the behavior of the wild girl expressed the benevolent instinct which, since the very origin of societies, has impelled man to help his kind.[41] By discharging the debt of a perverse Eve, this episode brought to light a notion of humanity that was moving away from the dogmatic pessimism which the Catholic church had advocated—the female sex was becoming naturally good. But not until Rousseau's *Discourse on the Origin and Foundations of Inequality among Men* was this really understood. The publication of the wild girl's story, forgotten for almost twenty years, followed the publication of Rousseau's famous discourse by just one year.[42] The fate of an individual who had accidentally been returned to nature provoked a wave of timely reconsideration about the human species' capacity for evolution. But it was Rousseau's model that inaugurated an unprecedented spate of interpretations of human history.

The luxurious and refined state of Western society, to which Montesquieu and Voltaire had rendered homage, became for the Genevan philosopher an object of mistrust and revulsion. In his first Discourse on sciences and letters, even as he recognized that scientific, artistic, and literary production were tied to economic surplus and abundance, he issued a condemnation of luxury[43]— an unequivocal condemnation that was restated in the *Fragments for Emile*, where Rousseau blamed luxury for all of society's evils.[44] The ideal of republican virtue guaranteed an equality that was irrevocably shattered by an accumulation of wealth, a wealth that corrupted the country's morals and incited its neighbors' envy. This theme fit in with Rousseau's nostalgia for the rustic simplicity of the state of nature. The archetypal image of the virtuous woman—as the antithesis of the artificial creatures being produced by the eighteenth century, stirred his imagination:

> I must not forget that precious half of the Republic which makes the happiness of the other; and whose sweetness and prudence preserve its tranquillity and virtue. . . . Happy are we, so long as your chaste influence, solely exercised within the limits of conjugal union, is exerted only for the glory of the State and the happiness of the public. It was thus the female sex commanded at Sparta; and thus you deserve to command Geneva.[45]

Yet Rousseau seemed to favor the political participation of women at the highest levels. In certain fragmentary texts antedating the *Discourse on Inequality* we find a similar attitude. In the essay "On Women" he writes,

> Let us first consider women deprived of their liberty by man's tyranny, men who are masters of all things, for the crowns, the duties, offices, the command of armies, are all in their hands, they made all this their own from the very beginning by who knows what natural right which I never could understand and which might have no other foundation than their greater strength. . . . If women had as much to say as we in the management of affairs and governing of empires, they might have developed heroism and great courage to a higher extent, and might have distinguished themselves more than men.[46]

Was this perhaps a reflection of a preoccupation Rousseau shared with Madame Dupin when he served as her secretary? Mme. Dupin had indeed planned a monumental work on women in ancient and modern history, and to this end she had gathered many documents. Some of the notes drafted in Rousseau's hand, abundantly annotated by Mme. Dupin, have survived, although in too disconnected a form to give us an accurate sense of the work:

> What is beyond doubt is that women could not have found a more worthy interpreter of their rights, a more sympathetic advocate to plead their case. . . . Madame Dupin would have wished that women's education be less superficial, that their studies be more serious, and that men do justice to their talents, their minds, their reason, and even to their bravery.[47]

Let us now explore Rousseau's political essays to see whether the natural woman took on greater appeal to him as a result of the historical injustices noted above. We also propose to see to what extent his project was to compare "man's man with natural man"[48] and to replace history's disfigurations with his notion of things as they must have been in the beginning of human existence.

In the first section of the *Discourse on Inequality*, Rousseau wrote about the original stage of humanity. The man-woman distinction hardly appeared here, except when he mentioned the privileged relationship of the human mother with her nursling. This presocial state is characterized as one in which individuals live in isolation, making it difficult to establish common behavioral norms. Rousseau rejected Locke's claim that nature intended the stable union of man and woman.[49] According to Rousseau, in that early time there was no reason for the sexes to seek each other: solitude was everyone's lot in the state of nature. Sexual difference took on meaning only in a subsequent phase of human history. The complementary functions that irrevocably demarcated the sexes evolved as populations became sedentary and established settlements. The first grouping in families initiated the division of labor along gender lines.

> The sexes, whose manner of life had been hitherto the same, began now to adopt different ways of living. The women became more sedentary, and accustomed themselves to mind the hut and their children, while the men went abroad in search of their common subsistence.[50]

Rousseau saw the family as the original model of political societies.[51] The family's organization prefigured the republican pact, in the sense that children stood equal before the authority of the father, whose moderation differentiated him from the arbitrary power that would characterize absolutism. Rousseau wished to distinguish his view of patriarchal power from a political tradition that had already been vigorously criticized by Locke in his *First Treatise on Civil Government*. Fathers exercised authority solely for the good of their children. What sovereign state could say the same about its rule over its subjects? The father's power, which Rousseau sanctified as benevolent and moderate, is nonetheless indivisible. Because of biological indispositions that regularly kept her from active life, the mother was denied equal authority with the father over their children.[52]

Rousseau's effort to dispute the idea that absolutism was the most natural organizing principle led him to regard the family as a unique and powerful counterexample. His argument on this point, it must be noted, differed from that of Pufendorf, who was more legalistic in his contractual definition of family relationships:

> When the further question is raised, as to which parent has the greater right over the offspring, the matter may be cleared up by drawing a distinction at the outset. For they either live within or without a state; and there is or there is not a pact between them. If the parents live without a state, in natural liberty, the offspring belongs to the mother, in case they joined themselves without any lasting pact. For in that state the father cannot be known but on the evidence of the mother.[53]

While the contract made between the father and mother determined jurisdiction over the child, Pufendorf held that in societies formed by men, the husband was normally the head of the family. The child would go to the mother only when no commitment had been made between the two persons beyond the act of copulation.

Championing the natural, Rousseau rejected this case. Pufendorf defined natural law on the basis of man's rationality;[54] this assumption yielded numerous prescriptions. Rousseau leaves behind Pufendorf's conception of natural law as depending upon reason. The dictates of natural law, for the author of the *Discourse on Inequality*, are based on "principles prior to reason": self-preservation and compassion become "the modernized form of natural law."[55] These two instincts which he attributes to humans in the natural state, forge a kind of immediate contact among individuals, a direct means of understanding. The body—"the only instrument the savage man knows"—lies at the center of Rousseau's representation of the evolution of the human race. How, then, does political society affect the body's expressive capacity? Does culture merely provide additional marks of sexual difference above and beyond the anatomical?

In the *Letter to d'Alembert*, in order to combat the perverse pleasures of the theater, which are incompatible with the sensibilities of a "citizen of Geneva," Rousseau gave a contemporary cast to man's original simplicity: he claimed that the integrity of the husband-wife relationship must be guaranteed by feminine modesty. Women's modesty signified their withdrawn domestic life; far from being a stiff expression of propriety, or a prejudice, it instead symbolized the voice of nature, scorned as this might be by Parisian society.

> If I add that there are no good morals for women outside of a withdrawn and domestic life; if I say that the peaceful care of the family and the home are their lot, that the dignity of their sex consists in modesty, . . . I will be immediately

attacked by this ephemeral philosophy which is born and dies in the corner of a big city and wishes to smother the cry of nature.[56]

So the condition of an entire society must be judged on the basis of women's morals. In arguing that natural modesty makes women suitable for domestic happiness, Rousseau paradoxically cited the dance of the Lacedaemonian girls at public festivals. To the pleasure of the darkened theater, he opposed this nude dancing which owed nothing to darkness or secrecy. By removing the body from the adornment and affectation that disfigured it,[57] he restored it to its original naturalness, while at the same time demanding flawless morality and strength of spirit from his compatriots: "But can it be thought that the artful dress of our women is fundamentally less dangerous than an absolute nudity the habit of which would soon turn the first effects into indifference and perhaps distaste?"[58]

Let us return to the development of humanity as Rousseau depicted it in the *Discourse on Inequality*. In the earliest times, individuals were dispersed throughout the forest, naked and equal. When the first groupings were formed, collective diversions came and ruptured this initial equality;[59] the desire to be seen and noticed introduced an element of social differentiation. Similarly, in the *Letter to d'Alembert*, it was the gaze that divided humanity into men and women, spectators and spectacle. For Rousseau, then, did sexual difference go hand in hand with inequality?

His "unveiling" of the female body is tied to his rejection of the artifices of civilization. While restoring to women their innocence, Rousseau emphasized their vulnerability; women are at the mercy of the citizens' good conduct. The attention he devoted to whatever turned appearance away from nature was fueled by a religious tradition that had long condemned costume and ostentation. Protestantism, however, brought forth a need to soften the contradiction between, on the one hand, a liberal theory of individuals which paid no attention to organized groups, and, on the other hand, the functional complementarity of men and women in marriage. Must we then read the *Letter to d'Alembert* as an echo of Calvin's sermon on women's modesty?[60] Calvin was similarly concerned to reconcile the equality of men and women before God with the temporal submission of women to men (in the form of the imposition of costume). But Rousseau's writing diverges from early Protestantism in an important way. In his meditation on adornment, he displaced the origin of evil onto civilization and history. Evil is external to God and to natural man;[61] while the inspiration for Calvin's sermon was the role of Eve's seduction in original sin. Even so, for both Rousseau and Calvin, the taste for vanity and ostentation that prevailed in relations between the sexes does battle with the order of Nature.[62] How can men and women in society be freed from this historical contamination and rediscover the natural order?

Rousseau's answer: through good education. Accordingly, advancing sound educational principles for both sexes was a major concern for him. He felt that boys would become stronger as a result of a pedagogical strategy of isolation;

the idea was to preserve the boy from any contact with the community.[63] But though the natural man is defined as a savage in the *Discourse on Inequality*, Emile is going to have to live in the world of society and lead an urban life. In order to do so he has to develop good judgment.[64] Puberty marks the end of the one-on-one relationship between the pupil and his mentor; desire for the other sex introduces a third player in the game. At that point the adolescent must encounter the world of society and learn its ways in order to regulate his own conduct. Here the "Creed of the Savoyard Vicar" figures into the adolescent Emile's moral and religious training. For Rousseau the major factor in raising man to this superior natural state is moral *conscience*, "making man like to God! . . . apart from thee, I find nothing in myself to raise me above the beasts—nothing but the sad privilege of wandering from one error to another, by the help of an unbridled understanding and a reason which knows no principle."[65] Rousseau replaces universal reason and intellect with a universal instinct that draws men together instead of separating them, an instinct whose rational style is quite striking. Seen in this light, man's humanity results from an apprenticeship. Since the natural state is considered innate, it has intervened at key stages in the evolution of the race in the form of an affirmation of faithfulness to self, which for Rousseau characterizes man's liberty.[66]

To invoke an "indestructible" original principle of equality underlying these changes in humankind, in order to discard contemporary values and discern what is permanent: such is the meaning of modern natural right. The search for a natural measure of man would guarantee the individual's independence. We may well ask whether Rousseau glimpsed any similar principles of such individual development for women; the answer lies in book 5 of *Emile*, which concerns Emile's female counterpart Sophie.

Although Rousseau made equality the cornerstone of his political thought, this right did not seem to apply to women. "Vague assertions as to the equality of the sexes and the similarity of their duties are only empty words."[67]

Despite many similarities between the sexes, there are ontological differences which called for an entirely separate pedagogical system for women. What was good for Emile was not for Sophie. Emile's mentor protected his charge in a manner conducive to spontaneity in his development. Sophie's treatment was quite different: she benefited from the oft-mentioned presence of her parents, who were, after all, very wise; she profited from family life. There Sophie learned the rules of proper conduct which were the main focus of her education. Feminine wisdom and the social customs of the day were transmitted from mother to daughter, and in this way Sophie's education acquired its cultural dimension. For example, in her conquest of Emile, Sophie found in her mother a guide for every moment.[68] What was this law of right conduct for Sophie which would make her into the ideal companion for Emile?

"I maintain that coquetry, kept within bounds, becomes modest and true, and out of it springs a law of right conduct."[69] Rousseau could not find praise enough for Sophie's naive artfulness in utilizing her charms to capture the heart of her lover. Taking up the topic of women's adornment again, but in a milder tone than in the *Letter to d'Alembert*, he found a middle ground in the practices of feminine seduction.[70] The essence of femininity lay in a balance between the woman's own self-esteem and her desire to attract a man's attention. This conception of right conduct, raised to the status of a law, ties in with the principle of political equality. It is as if Rousseau's universe permeated his characters, from whom all excess was excluded, and who were pacified by the didactic narrative. A balance between seduction and modesty characterized Sophie's education, whose single goal was marriage. The father's discourse on marriage, like the brilliantly wrought "Creed of the Savoyard Vicar" earlier in *Emile*, is written as an intervention by a character in direct discourse. The father's conception of marriage is inscribed within Rousseau's ongoing eulogy of the natural order, and leaves his daughter free to choose her own husband. "I propose an accord between us which shows our esteem for you, and restores the order of nature between us. Parents choose a husband for their daughter and she is only consulted as a matter of form; that is the custom. We shall do just the opposite."[71]

For the woman, natural law means (solely) the freedom to choose a marriage partner, a crucial condition for happiness. But here Rousseau does not go beyond a moral critique of forced marriages, already voiced many times over. The freedom in marriage agreed upon between father and daughter is quite illusory. Apart from her liberty to choose, the conjugal state consists in the woman's total dependency on her husband. In affirming this submission, Rousseau's tone is declamatory: "When Emile became your husband, he became your head, it is yours to obey; this is the will of nature."[72] Inevitable fate of the female sex, chained to a division of the world to which she has not agreed! "The woman . . . must limit herself to the administration of the household, not meddle with what is outside, remain shut inside the house, and, mistress of everything around her, always obey the absolute law of her husband."[73] The exclusive realm for her talents, the circle of domestic activities, must not provide any pretext for altering this hierarchy. Human endeavors are classified in two spheres, according to whether they are associated with the public space of social and political life or the private space of the home. This is an airtight classification, forbidding any transfer of role or status.

Under this symmetrical system, the birth of illegitimate children means catastrophe. It unavoidably entails the destruction of the family unit, since it testifies to the existence of equal moral freedom and freedom of action for husband and wife.[74] The husband has to keep his wife's fertility under constant surveillance, and her moral behavior must be reined in from an early age. Confining wives physically to the home has proven to be an ineffective measure in the combat against women's infidelity. A better strategy is psychological. Pierre Burgelin, in an article on the education of Sophie, has remarked: "*Télémaque* is the only book Sophie read, by chance, just as *Robinson Crusoe* was for a long time Emile's only book. . . . Consequently Emile identifies with a solitary hero capable of adapting to anything, and Sophie identifies with a nymph in love."[75] This is a fitting illustration of women's ontological dependency. By virtue of her imagination, Sophie thereby becomes accustomed to meeting her husband's needs. But the husband can also transform himself into a pedagogue, drawing from the authority of knowledge a new justification for controlling his wife. We shall not dwell further on the pedagogical techniques that Rousseau perfected to assign women to the status of satellites orbiting around men. In all events, a space of liberty, the precondition for any political equality, was denied them.

Affirming the existence of rights anterior to society—the natural state—was a way for Rousseau to show continuity between private individual and citizen. Each would find his place in civil society by means of cultivating moral instincts. For women, this moral development consisted of little more than learning to adapt to the ordinary demands of life in society. The law of proper conduct dictating their behavior was a virtual parody of moral laws; at best, it reflects Rousseau's own pleasurable fantasies about women. How could his political liberalism accommodate such discrepancies between the destinies of men and women?

Rousseau conceived of the formation of societies as a gathering of individuals. By means of the social contract, each man became an equal party to the general will, thereby preserving his individual liberty. But conversely, on the question of the political and social place allotted to women, there surfaces a logic of constraint that focuses on a representation of the female body's organic functioning. Rousseau the moralist fades before Rousseau the physiologist. While his work sometimes asserts a causal connection between women's physiological particularities and their necessary political and social subordination, he passes his ultimate judgment on women by moralizing about their carnal specificity. This moralizing, in the section of *Emile* concerning Sophie's education, results from considering all the dangers that female sexuality could bring about, and which must be fended off by severely restricting women's actions. Rousseau takes exception to the idea of continuity between the animals and man. ("No purely material creature is in itself an agent, and I am.")[76] His Savoyard vicar rejects the idea that humanity is subject to materialistic determinism; he challenges the anthropological hypotheses of Buffon's natural history.[77] Man is typified by free agency. For Rousseau the woman's sexual vulnerability and fertility oblige her, in the public interest, to behave with strict modesty and reserve, because an illegitimate child resulting from an indiscretion would endanger both the familial and political orders. Although she *chooses* this restraint, her choice tragically quells any personal aspirations for freedom.[78] Rousseau's recasting of the damaging effects of sexual attraction allows him to validate the secular domination of men over women. The protection of the family, in its role as the natural unit of society, imposes duties on women; but they are not accorded rights in proportion to their duties. Rousseau's political thought reveals his inability to imagine women participating in civil and political life. In his writings on practical legislation—"Constitution for Corsica," "On the Government of Poland"—he assigns no political status whatsoever to the female population.

III.

The marquis de Condorcet, employing a deductive form of reasoning dear to the Cartesians, criticized the antinomy created in Rousseau's philosophical and political thinking by the latter's patriarchal conception of natural right, and undoubtedly aggravated by his obsession with the workings of passion.

"I must take exception with you on this," wrote Condorcet in the second "Lettre d'un bourgeois de New-heaven à un citoyen de Virginie" (1787):

> We want a Constitution whose principles are founded solely on the natural rights of man, anterior to social institutions. We call these rights natural because they derive from man's nature—that is, capable of reasoning and of acquiring moral ideas. An evident and necessary consequence is that he must enjoy these rights, and must not be deprived of them unjustly. . . . Is it not as sentient beings, capable of reason, that men have rights? Women therefore must have absolutely the same rights, and yet never, in any so-called free Constitution, have women exercised the rights of citizenship.[79]

Not content merely to point out how irrational it was to exclude women from urban life, he went on to condemn his compatriots' eagerness to contrive repressive laws: "So do you think it necessary specifically to forbid citizens by law from doing anything that would be a ridiculous choice or action, like choosing a blind man to serve as court secretary, or having one's field paved over[?]"[80] The inequality of women's intellectual abilities (if, indeed, such inequality existed) resulted from the education they were subjected to from the start: "I do not believe that one can find a a single difference between women and men that is not the result of education."[81] It had long been understood that girls' education was a mainspring of female subordination. Madame de Lambert, Fontenelle's companion, gained celebrity by denouncing the male tyranny which had robbed women of the use of their intelligence and had ridiculed those women who tried to overcome obstacles to their education. But the philosophical implications of natural right served to revive the debate. It was less a matter of proposing a scheme to remedy the traditional inadequacies of women's education than of evaluating the causes of female inequality, that is, of determining how much was attributable to nature and how much to civil society.

Choderlos de Laclos, on the occasion of a competition sponsored by the Academy of Chalons-sur-Marne in 1783, wrote an essay on "the best means to perfect women's education."[82] Here he rejected the strategy of merely adding positive content to female education. "There is no way to perfect the education of women" short of "a great revolution." Borrowing Rousseau's notion that the natural state was preferable to corrupted civilization, he compared "natural woman" to woman in civil society; then he proposed to explore in greater depth the idea of the free woman. Rousseau had deliberately forsaken such an exploration on behalf of Sophie's companion Emile, the natural man. Despite its brevity, Laclos's essay bears witness, on the eve of the Revolution, to a keen political awareness of an educational system that fostered inequality.

Condorcet's reflections on the feminine condition were tied to his stated desire to reorganize the kingdom by endowing it with a modern constitution. His essay on the constitution and the functions of provincial assemblies supported and extended Calonne's reform, which would have created provincial assemblies in all French provinces that lacked *parlements*, with the goal of rationalizing taxation. Influenced by physiocratic ideas, Condorcet considered the landowner to be the true citizen. "Inasmuch as a country is a territory circumscribed by boundaries, one must regard landowners as being the only true citizens."[83] In *La Vie de Turgot* Condorcet specified, according to categories used in natural right, what is meant by property:

> Property is nothing more than the free disposal of what one legitimately owns. In the state of nature, everything one possesses without having taken it from another forms this property; in the social state, it becomes that which one receives from one's family, that which one acquires by work, that which one obtains by agreement. Laws regulate the manner of exercising this right, but it is not due to laws that one holds it.[84]

According to this view, women landowners should not under any pretext be denied the vote for the provincial assemblies, which in Condorcet's scheme of a hierarchy of assemblies would assure a fair representation of property-owning citizens on the national level. Should we then see Condorcet as the spokesman for an ideology that would limit perspectives for a social revolution to the interests of notables?

Condorcet's adherence to Turgot's ideas about economic liberalism gives his politics a profoundly progressive thrust. The idea of property as the basis for suffrage seemingly assured a social fluidity that would precipitate the decline of a society organized according to orders, just as the removal of traditional hindrances to the market economy would assure an expansive economic vigor. The antagonism existing among the social classes would be resolved by improved living conditions and increased wealth. Despite the importance of equality for the revolutionary *philosophe*, unequal wealth did not contradict natural right in his view, since it is a "necessary consequence of the nature of man and things."[85] Differences in the social functions of individuals were seen as part of the natural order. Every individual accepted this distribution of wealth in order to preserve the general prosperity. In a 1793 article Condorcet developed the idea that "all classes of society share a single common interest." (This politically ecumenical economic liberalism would be dissipated in the nineteenth century by the structure of a strongly inegalitarian society.) At the same time his defense of liberalism suggested that too much equality could be harmful. "It is not a question of maintaining too great an inequality, it is only a matter of leaving everything up to the free will of individuals, to assist, with sensible institutions, the inclination of nature, which leans toward equality but which stops at the point where it would become harmful."[86]

In 1793, it was not untimely to distinguish between a *liberal* conception of economic and political society, concerned to preserve the liberty of all, and a democratic conception with a "totalitarian" tendency. Indeed, to return to our reflections on the female condition, let us focus on the subject of the indissolubility of marriage, and cite an example of such latent "totalitarianism" on the level of ideology. Condorcet was an advocate of divorce;[87] his wife Sophie de Grouchy de Condorcet, after translating Adam Smith's *Theory of Moral Sentiments* into French, put forth some daring arguments concerning trial marriages:

> Let us imagine that divorce is permitted among all nations; let us even imagine that in favor of human weakness and the more enduring needs of one sex, that it were possible, as in Rome, to form temporary unions which the law would not condemn, and whose conditions the law would determine; then, we see . . . that most of the unfair actions which love . . . can cause, would not longer have grounds for happening.[88]

This desire to free men and women from an institutional constraint which they no longer want would have completely mystified the future Convention delegate Saint-Just, if we take seriously a comment in his 1791 *Esprit de la Révolution et de la Constitution*: "What could they have been thinking of, those who wished to allow divorce in France, and under what kind of delusion were they laboring? No more was spoken of it . . . "[89] On the other hand, he revealed himself elsewhere to be an advocate of temporary marriage of a more authoritarian sort. For example: "Spouses who neither bear nor adopt children in the first seven years of their union must be separated by law and must leave one another."[90]

The opposition we have seen between the "liberal" and "statist" views of democracy would subsequently shape the history of France's institutions. But what is distinctive about Condorcet's liberal individualism is its conception of an equilibrium between justifying private ownership and the integrity of the human person, the mastery of one's faculties and one's work.

In his "Essai sur la Constitution et les fonctions des Assemblées provinciales" (1788), Condorcet took up the idea formulated earlier in his "Letters from a Bourgeois of New Haven" on women's right to citizenship. General custom excluded women from the conduct of public affairs, and natural right could not be called on for a precedent. But Condorcet maintained that because women were reasonable and sentient beings, they deserved, in spite of custom, to enjoy political status. While it seemed to go without saying that "monks, servants, and men condemned for crimes" were to be excluded, since they did not possess an autonomous will ("volonté propre"), this argument could not logically be extended to the entire female population. Didn't the provisional ruling on the elections to the provincial assemblies grant a proxy vote to women fiefholders?[91] Condorcet later came out against all electoral property qualifications, and called for universal suffrage.[92] During this prerevolutionary period, Condorcet's feminism was rooted in a philosophy of human understanding popular at the time; this led him, as it had Locke and Rousseau, to see education as a crucial and irreplaceable influence on the individual.[93]

His famous essay, "On the Admission of Women to the Rights of Citizenship," which appeared in July 1790 in the *Journal de la Société de 1789*, brought together his previous thought on women's political status. The very title emphasized his global approach; not content to acknowledge each right as a separate issue, he demanded women's right to participate in every aspect of society. In order to sway public opinion as effectively as possible, Condorcet broke from the perspective promoted by the eighteenth century's sensationalist theories, which forged an association between nature (in the restrictive physiological sense) and women's condition. Because of this particular linkage of woman to nature, physiology had become the elemental determinant of women's civil status.[94]

> It would be difficult to prove that women are incapable of exercising the rights of citizenship. Why should individuals exposed to pregnancies and other passing indispositions be unable to exercise rights which no one has ever dreamed of witholding from persons who have the gout all winter or catch cold quickly?[95]

Condorcet's argument was polemical in style. After ridiculing the arguments of those who wish to justify the continued subordination of women, he queried women's abilities, their supposed absence of genius, and the intellectual inferiority ascribed to them, to conclude that the unequal shares designated for the sexes only demonstrate "inferiority and superiority." By means of contrasting examples, he anticipates not only women's exercise of political rights, but also their access to the most honorable positions in public service. "Can it be supposed that Mistress Macaulay would not have expressed better opinions in the House of Commons than many representatives of the British nation?"[96] The incompetence of men bears witness all too often to the arbitrary nature of their privileges. But legislators should not be concerned with individuals' particular characteristics, nor even with establishing a hierarchy among various social groups. Condorcet wanted to reassure his readers regarding changes in morality ("It is unnecessary to believe that because women could become members of national assemblies, they would immediately abandon their children, their homes, and their needles.")[97] But he was uncompromising in his respect for the constitutional principle of equality, which demands the introduction of rationality into the organization of society: "Either no individual of the human species has any true rights, or all have the same. And he who votes against the rights of another, of whatever religion, color, or sex, has thereby abjured his own."[98]

Religious fanaticism and moral intolerance have transformed numerous law-makers into persecutors. The modern lawmaker had to draw the line between the realm of morality, that of personal liberty, and that of legality. For Condorcet, the evaluation of these distinctions took on the character of scientific exactitude.[99] In assessing the variety and complexity of human behaviors, he deemed it important to keep track of the frequency of their occurrence, the stability of certain phenomena, the fortuitous character of others. This mathematical reduction of the real determines when a law could and should intervene. In Condorcet's writing, every commentary on mores is accompanied by the scientific and moral scruple of making laws advisedly. We shall cite three examples, remarkable for the modernity of the point of view he defended, to illustrate his approach.

In Condorcet's *Vie de Voltaire*, rape is discussed in an appended note:

> Rape is a real crime, even when considered independently of all the ideas of honor and virtue that have been attached to chastity. It is a violation of the ownership each has of himself; it is an outrage done to weakness by strength. It must be punished like other assaults to personal safety, murder aside. To prove that a rape has been committed is not impossible; there may be such proofs as leave no doubt, and on the basis of these proofs the criminal may be condemned.[100]

Thus, by virtue of the individual's natural rights, rape is recognized as a crime and not as an unavoidable fact of social life.[101] It is necessary for a rational chain of proof to be established in order to punish the criminal.

On the other hand, in Condorcet's view, sodomy is not to be condemned, since it belongs within the purview of each person's liberty.

> That which involves no violence cannot be subject to criminal laws. It does not violate the rights of anyone else. Its only effect on the social order is an indirect influence, like that of drunkenness or gambling. It is a vile and disgusting vice whose true punishment is contempt; punishment by fire is an atrocity.[102]

Antoine de Caritat, marquis de Condorcet, descended from an old French family of the Midi, a family which in the sixteenth century had embraced Calvinism,[103] and which in the seventeenth century, whether by will or by force, abandoned Protestantism and reconverted to Catholicism. Sensitized perhaps by his family's past, and following in the wake of Voltaire's calls for religious tolerance, Condorcet took up the cause of the Protestants. He expressed violent indignation at the religious persecutions during Louis XIV's reign. These persecutions dishonored not only the condemned Protestants, but also reflected back on those responsible for such degradation of the human spirit. With a wholly contemporary perspicacity, Condorcet pointed out that cruelty toward women could be explained in terms of the perverse gratification it provided.

At Uzès, eight girls between sixteen and twenty-three years of age were bared
up to the back and whipped, in the presence of the town judge and the major
of the regiment of Vironne, by nuns who performed the torturers' duties with
most revealing zeal. The idea of half-naked girls being whipped by nuns before
men must have disconcerted the prudery of Madame de Maintenon, but even
Aubigné's granddaughter did not dare to plead on behalf of the Protestants; she
feared compromising her influence vis-à-vis that of the Jesuits, who shared with
her the honor of inspiring Louis XIV with bad laws and ridiculous decisions.[104]

This work on "the state of the Protestants" sheds light on the nature of
Condorcet's intellectual, moral, and political commitment. The Protestants
were as victimized by Catholic barbarism through physical cruelty as they were
in their social and professional lives through forced exile. And on the horizon
of his analysis of the condition of French Protestants, Condorcet saw America,
land of tolerance and political liberty! On a topic no less inflammatory than
religion, this man of science dared imagine new relations between the state,
society, and individuals. He emphasized the distinction between administrative
authority delegated to the state and public religious worship which would subject individuals to a religion they might not subscribe to. The collective practice
of religion should rely solely on the association of individuals who meet of their
own free will for this purpose. The state, for its part, should assure the peace
and safety of the other citizens by vigilance identical to that which it exercised
in other areas.

Condorcet's last work was the *Sketch for a Historical Picture of the Progress of
the Human Mind* [*Esquisse d'un tableau historique des progrès de l'esprit humain*].
Though written in hiding during the Terror, just a few months before his arrest
and execution, the *Sketch* lets nothing of his precarious situation show through.
It again clearly shows his desire to give scientific validity to laws. Condorcet
dreamed of an application of mathematics to social facts, seeing this as essential
to human progress. "Have we reached the point when we can reckon as the
only foundation of law either justice or a proved and acknowledged utility
instead of the vague, uncertain, arbitrary views of alleged political expe-
diency?"[105] But hackneyed terms might fail to evoke the originality of this approach to law for the modern reader, and so we prefer for the moment to leave
aside his final, fearless work written in a supreme and implacable effort to believe
in humanity. Let us rather look at Condorcet's evolving palette of writing which
elaborated on its subject via successive brushstrokes.

The *philosophe* Destutt de Tracy appended to his commentary on Montesquieu's *Spirit of the Laws*[106] some notes by Condorcet about the twenty-ninth
book of that work, entitled "On the Manner of Drafting Laws." The severe
criticism Condorcet leveled at Montesquieu's text gives us an idea of the distance
separating their respective interpretations of political freedom and the role of
lawmakers.

For Montesquieu, the legislative body must always act moderately, because
in a monarchy, individual freedom is safeguarded by the balance among the

government's different branches. Imperfections in laws often escaped lawmakers. In order to refine the legal system, according to Montesquieu, one had to proceed by keeping in mind the diversity of national temperaments and histories, among other factors. Nothing could be further from Condorcet's rationalist and utilitarian perspective than this comparative methodology. For this revolutionary *philosophe*, there is only one criterion for examining the relevance of old laws and appraising the efficacy of new laws. *Simplicity* is what he "scientifically" chose to guarantee justice and happiness to all citizens. Montesquieu's "historicism" became synonymous with resignation to injustice. With an ardor that could scarcely be contained, Condorcet wrote, "It is not in a spirit of moderation but in a spirit of justice that criminal laws must be gentle;"[107] even as he professed unqualified admiration for the author of *The Spirit of the Laws*.

In this regard, the conception of history that Condorcet developed in his *Sketch for a Historical Picture* approaches the anthropology Rousseau espoused as he was looking for a remedy to the imperfections of modern civilization and sought out the presocial original man. Condorcet's resolute modernity, however, transformed the meaning of this journey back in time; for him the point was to show that the evidence of human perfectibility could be found everywhere. By generalizing the individual's intellectual and moral abilities to the scale of universal history, Condorcet showed his unswerving confidence in scientific progress. These two registers of human thought and action were profoundly intertwined. His political individualism reflected his adherence to the scientific clarification of the universe; his commentary on the monadism of Leibniz—"He cut the knot which the most skillful analysis would never have been able to untie and constructed the universe from simple, indestructible entities equal by their very nature"[108]—could apply equally to his own vision of the body politic. Alongside the traditional themes of natural right, that is, the freedom and safety of the individual and his property, Condorcet added "the right to equality." "Only the last of these rights needs to be explained. The equality which natural rights require among men excludes any inequality which is not a necessary consequence of the nature of man and things and which would consequently be the arbitrary product of social institutions."[109] Political equality was based on the natural framework of the universe. Inequality in constitutional rights thus amounted to an alteration of the principles of nature.

In view of the coherence of Condorcet's philosophical system, we may well question the ultimate eclipsing of women's citizenship in his 1793 Constitutional Plan. To what extent Condorcet agreed with this attack on the constitutionality of his political principles is in doubt, considering that he still affirmed in the *Sketch for a Historical Picture* that "among the most important causes of the progress of the human mind that are of the utmost importance to the general happiness, we must number the complete annihilation of the prejudices that have brought about an inequality of rights between the sexes, an inequality fatal even to those whom it elevates."[110]

Franck Alengry, author of a vast study on Condorcet and the Revolution, has noted this inconsistency, attributing it to the influence of "ambient prejudices." "It is probable that he thought . . . in the presence of the working-class women who loudly acclaimed Marat in the galleries of the Convention that the general state of morals did not yet allow for women's regular participation in the exercise of national sovereignty."[111] In Condorcet's draft of the "Declaration of the Rights of Man" (1789), the equality of the sexes in matters of civil rights was clearly asserted; as for political rights, he unreservedly advocated universal suffrage:

> All citizens, without distinction, will have an equal part in rights of citizenship, that is, in the election of representatives or generally all those to be elected by the citizenry; also, in the decisions on matters concerning which all citizens must judge, with no inequality other than that which results from the necessity of establishing divisions and their subdivisions.[112]

Even if women's political rights are not explicitly mentioned, it is difficult to believe—without attributing to Condorcet an inconsistency that is not at all characteristic of him[113]—that he could have intended to deprive women of their political capacity without a word of explanation. On the other hand, in his Constitutional Plan presented to the National Convention on 15 and 16 February 1793, no mention is made of women's citizenship. At the time of the discussion, Lanjuinais, spokesman for the Commission of Six which succeeded to the committee appointed by the Convention, commented on Condorcet's silence regarding Title II of his draft, "De l'état des citoyens et des conditions nécessaires pour en exercer les droits" [On the status of citizens and the necessary conditions for exercise of their rights]: in principle he accepted the admission of women to the rights of citizenship, but not right away: "Defects in our educational system necessitate this delay, at least for a few years."[114] Lanjuinais's remarks were perceived as evasive. The convention delegate from the Côtes-du-Nord, Pierre Guyomar, protested against this postponement of political rights for women, and voiced his disagreement in a document entitled "Le Partisan de l'égalité politique entre les individus, ou problème très important de l'égalité en droits et de l'inégalité en fait" [The advocate of political equality among individuals; or, The very important problem of equality in rights and inequality in practice].[115] In this pamphlet, Guyomar turned to the notion of the "individual" in order to remove the ambiguity of the word "man" as a blanket term for all human beings. Examining the nature of the difference between the sexes which sometimes justified unequal treatment, he exhorted the Assembly: "Choose between them[116] in good faith; the difference between the sexes is a better founded distinction than the color of negroes as a prerequisite for slavery."[117] Even so, Pierre Guyomar was interested in admitting women only to primary assemblies, once a better education had taught them to think for themselves.

Despite this ultimate failing which could be attributed to a general lassitude in Condorcet, his desire to emancipate women from the burden of their legal incapacities remained exemplary for the period. It was quite isolated as well, until his political brief was joined by the demands of women themselves during the Revolution. We must note that revolutionary women took up the issue of women's political rights only after the publication of Condorcet's 1790 article "On the Admission of Women to the Rights of Citizenship."

IV.

Each in its own way, the works of the philosophers Montesquieu, Rousseau, and Condorcet shaped the conditions of the individual's civil and political enfranchisement. In this context the social and political emancipation of women was taken up by the three with varying intensity. More than any other question, women's equality was the focal point of projected values, both personal and collective, which considerably curbed the scope of its development. What were these limitations in each case?

Montesquieu's confidence in constitutional monarchy took back from the individual-subject some of the benefits of his initial recognition. An analysis of despotism as the degenerate form of one man's sovereignty remained the cornerstone of Montesquieu's thought. Himself a member of a nonegalitarian society, Montesquieu conceived political freedom as based on a governmental institution with balanced powers. He did not see republican equality as the system of the future for the leading nations. What stands out in his writing on women's condition are the passages where he denounces the despotic authoritarian relationship as an attack on the woman's dignity as a human being. Couldn't this oriental form of power extend to Western civilization? The notion of sexual equality was not clearly defined in his political doctrine, which was overshadowed by a patriarchal conception of family life.

As we know, Rousseau gave the fight for equality a central position. His rejection of parliamentarianism led him to consider the individual as the key element of political society. To the individual, then, Rousseau attributed rights and duties. But his conception of the individual's political existence did not extend to everyone. Despite some ambivalence on his part, women remained excluded. Influenced by his personal desire with respect to women, a desire strongly present in his writings, he held that all value systems differentiate between the sexes in apportioning rights and freedoms. What was good for men's realization was not good for women. Two universes were juxtaposed, and their coexistence conceptually prevented him from extending political equality to include gender equality. This structural feature of Rousseau's thought kept his political system, also, bound to a patriarchal ideal of the family, to a fragile conception of domestic happiness without which man could not lead a balanced life.

In extending the exercise of citizenship to women, Condorcet supplied a salutary corrective to Rousseau's politics. Equality, which for him was one of

the principal resources of the nation's life, should not contribute uniformity
of individuals' actions in society. His conception of the public good came close
to Rousseau's idea of the people's sovereignty. But his belief in the greatest
possible equity in individuals' share in the general good was not matched by
his idea of the legislator's work as striving to impose an ascetic ideal onto the
people. Indeed, with Rousseau, the conformity of nature to virtue had introduced a principle of transcendence (reflected in the Montagnarde Constitution
of 24 June 1793, which proclaimed the existence of the supreme Being). Condorcet's vigilance over the legislature's interference with personal morality arose
from a conception of freedom which involved the "liberation of spontaneity"[118]
and respect for human initiative. This tolerance for individual differences, which
the state had to take care not to crush, allowed him to imagine the integration
of women into national political life.

V

WOMEN AND THE FRENCH REVOLUTION

Marie-Charlotte Pauline de Lézardière was the author of an untimely treatise, *Théorie des lois politiques de la monarchie française* [Theory of political laws under the French monarchy].[1] Untimely, in that her attempt to revive the founding laws of monarchy, those which delimited the king's and his subjects' respective rights, appeared at a moment when revolutionary events had rendered obsolete any such philosophical rehabilitation. Her project was informed by the same impulse that lay behind Chancellor Maupéou's struggle to disentangle Louis XVI from the *parlements*.[2] Discredited by two centuries of arbitrary governing, the monarchy needed to return to the liberal foundations of its original pact with the French nation.

Lézardière was doubly hurt by the Revolution: as an author, she saw the first two parts of her work nearly wiped out when her publisher's premises were ransacked, leaving available only a very small number of intact copies; and as a member of the nobility from Vendée, she was forced to emigrate after her family was decimated by the Terror. Although she continued her work after returning in 1801,[3] her political theories fell on deaf ears in France under the Premier Consul. Her *Théorie des lois politiques* was republished in 1844, nine years after the author's death, under the auspices of Guizot and Villemain (who were ministers of foreign affairs and public education, respectively). This new edition included a third section by Lézardière that had not been included with the original two parts. A fourth section, covering the period from Philippe le Bel to "modern times" and reputed to contain the author's strongest political assertions, was completely lost.

Elie Carcassonne's book, *Montesquieu et le problème de la Constitution française au XVIIIe siècle* [Montesquieu and the problem of the French constitution in the eighteenth century], traces the evolution of aristocratic conceptions of history up to the Revolution.[4] As an heir to Enlightenment philosophy, Lézardière figures prominently in Carcassonne's study of subsequent political developments of Montesquieu's thought. In addition to Carcassonne's work, unpublished writings discovered in the National Archives permit us to reconstruct the contemporary arguments that informed Lézardière's thought. Biographers of Lézardière[5] have openly reminded us that her historical work was made possible only through the good graces of Malesherbes, who was also the protector of the editors of the *Encyclopédie*, a defender of freedom of the press, and an advocate of civil rights for Protestants. This privileged sponsorship gave our author access to books in the king's library. Malesherbes's protection acquires its full significance when considered in light of his actions as president of the *Cour des Aides*, favoring those institutions that limited the king's absolute power: the *parlements*, the various justice courts, the Estates General.[6] But what relation does Lézardière's work have to this political crisis—beginning with the dissolution of the *parlements* and continuing to the brink of the meeting of the Estates General—which shook the country's institutions to their foundations?

In her *Théorie des lois politiques*, Lézardière appropriated an idea expressed many times in Montesquieu's *Spirit of the Laws* concerning the freedom of northern or Germanic peoples: modern monarchies were deemed free to the degree that they embodied the spirit of their Germanic forerunners. The laws and institutions imposed by the Roman Empire on its provinces perverted the ties between princes and people, to the latter's detriment. Thus, according to Montesquieu, the Roman Empire reproduced the extortions and abuses of power characteristic of Oriental despotism. On the other hand, Mlle. de Lézardière continues, Germanic traditions of independence (such as the one calling for all free men to meet each month and discuss public affairs)[7] prefigured for Lézardière the contemporary aspirations of a "National Assembly." This idealized portrayal of popular monarchy, concerned with the widest possible participation in public life, showed precious little concern for the absence of women. Women's participation in politics might have been inconceivable under Charlemagne; but was it so inconceivable for this young woman who defied the conventions and prejudices of the second half of the eighteenth century in order to dedicate herself to the study of political science?

Among the praiseworthy qualities of the Germanic people mentioned in *Théorie des lois politiques* is their respect for marriage and monogamy. In the whole of Lézardière's work, however, we find only vague indications of the author's opinions concerning women's political role. She scarcely mentions the Salic law, the Germanic civil law which was subsequently adopted as a founding law of the French monarchy, justifying the exclusion of women from succession to the throne. In a work that did not see publication during her lifetime, *Tableau des droits réels et respectifs du monarque et des sujets depuis le fondement de la Monarchie française jusqu'à nos jours*,[8] Lézardière severely criticizes Queen Brunehaut's crimes, as if women's access to political power could only lead to catastrophe, and as if there were a basic incompatibility between the dominant traits of womanhood and the demands of governing. She writes: "This ambitious and miserly woman wanted to appropriate fiscal revenues only to squander them according to her whims. . . . The nobility was indignant to see its most important possessions, its dignity, its very state become the toy of a capricious woman tarnished by so many crimes."[9] Thus, Lézardière's assessment

differed from Montesquieu's, which was considerably less severe toward the
Queen's crimes:

> It seems extraordinary at first that this queen, who was daughter, sister, and
> mother to so many kings, a queen to this very day celebrated for achievements
> worthy of a Roman Aedile or Proconsul . . . endowed with qualities so long
> respected, should suddenly see herself exposed to so slow, so ignominious and
> cruel a torture.[10]

Lézardière's insensitivity to the biases against women inherent in the country's founding laws and public offices, as well as her willingness to adopt theoretical positions that were disadvantageous to women, have symbolic import.
They reveal the difficulty she had with having to belong to an excluded group.
Her protoromantic ideal, combining a desire for equality with a love for warlike
freedom, could not accommodate itself to such objectification of her own destiny in such a limited manner. At the risk of being reminded of her own modest
duties, she preferred to take responsibility for the misogynist prejudices of the
French parliamentary tradition. Remember that the Edict of 28 June 1593, condemning "government by women," had become a fundamental law of the land.
It remained no less true, however, that it was to a woman that we owe one of
the most systematic expositions of liberal monarchy ever composed during these
years which were so critical for the country's political institutions. What was
this doctrine of monarchical liberalism?

Taking up Montesquieu's emphasis on the importance of intermediary bodies
in monarchical government, Lézardière defined the functions of the *parlements*
thus:

> The French Constitution, which consecrated both the prerogatives of the throne
> and the rights of the people by a single principle, placed an intermediary body
> between the throne and the people, in order to protect the throne's prerogatives
> against attacks by its subjects, and to guarantee the subjects' rights against the
> throne's onslaughts.[11]

In its relation to these two basic entities of the French nation, the *parlements*
were heir to the royal court. Their function was to work with the king to
implement edicts regarding justice and police, endowing these regulations with
legal authority simply by recording them. Despite this power, they could not
presume to change the kingdom's fundamental laws, nor to nullify decisions
made by the Estates General. In fact, through various means (depending on
the period), the nation expressed inalienable rights through such bodies as the
"placités généraux" [public trial courts], the seigneurial assemblies, and the
Estates General. The history of these political bodies not only asserted the
precedence of the nobility's power over the king's, but also expressed all free

men's respect for civil and penal laws guaranteeing "property, security, and the liberty of its citizens."[12]

This evocation of the "rights of man" by an ardent monarchist may come somewhat as a surprise; but Lézardière employed just such democratic terms to describe the legislative power of these assemblies. In the "Remonstrances de la Cour des Aydes," addressed to the king on 18 February 1771, a similar argument was used to declare the unconstitutionality of the Edict of December 1770, which had declared the dissolution of the *parlements* and courts of justice: "There exist in France, as in all monarchies, inviolable rights that belong to the nation. We will not have the temerity to discuss exactly how far they extend, but simply put, they exist."[13] A common front against the king's arbitrary power was established between the aristocracy's interests and those of the magistracy. Thus the idea of a positive constitution had worked its way into this institutional crisis; and the conflicting efforts of the various bodies to protect their respective interests gave way to the idea of sovereign representation.

In her *Essay sur le rétablissement possible de quelques points essentiels de la constitution politique de la France* [Essay on the possible reestablishment of some essential points of the political constitution of France], Lézardière emphasized the need to form provincial "Estates" in the provinces where there were none, within each of which would be separate bodies.[14] Her insistence on including all social groups, even those in the lowest orders, arose from a desire to gain the greatest possible national representation. Her *Théories des lois politiques* reflects this desire. Lézardière advocated that both ordinary priests within the clergy and peasants from within the Third Estate be represented. The two orders of the clergy and the Third Estate had until then only admitted city dwellers to the existing provincial Estates. She wrote, "All citizens who constitute the people properly speaking, should equally enjoy the right to name representatives for the Third Estate."[15] This monarchical populism led Lézardière to prefer a single National Assembly on the model of the "placité général," giving greater representation to all the nation's social groups than had the Estates General of old France.

Thus, the political liberalism of Lézardière, like that of Montesquieu, was expressed through a constitutional conception of liberty which drew its legitimacy from national representation. The individual, as the political unit in the social contract between people and prince, seemed deprived of any positive aspects. While the political capacity of the free man was embodied, for Lézardière, in the citizen—whether in a monarchy or in a republic—the notion of the citizen remained nonetheless strictly subordinate to the "Bodies." Writing about the "rights of the social bodies of the people," her reorganization of the nation into Estates and their component social groups privileged communities over individuals. Thus the author's indifference to sexual discrimination, as reflected in this work's attempt to reconstruct the nation's history, may be more correctly seen as the consequence of a conceptual system that was ill-equipped to handle the idea of individual freedom.

Noblewomen possessing a fief and women belonging to ecclesiastical com-

munities were able to designate a *Procureur* (or delegate) in their respective
orders to represent them at the Estates General of 1789. This was decided in
"La Lettre du Roi pour la convocation des Etats Généraux, le 27 avril 1789."[16]
Such limited participation concretely illustrates the minimalization of women's
social and political roles at a time when representation of the orders themselves
was being challenged (particularly through the question of a twofold increase
in Third Estate representation).

The government's regulations concerning the representation of women rein-
stituted the traditions of earlier Estates Generals, according to which the nobility was personally convened by the *Bailli* at the General Assembly of the
Bailliage,[17] more because they were owners of fiefs than because of their noble
titles. Historian Jacques Cadart writes that according to this tradition, minors
and women were represented by delegates.[18] This electoral system stipulated
that elections in large cities be based on corporate or guild structures (according
to article twenty-six of the royal summons), a stipulation that would have
permitted women's guilds to be represented. But Paris, with its numerous wom-
en's guilds, was given a different electoral system because of the great density
of its population. The first stage of the elections allowed only a restricted con-
stituency: twenty districts for the nobility and sixty districts for the Third Estate.[19] The *cahiers de doléances* [grievance registers], written by the women's
communities, testify to their disappointment at being deprived of representation at the 1789 Estates General.

> The community [of women's guilds], out of respect for the king's orders, did
> not wish to complain against inviting representatives to the Estates General based
> on districts, even though according to regulations it was to be done by the guilds.
> But this large community, which annually pays a considerable sum to the king
> both in taxes and in governing privileges along with other powers, hopes to be
> represented.[20]

Providing the nation with financial sustenance made the women of these
guilds aware of their right to participate in the country's public life. Although
the women's grievance registers were most often used to defend a specific guild's
interests (e.g., calling for royal protection against unfair competition), the
women's guilds frequently reminded the king of their financial contributions
to the crown. Religious communities who also drafted such grievance registers
traditionally referred to local economic or financial preoccupations without
addressing national concerns.[21]

A bourgeois woman from the Caux region, reputedly the author of a "Cahier
de doléances et réclamations des femmes" [Register of women's grievances and
complaints], attempted to bring out the political and social implications of the
upheaval caused by the king's convocation of the Estates General: "It is in this
time of general revolution that a woman, stunned by the silence of her sex
when there is so much to say . . . dares raise her voice to defend the common
cause."[22] The notion that an instrument such as the grievance register, which

was supposed to voice the concerns of a regional assembly, could be used by an individual in this way, might understandably worry the authorities. Known only as Madame B . . . , the author strategically added a political argument to the traditional ones in support of women's virtues. She compared by turns the servitude of women with the slavery of Negroes, and the delegation of votes between sexes to the transmission of political power among the three established orders. Finally, she demanded that women from the Third Estate be represented at the Estates General, not only in the name of equality between the sexes, but also because they paid royal taxes.

Sending out a call to the "filles cauchoises" [girls of Caux], this woman indicated in her writing that she was well versed in the history of her region. She offered suggestions on a local level to reduce the national debt, even as she promoted Third Estate demands (such as expanding taxation to the two privileged orders to make it more equitable). By pointing out the irregular legal status of some church possessions, she indicated both to the king and to public opinion that there were properties which could be confiscated "in order to contribute to the common good."

Madame B . . . displayed a remarkable sense of determination in her register. In the manner of the Enlightenment philosophers, she denounced the abuses suffered by women of the Third Estate. Her own commitment was sustained by recognizing the potential of women as a politically unified body, a potential she invoked throughout her text. On the eve of the Estates General meeting, however, uniform representation by sex within an order as large as the Third Estate was infrequent, so much had the different living conditions of the various groups given them conflicting interests, thereby fragmenting them into many subgroups. Even so, other women from the Third Estate petitioned the king, asking him to redefine the division of social roles between the sexes; they also demanded protective laws for the so-called female occupations and free schools for all women.[23] The contradiction between a demand for greater parity in the social realm and a demand for special protection for occupations specific to their gender was resolved for these women by a self-imposed limitation of their activity in both domains. Was the demand for a competitive norm in educational and professional spheres due to a resigned but perceptive understanding of the possibilities for change in this area?[24] Or did it reveal the inherent difficulties that forms of political expression under monarchy have in imagining uniformity?

These writings also provoked a parodic literature, representative in its way of the fluid political atmosphere. The enterprising pamphleteers made use of the women's demands to direct their own attacks against the monarchy's administration, sometimes adding a liberal dose of humor. Under the pretext of commenting on women's role in public life, the pamphlet "Remontrances, plaintes et doléances des dames françaises à l'occasion de l'Assemblée des Etats Généraux" [Admonishments, complaints and grievances of French ladies at the Estates General assembly] denounced the harmful activities of favorites at the royal court. In the lush and openly anticlerical popular diction of "Le Cahier des dames de la halle" [The *cahier* of the market ladies], the authors lashed out against the abuses of the fiscal policy of the *ancien régime* directed by the *Ferme Générale*, as well as against the inhuman public health conditions at the Hôtel-Dieu.[25]

Women were not represented at the Estates General of 1789. On a local level, however, the newly installed electoral system required everyone to voice a position on the monarchy's arbitrating role between individual and collectivity. This national referendum contributed indirectly to the shaping of women's political consciousness, giving them a sense of group solidarity that distinguished them from the rest of humanity. In the years of political instability preceding the convocation of the Estates General, other commentaries in support of women had been published. Mademoiselle de Coicy, for example, in drawing up a list of the offices barred to women due to the simple fact that they belonged to a celebrated but powerless sex, marked the extent of women's social and political exclusion.[26] She duly noted that women's social treatment became increasingly unjust and unequal the higher one went in the social hierarchy. Madame Gacon-Dufour, a reader for Louis XVI, had the indisputable merit of showing her impatience with the silence imposed on women. However, the tone of her writing remained on the worldly level of personal quarrels. She writes: "How could the Chevalier de Feucher have the temerity to say we are to blame for moral corruption? It is inconceivable to me."[27]

Olympe de Gouges's "Lettre au peuple ou projet d'une caisse patriotique par une citoyenne" [Letter to the people, or plan for a patriotic fund by a woman citizen], intimated how national movement could affect the ripening of issues related to women's emancipation.[28] Gouges interpreted a minor altercation one evening—involving a crowd with firecrackers which forced a grocer to hand out torches—as heralding outright civil war; and in response she offered the nation her plan for national solidarity. According to this plan, the country's large budgetary deficit required the levying of a "patriotic tax" on all citizens regardless of order or privilege. Although not overlooked completely, the specifically female contribution to this project remained poorly defined. On closer inspection, however, we see that her argument was based on a relationship she posited between the naturalness and the feminine simplicity of the people: the people embodied the possibility of spontaneous collective action. Because prejudices prevented women from acquiring political acumen, Gouges mined her own femininity for the basis of a new legitimacy.

Did the transformation of the Estates General into the National Assembly, and then into a constitutional National Assembly, bring any changes to the political representation of a group so traditionally marginalized by national institutions? Documents on this question are few and far between. The patriotic gift, one of women's most constant contributions to the national cause, sometimes served as a basis for arguing in favor of changing their condition.[29] Since their merit no longer needed proving, why should they be excluded from the social and political renewal sweeping the country? A few motions and speeches continued to condemn royal despotism by denouncing an equally abusive domination—paternal and conjugal despotism, which could attack the personal liberty of women at any moment by having them locked up in convents.[30] Forcing women into religious vocations seems to have been one of the most hated practices of the *ancien régime*. For all their virulence, the authors of these condemnations were nevertheless reluctant to endorse women's participation in the country's institutional reorganization. Attempts to rally and unite this "peuple de femmes" showed how difficult it was for women to imagine group solidarity. Could the old communitary forms of guilds regroup a population whose sole social reference point was the family?[31]

Mademoiselle Jodin, the daughter of a Geneva clockmaker and collaborator with the *Encylopédistes*, gave greater concrete substance to women's demands for citizenship than any previous woman writer. According to the political model of popular sovereignty, but with respect to civil legislation aimed particularly at women,[32] Jodin proposed the creation of a special tribunal designated only for women and administered by them. To recognize the differences between the sexes was justified on a legislative and juridical level, according to Jodin, by the pressing need to put an end to public disorders due to corrupt morals, which police were wrongly blaming on women alone. Responsibility for these debauches—"one portion of our sex devoted to the excesses of yours"—was to become the object of a rigorous investigation in the name of the public good. Well read in Jean-Jacques Rousseau, Jodin believed that a healthy political body required a moral social body. But contrary to the Genevan *philosophe*, who thought women should be confined to a strictly domestic universe, Jodin endorsed women's participation in forming the new civil society.

Assembly president Linch asked Jodin to reorient her argument to treat only moral questions, commenting that "it would do justice to your writing if your proposal for a tribunal were to be introduced by a sort of moral code designed specifically for the more amiable half of humankind." Despite Linch's ambiguous reception, Jodin's effort to rehabilitate women at least anchored moral reform within the framework of national institutions. This conception of liberty, inherited from Montesquieu, abandoned philosophical speculations, and any other discussion for that matter, which was not grounded in these institutions. In Jodin's mind, "marital bliss" was tied to the idea of a law for divorce. Such was the meaning of her response to an administration which was more concerned to rid itself inconspicuously of an annoying demand to share power than to seriously consider her proposal.

Among the first efforts of the National Assembly was to propose, on 27 July and 28 August 1789, that the Salic law be renewed.[33] On 22 December 1789, it ratified a plan to organize judiciary power which also excluded women. Proposed by the Constitutional Committee, this project renewed the administrative definition of electoral and voter eligibility making up the base for national representation, and it did not give women any electoral role. Although this right had been accorded to women of the nobility who owned fiefs by the royal order of 24 January 1789, it was now suspended as an elitist privilege. The "Declaration of the Rights of Man and the Citizen," promulgated on 26 August

1789, consecrated this same exclusion by omitting any mention of the rights of women citizens. Given this background, and with an Assembly so little equipped to consider women's civil rights, the "legislative prospects for women" were not likely to get beyond a *petitio principi*. But out of the anonymous crowd of women participating in the revolutionary days of October, a few would emerge to become the revolutionary symbols of women's emancipation.[34]

Théroigne de Méricourt offers a celebrated example of this mythical crystallization process that transformed people into legendary heroines. Her adventurous life lent itself to this: a dubious past as a demimondaine, a brief political career (1789–92), and her insanity and consequent incarceration for long years until her death in May of 1817, add up to a complex and puzzling historical figure. If the reports in her autobiography can be trusted, Méricourt's real contribution to the revolutionary days of July and October 1789 amounted to little,[35] although the circumstances under which she wrote must be taken into account. Her abduction by French royalists on the Austrian emperor's payroll, along with the severe conditions of her incarceration, might have led the young woman to play down her role in the Revolution. Whatever the case may be, this woman from Luxembourg (mistakenly identified as a "belle Liègeoise") advocated a militaristic feminism. There were women soldiers in the Revolution,[36] and Méricourt was not alone in wanting to arm other women. On 6 March 1791, a delegation of women led by Pauline Léon requested authorization from the National Assembly to arm women. "Yes, Gentlemen, we need weapons; and we have come to ask your permission to acquire them."[37]

In Théroigne de Méricourt's extant speeches, this militaristic feminism was intimately bound up with the desire to integrate women into all levels of public affairs. Women's nonparticipation in the army was the most palpable manifestation of women's exclusion from public life. Méricourt deplored this exclusion, writing:

> women citizens, why not compete with men? Are they the only ones entitled to glory? No, no . . . and we, also, want to earn a civic crown, and we covet the honor of dying for a liberty that is perhaps more dear to us than to them, since the effects of despotism still weigh more heavily on our heads than on theirs.[38]

Méricourt's subsequent address to the forty-eight sections of Paris proposed the appointment of six women from each section as mediators to settle conflicts dividing the citizenry.[39] This Amazon warrior's ambition to give structure to women's presence in the sections demonstrated a certain constancy to her actions, if not an integrated strategy. Camille Desmoulin's undoubtedly embellished account of Méricourt's arrival at the Club of the Cordeliers[40] testifies to the latter's political and oratorical skills. Méricourt made the spectacular proposal—sure to catch her listeners' attention—that a "Temple of Liberty" be built where the Bastille once stood. Along with this project she requested admission to the district in an advisory capacity. Though her first motion was accepted with enthusiasm, her request for membership in the famous club was almost unanimously rejected. The club's assembly succinctly defined the permissible boundaries of women's political activity:

> Mademoiselle Théroigne, and all others of her sex, will always be free to propose what they believe to be to the country's advantage; but concerning the question of state, of whether to admit Miss Théroigne to the club with consultative powers only, the assembly is unable to take a position and there is no reason to discuss it.[41]

To borrow a phrase from Camille Desmoulin, "The Sabbath Queen could not get the better of the Solomon of the district." In other words, her oriental sumptuousness could not bend the deputies' inflexible misogyny.

Léopold Lacour's well-documented biographical study of three women of the French Revolution (Olympe de Gouges, Théroigne de Méricourt, and Claire Lacombe) makes the case for considering Méricourt's revolutionary activity as a "parliamentary commitment," rather than as street activism.[42] Her conscientious attendance at the National Assembly, though difficult to trace today, may provide a deeper understanding of her support for the Revolution. What were the philosophical grounds informing her actions? In a given situation, her sense of the just and the unjust is mediated by an appeal to reason. Did this reason represent anything else for Méricourt than a simple rhetorical effect reflecting the tastes of the day? Was it "reasonable" for women to defend their rights merely because it was legitimate to do so? This search for legitimacy, which Méricourt pursued until insanity overtook her, tended to confuse the personal expression of transcendental moral laws with legislative activity in the National Assembly. Such confusion was typical for her period, but it emerged in Méricourt's work as a bastardized version of a major Enlightenment theme: natural rights.

In a pamphlet dedicated to the queen,[43] Olympe de Gouges, that other Amazon of the Revolution, extended the Enlightenment social code of individual freedom to women.[44] Her "Déclaration des droits de la femme et de la citoyenne" [Declaration of the rights of woman and the woman citizen] is an exceptional document in the history of ideas.[45] However, it went practically unnoticed by the author's contemporaries. Patterned after the "Declaration of the Rights of Man and of the Citizen," this manifesto contained a short preamble, seventeen articles, and an afterword, containing a note that dates its composition to a few days before the king's acceptance of the 1791 Constitution. In a singularly aggressive tone, Gouges's foreword chastised the men of the Revolution for their effrontery in claiming equal rights for the male sex only, thereby setting man—and only man—apart from the animal and vegetable world. She used the notion of nature's harmony to announce and affirm women's natural rights, claiming that domination over women had broken the universal equilibrium. Gouges's indignation at male presumptuousness led her, despite the scope and difficulty of the task, to demand that reparations be made to the sex that was "superior both in beauty and in courage." Such was the scenario that this woman, whose pronounced taste for patriotic ceremonies never abated throughout her political career,[46] imagined as the opening of her manifesto!

In the main body of her text, Olympe de Gouges was content largely to recapitulate the "Declaration of the Rights of Man and of the Citizen." But the changes she brought to it, however slight, require a careful examination of each article in turn. The declaration's preamble inventories the categories of people concerned: "Mothers, daughters, sisters [and] representatives of the nation demand to be constituted into a national assembly." Thus it is by way of the matrilineal line (notice the absence of any mention of wives) that the author envisioned the national grouping of women. Uniting women was necessary in order to make the transition from a strictly domestic life to a public one. What would call someone to this public life?

Again in the preamble, Gouges replaced the original declaration's "the authoritative acts of the legislature and the authoritative acts of the executive" with the formula "the authoritative acts of women's power and the authoritative acts of men." But does this mean she was attributing legislative power to women and the executive to men, according to the principle of separation of powers?

Change laws in order to change life: did the call to redistribute power along gender lines indicate the state of mind of a group so long subjected to legal brutality that different living conditions were only imaginable through different laws? The executive function, incarnated in the person of the king, was only obscurely understood by the people. It carried on a masculine tradition uninterrupted by the Revolution. Was the author trying to clear up this obscurity by addressing herself to the queen? Olympe de Gouges's most noteworthy contribution, moreover, is found in her statement on the rights and obligations of the woman citizen: if she added "Justice" to "Liberty" in article IV, in order to delimit the individual's activities in relation to the community, in article VII she proceeded to revise the definition of law. By eliminating the protective and repressive aspects of law that particularly affected women, Gouges emphasized the positive consequences of the equality principle: women's access to public offices and responsibilities. In taking into account the eighteenth century's emphasis on public equality, this new access signaled a rehabilitation of women's dignity. Fear of being excluded from the whole of society, or even of being singled out for special treatment, may have led the author to occasional clumsiness of style, unintentionally reintroducing the idea of woman's exceptional status and sexual inequality. "No woman is immune," she affirmed in article VII, incisively expressing the necessity for women's total submission to the rigors of the law. But so deeply had she internalized discriminatory treatment that the phrasing of the following article could be interpreted as suggesting that the law be applied in a way that was particular to women—which surely goes against the general sense of Olympe de Gouges's ideas. Her belief in an ideal justice that always functioned perfectly led her to oversimplify at times, and she gave only short shrift to the principle of "in-

nocent until proven guilty." Nothing was more foreign to her than the deliberate and careful inquiry of the vigilant legal mind that must remain open to
all the possible meanings of a text. In article X, her legislative preoccupations
included a discourse on history: "Woman has the right to mount the scaffold;
she must equally have the right to mount the rostrum." This brilliant phrase,
reverberating through the centuries, instituted a feminine historical subject. In
bringing together two situations atypical for women (capital punishment and
public speaking), the author opened up the understanding of rights and obligations to a new field of interpretive possibilities. The logical consequence of
women's right to die for their country was the right to throw off the docile
silence imposed on them. The demand for this political voice was not long in
coming. On the question of freedom of expression, Olympe de Gouges used
direct discourse—a woman citizen's voice—to comment in article XI[47] on paternity suits, saying that in order to clarify social and family structures, it was
of the highest importance that women take this painful step and force the male
world to face up to its responsibilities. Whether her own illegitimate birth was
real or imagined, Gouges shared the preoccupations of a large number of
women. One of these women, Madame Grandval, wrote in a petition to the
National Assembly that according to natural law, illegitimate children have a
right to paternal inheritances. Gouges's impulse to clarify family and social
relations and her desire to foresee and prevent conflict led her in the postscript
to the declaration proposing a social contract between man and woman, in
order that nothing be left to chance between spouses, or between parents and
children. The claim to personhood for the female citizen represents a collective
realization by women of their power as a group subject. Olympe de Gouges
used the expression "the mass of women," indicating that the female citizen
was not merely the author's puppet.

The new era of rationalism had held out the potential for women to free
themselves from the persecutions they had suffered for centuries. The political
revolution that followed this would-be philosophical revolution extinguished
such hopes of freedom. "Oh, women, women! When will you cease to be blind?
What advantage have you received from the Revolution?" wrote Gouges in the
postscript of her manifesto, less than two years after the storming of the Bastille. But does this "tocsin of reason" sound like fanaticism, or rather does it
warn of other dangers? Though commonly described as a fiery, ostentatious
southerner with scant education, Gouges had to face the difficult task of re-
versing a principle against itself. The union of reason with liberty had only led
to renewed domination; a democratic government now sanctioned revolutionary men's brigandage of women's rights. Gouges called on women to unite
under the banner of Philosophy; but this "share" in "the treasures of the Supreme Being," which she depicted as the peaceful sign of man's rational recognition of woman, should not be taken at face value. She realized that reason
was a two-edged sword which, even as it may deliver us from the fear of un-
thinking nature, also permits the misuse of this nature against half of humanity;
and it is this realization that added a combative dimension to her words. Was

the utopia of reason defeated? The author's agile description of the "slave power" that certain women in the past had developed through scheming and calculating; her insistence on proving "the force of reason"; her implacable effort to vanquish the adversary in an almost seductive mode—all of these indicate that the real issues of this manifesto, despite the author's conciliatory protests, should be seen in a context of psychological warfare between men and women. Her serpentine ability to play now the role of conqueror, then the conquered, had a way of heightening the tension, even as she exposed the mechanisms of this power relation. But what concrete battles did Gouges have in mind? To upset the usual interplay of political factions, by persistently pro-claiming her positive and negative positions, and by proposing a referendum on the choice of government,[48] she openly proclaimed her likes and dislikes,[49] and disrupted the normal interplay of the political factions. The acts of this Amazon strategist were those of a solitary propagandist. Though Pierre Chau-mette, leader of the Hébertiste faction, wrongly credited her with founding women's clubs,[50] he (and others) recognized in her the charisma of a head of state[51]—and it is this charisma which would ultimately lead Gouges to the guillotine. "She tried to be a statesman and it appears that the law has punished this female conspirator for forgetting the virtues appropriate to her sex," wrote *Le Moniteur* in the guise of an epitaph, twenty days after her death. The political and philosophical notion of natural rights had evolved, in the course of revo-lutionary events, from the demand for civil equality for everyone, toward the predominance of a masculine norm. Olympe de Gouges's execution was an-other of the bloody episodes in the Revolution's usurpation of women's po-litical rights.

The writings of the Dutch propagandist Etta Palm d'Aelders drew on the same liberal conception of the Revolution which Gouges was able to formulate for women in the "Déclaration des droits de la femme." In her numerous speeches to the "Cercle des Amies de la Vérité" [Circle of the friends of truth], nation, law, and inalienable natural rights were the most common themes she invoked. But her borrowings from Enlightenment philosophers remained un-imaginative. The egalitarian individualism which subtended her constitutional feminism drew its models from Roman history (Cornelia and Clelia, among other classical figures), as well as from the history of the free Celtic and Scythian tribes. One can detect in the latter the faint echo of a national Gallic tradition, made up of a mixture of liberty and bellicosity. "The blood of the ancient and valorous barbarian tribes courses through my veins, and I am ready to spill it for the freedom and happiness of the French people,"[52] she wrote somewhat pompously in a letter to the municipality of Creil-sur-Oise, thanking it for hosting the Society of Amazon Citizens.[53]

The actual historical enactment of her feminine patriotism was never put into practice. Etta Palm's most concrete political contribution was her founding of the "Amies de la Vérité," a federative network of women's organizations, the central chapter of which invited all fraternal societies from the 83 depart-ments to begin a dialogue with them. She understood the need to give women all over the country a moral and patriotic education, with the aim of fostering the social cohesiveness so indispensable to the Revolution's success. Regenerating moral standards seemed the best way to guarantee national domestic peace. The women's organizations would lavish care and assistance on the poorest sectors of society, sectors which represented potential dangers to the new social order. "These circles of women could be charged with overseeing the establishment of wet-nurses . . . [and] public education. . . . These women's clubs could be charged in addition with investigating the conduct and the need of unfortunate people requesting aid from the Section."[54]

But Etta Palm's outline of possibilities for women's social influence ran up against a wall of general indifference. Her French organization stagnated when, after violent attacks provoked by her activities,[55] she left France around January of 1793.

The historian Albert Soboul has demonstrated the existence of a "sans-culottes feminism," paradoxical as this notion may seem.[56] Marie Cerati's monograph on the Club of Republican *Citoyennes* sought to demonstrate the consistency of this group's activities during the Revolution.[57] Above and beyond her strictly biographical research, the challenge she faced was to explain the interrelations of this organization with other popular movements, and with the struggles among factions in the Convention. Additionally she felt the need to investigate the nature of revolutionary masses, as well as popular movements in general! Marie Cerati's book assumed an opposition between a liberal feminism, supported by a few eccentrics, and a mass feminism, exemplified by the Club of Revolutionary Republican *Citoyennes*. This presupposition problematized her own historical approach, in that her detailed account of such important activists as Claire Lacombe and Pauline Léon gave us an analysis of the role of an elite group, not a more broadly based popular movement. The rank and file women of the Revolution still await their historian.[58] In the meantime, we must limit ourselves to a brief outline of the political concerns that this group, in the name of women, helped to define.

On 13 May 1793 *Le Moniteur* described the formation of the Republican *Citoyennes* in this way:

> Several women citizens presented themselves to the city offices and in accordance with municipal police law, they declared their intention to assemble and form a society to which only women would be admitted. This society's goal is to deliberate on the means to foil the projects of enemies of the Republic. It will be named the Republican Revolutionary Society and will meet at the Jacobins' Library on rue St. Honoré.[59]

Was the founding of this society part of a Jacobin strategy to discredit and ruin the Girondins? The Revolutionary Republican *Citoyennes* were not satisfied with sending peaceful petitions to obtain the prosecution of the Gironde leadership;[60] they organized a veritable campaign against all adversaries of the Montagnards.[61] For this reason, they whipped Théroigne de Méricourt in front of the Convention's vestibule and labeled her a "false patriot" on 15 May 1793,[62] despite the civic crown the Federates had bestowed on her just one year earlier.

Trouble arose when these women of the people opposed the provincial delegates' right to distribute entry passes to the Convention on the grounds that it was nonegalitarian. Was this disruption due to the mobilization of these women who, since February, had fought with increasing violence against the high cost of provisions and demanded that bread prices be controlled?[63] Or was it rather the result of Jacobin manipulations to take advantage of the popular movement in order to advance their own objectives? The Revolutionary Republican *Citoyennes*' activities raise the thorny question of the nature of the Jacobin alliance with the sans-culottes. In an excerpt from the minutes of "the General Assembly of the Commissioners of the constituted authorities of department and sections of Paris,"[64] the sans-culottes women were praised for their part in the May 31 and June 2 protests, organized by the Parisian sections, which were decisive in the Montagnard victory over the Girondins. Their contributions were thus noted: supporting the people's patriotism by organizing civic ceremonies to help solidify the masses, and overseeing the popular protests of women angry with monopolies (the laundresses and women fish vendors for the most part). These popular uprisings had been unanimously condemned by the Jacobin Club and by various factions of the Convention who held them to be aristocratic plots and counterrevolutionary intrigues.

The recognition of women's civic importance was not limited to praises of the Republican *Citoyennes*. The sans-culottes had admitted women into their grass-roots organizations;[65] and women were strongly encouraged to participate in the debates that were taking place in the primary assemblies of the sections before the voting on the Constitution. Women thus participated in the primary assemblies, and in votes by acclamation; but none took part in roll-call balloting.[66]

Because militants of the period were more inclined toward action and proclamations of principles than introspective reflection, texts revealing the ideological makeup of this group of women are rare. However, one influential member of this group, Pauline Léon, did write a short account of her participation in the Revolution while detained in the Luxembourg prison. In this account she justified her stand in the struggle against the Girondin faction, whose federalism threatened the Republic's integrity. She proclaimed her confidence that the Constitution of 1793 would be able to resolve the country's organizational problems—an attitude consonant with the democratic ideology of the sans-culottes. She wrote:

> It is within the popular-based societies, and under the gaze of a great mass of people, that I showed my love for my country, that I spread the principles of sweet equality, and that I supported the Republic's indivisible unity; it was there that I vowed to curse the villainous Roland, Brissot, and the whole federalist aftermath, where I finally took up the defense of all the persecuted patriots such as Robespierre and Marat. It was in the sections in the Faubourgs Saint Antoine

and Marceau, at the central club, and in the presence of deputies from all the sections and popular societies, that I encouraged, with all the energy of which I am capable, the holy insurrection which, by freeing the Montagnards from their shackles, would give birth to the Republican Constitution.[67]

The struggle against the Girondins inspired in these republicans a vivid language that constantly affirmed the authority of the people's power, giving recognition to the instances and places of its expression. Was it the indifference of the Convention delegates to women's demands that accelerated the ideological evolution of this group toward Jacques Roux's economic socialism and his campaign against hoarders? Did it alienate them from the objectives pursued by the Montagnards in favor of the "Enragés,"[68] who intended to push the Paris Commune and its sections to insurrection? The Constitution vote in the sections reignited women's righteous discontent with their political status. We see evidence of this in the demand of a woman from the Beaurepaire section: "Women are not taken into account in this political system. We request primary assemblies, and since the Constitution is based on the rights of man, we demand full participation in them right away."[69] To this political atmosphere we can add the propagandistic effort that Jacques Roux directed on women's behalf, convinced as he was that they had a major role to play in the Revolution.

As of July 1793 the tone was set; the Republican *Citoyennes* vehemently demanded the application of the constitutional laws: "We have come to request the enforcement of the constitutional laws. We were not the first to accept this constitution only to see anarchy and intrigues endlessly prolonged. . . . Ah delegates, is this how you deceive the people? Is this the equality that was to form the basis of their happiness?"[70] The Republican *Citoyennes* confronted the lawmakers on behalf of the entire nation; and backed by the sections, they threatened the government with the thunder of popular insurrection. Taking up one of the sans-culottes' characteristic tenets, they would not tolerate any infringement on popular sovereignty; and though the sans-culottes appeared somewhat more liberal than the Jacobins on this point, the male vote hardly welcomed the proposition with open arms. Women from the "Rights of Man" section delivered a speech to the Republican *Citoyennes* in which this masculine resistance was evident: "*Citoyennes*, the clamor of small minds surprised by the new and unfamiliar, and the rumblings of the envious, already wish to put shackles on your Constitution. Answer them with your disdain and carry on with courage."[71]

The voluntarily gender-free wording of the 1793 Constitution kept things ambiguous. By invoking the right to revolt (as provided for by article XXXV of the Constitution), these women were resisting the marginal status to which they were being relegated, and were symbolically appropriating the political authority of the Revolution. Can we interpret the threat these women posed as issuing from the *Enragé* Leclerc's personal relationships first with Claire Lacombe, and then with Pauline Léon? Perhaps. But the idea that they were manipulated by Leclerc,[72] on the other hand, denies these women any political autonomy or maturity.

From the very first days of the Revolutionary Republican *Citoyennes*, the forms taken by their popular protest revealed a suspicious attitude toward the Convention and its members. Did they gain more confidence in representative government once the Convention was purged of the Girondins? The disturbances they created in the streets and markets concerning the *cocarde* (the red, white, and blue rosette worn as the symbol of women's adherence to the Revolution) expressed their desire for direct democracy, in which the rule over the people should be in the hands of the people themselves. "The *cocarde* is the veil behind which the malicious are hiding their perfidious plans," wrote Latour-Lamontagne, an observer with little sympathy for the *citoyennes*' excessive zeal. Mass movements endangering the government's stability and predictions of more revolts were hardly expressions of civic pride! All these women of the people, of whatever stripe, were united by the need "for a new order of things to pull them out of the destitution in which they find themselves"; they complained about "all the constituent authorities, without exception, demanding a change of personnel of the Convention, the administrations, and the tribunals."[73] The Convention's decision of 21 September, requiring everyone to wear the *cocarde*, did not placate them. On 22 September, Latour-Lamontagne noted:

> the *cocarde* still divides women . . . the enemies of public tranquility flatter women's vanity, trying to persuade them that they have just as much right as men to govern their country, that the right to vote in the sections is a natural right that they must claim, and that in a State where the law consecrates equality, women can aspire to all civil or military occupations.[74]

The debate over the wearing of the *cocarde* seems to have crystallized a feeling of injustice, shared by many women. The *cocarde* issue became a sort of statement on women's political status: for some, wearing the revolutionary symbol emphasized women's political clout, while others rejected it as the pathetic symbol of a power that was already lost. Both positions questioned the government on the anticonstitutional nature of the situation. The taste of equality experienced by the sans-culottes was threatened by the all too many restrictions to which women were subjected in the social, political, and even military spheres. Adequate documentation is lacking to accurately gauge the threat to the government posed by the women's discontent. In any event, the fear of a popular revolt triggered by women made itself felt, and retaliatory measures were taken. The Jacobins aimed slanderous denunciations at the Revolutionary Republican *Citoyennes* in an attempt to discredit them. And on the eighth day of the second month in Year II, a woman petitioner asked for the abolition of all women's societies that had organized themselves as clubs.[75]

The deteriorating relations between the Jacobins and the women's societies exposed the real sexism of the revolutionaries. It is true that François Chabot, who was primarily responsible for accusing Claire Lacombe, had accorded political rights to mothers in his draft for the French constitution. But despite such short-lived attempts to bring women into public affairs, the Montagnards imperiously voiced their desire to eliminate women—now seen as an undesirable element—from the political stage.[76] This attitude led them to a blanket condemnation of all women. The recent memory of Marie-Antoinette (the "Austrian She-Wolf," beheaded on 16 October 1793), against whom the writings of Père Duchesne[77] had helped to hone popular opinion, nourished a sort of contemporary version of original sin. Père Duchesne petitioned: "We demand the abolition of all women's societies that have formed into clubs because it was a woman who caused France's unhappiness." Claire Lacombe vigorously rebelled against such insidious logic, which sought to equate femininity with monstrousness in order to discredit her group's political initiatives:

> Some slanderers, unable to attribute any crimes to us, have dared to compare us with the Medicis, with Elizabeth of England, with Marie-Antoinette, with Charlotte Corday. Ah, there nature did assuredly produce a monster who deprived us of the Friend of the People. But what crimes have *we* committed? Was Corday a member of our Society? Ah, we are more generous than men. Our sex has produced but a single monster, while for four years, we have been betrayed and assassinated by the countless monsters produced by the male sex.[78]

Oratorical prose of the Revolution was characterized by excess, echoing the general insecurity wherein individuals often found themselves victimized by rumor and intrigue. A street incident (whose causes remain unclear) involving a confrontation between the Republican *Citoyennes* and the *poissardes* [fishwives] over the wearing of the *cocarde* and the red Phrygian cap, provided the occasion for the *hébertiste* Chaumette to pronounce an entire discourse on womanhood.[79] These women decked out in red bonnets, he said, were an outrage to public morals. Invoking Rousseau's division of the private and public realms according to sex, Chaumette preached the absolute exclusion of women from public life, in the name of modesty and decency. Henceforth, the names of such public enemies as Marie-Antoinette, Olympe de Gouges, and Madame Roland[80] would be officially invoked to send women packing back to their housekeeping: any transgression of the "natural order" was punishable by death.[81]

Soon after the women's societies were abolished, Jean-Baptiste Amar, acting on the authority of the Committee for Public Safety, crushed any remaining women's hopes for a share in political life, and put to rest any lingering doubts there may have been about the Jacobins' intentions. Amar spoke to two questions, taking the high ground of principle: "(1) Can women exercise political rights and take an active part in governmental affairs? (2) Can women deliberate together, when grouped into political associations or popular societies?"[82] Invoking widespread public opinion to counter the demands of women who took the "Declaration of the Rights of Man" as their charter for liberation, Amar denied them participation in public affairs in any form. According to Amar, women must be kept to their assigned social functions of mother and house-keeper to ensure society's general order: "Each sex is called to the kind of occupation that is suitable to it; its activity is circumscribed within this circle beyond which it may not go, because nature, which placed these limits on mankind, commands imperiously and is subordinate to no law."[83]

The laws of nature take precedence over those of men. The affirmation of this hierarchy put an end to all women's hopes for sexual equality, hopes that had been nourished by the idea of popular sovereignty. The discourses on female incompetence took hold once again.

George Rudé notes: "The popular insurrections of 12th Germinal and 1st–4th Prairial of the Year III [1 April and 20–23 May 1795] marked the final, and the most considerable, effort of the Parisian sans-culottes to impose their will on their rulers as an independent political force."[84] Women from the Paris suburbs, prohibited from holding meetings and reduced to political nonexist-ence, besieged the Convention. On the 1st Prairial of Year III, they demanded "bread and the democratic Constitution of 1793." The minutes of the National Convention meetings attest to the disturbances they caused during these days of uprising. The women had indicated their hostile intentions by meeting in the Gravilliers section on 16 March; on the 1st Prairial (20 May), it was again the women who led the men of the sections to march on the Convention. Though women had traditionally taken part in food riots, their participation here signaled an urgent demand for direct democracy. This was duly announced under title VII of the proclamation written by the insurrectionists: "Male and female citizens of all sections without distinction will go out from all points in a brotherly disorder . . . so that the scheming and perfidious government can no longer muzzle the people as it has in the past."[85] This tardy sans-culottes feminism, which had earlier produced the Revolutionary Republican *Citoyennes*, was characterized by distrust of a representative system that remained beyond the people's control, and by the belief in the equal right of both sexes to manage their own living conditions. Like the Montagnards, the Thermidorians,[86] who had taken over the government in mid-1794, restricted women to an exclusively domestic position by forbidding them access to the street:

> The National Convention decrees . . . that all women must withdraw into their respective households until otherwise notified. Any women found in groups of more than five on the street one hour after the posting of this decree will be dispersed by armed force, and will be subsequently placed under arrest until public order has been restored to Paris.[87]

As if no intersection between women and the public welfare could be possible, this emergency measure also identified the female masses as a force capable of disrupting the state.

Thus, unable to resolve the contradiction between women's widespread par-ticipation during the days of insurrection and the familial conservatism of the male-dominated Assemblies, the men of the Revolution drew a dividing line between the public and private spheres which women were not allowed to cross, despite the bold attempts made by liberal feminists, and despite the impulse to generalize and institute the rights that the feminine sans-culottisme had so tenaciously fought for.

The French Revolution resonated throughout Europe. The early days of the Revolution provoked impassioned partisan stands. Commemorating England's Glorious Revolution of 1688, Doctor Richard Price, one of the theoreticians of the American Revolution, delivered a "Discourse on the Love of Our Country,"[88] in which he paid tribute to the French revolutionaries and expressed the wish that the principles of the "Declaration of the Rights of Man" would spread to England. The storming of the Bastille, once the initial astonishment passed, had given him great hope. This speech, delivered in the Old Jewry Meeting-House before an audience largely composed of dissidents and liberals, was charged with emotion. Could the French Revolution be the first sign of emancipation of the masses around the world? Could England remain untouched by this vast movement?[89] What did Richard Price mean by "love of country?" Critical of a narrowly defined nationalism, Price thought that once France became a constitutional monarchy, a reconciliation would occur between the two countries that could enable far-reaching political reform throughout continental Europe. By invoking the origins of England's constitutional monarchy, created out of a revolution that had been capped by the adoption of written law (i.e, the Bill of Rights), and by recognizing the right to resist abuses of power, as well as the individual's public liberties guaranteed by the balance of powers, Price positioned himself squarely within the Lockean tradition. These three principles[90] should be disseminated through the creation of societies in the provinces; and a decision toward this end was made that very day to lay the foundations for a new national and international solidarity. Presided over by Sir Charles Stanhope, these "Britons and citizens of the world, the Society of the Revolution," whose concerns Price voiced, congratulated the French National Assembly on its country's revolution.[91]

One year later, Price urged, "May Great Britain's Parliament become a National Assembly"; was he hoping for the violent overthrow of his own country's political institutions? Political thinkers in the two countries confronted very different circumstances. In England, the Glorious Revolution of 1688 had demonstrated that political institutions were flexible and could be modified. In France, however, the abuses of the *ancien régime* led the country to a more drastic series of changes. Within the English political context, Richard Price only wished to bring greater equity to national representation which, despite the system's defects, the English Parliament supported.

Price's political moralism never cost him his moderation, although Edmund Burke's subsequent response to Price would indicate otherwise. A year later, in fact, Burke showed his anxiety about the potential implications of the society's manifesto on the French Revolution, though he himself had defended the American one. In a work famous for its intransigent condemnation of the

French Revolution,[92] he answered Price's speech point for point. According to Price's assertions, the legitimacy of English royal power rested on an electoral principle which only needed to be revived. Burke argued, in contrast, that succession to the English throne had always been determined by heredity and written into law. The transformation in France of the Estates General into the National Assembly appeared to Burke as an unacceptable act of self-legitimation. Burke spoke out for a conservative liberalism that considered hereditary property the exclusive base for legitimacy. The demand for equality, so popular in France, represented for him a leveling of social and political values which could only end in the loss of freedom for all men. Inequality was the condition of existence for a free society which, in order to function well, required "equal rights but not to equal things."[93] In the ideological leveling of the French theorists, "the right of the people is almost always sophisticatedly confounded with their power,"[94] revealing the social standing of the country's new ruling professionals.[95]

Did Burke subscribe to the theory of natural rights? When he affirmed that all men could reap the fruits of their own labor, or when he stated that the ability to pass on property through family inheritance was the foundation of the state's political representation,[96] he was using the language of natural rights. On the other hand, Burke also exhibited a historical realism that was very distant from Rousseau's philosophical and political radicalism when he denied the original purity that gave these rights their legitimacy. "Indeed in the gross and complicated mass of human passions and concerns, the primitive rights of men undergo such a variety of refractions and reflections, that it becomes absurd to talk of them as if they continued in the simplicity of their original direction."[97] The political was not to be extricated from the weight of tradition and history. For those tempted to forget, the English Revolution was a reminder of the modern principles of the constitution of political power. For Burke the state or civil community was contractual in nature; but this contract went beyond the immediacy of any individual's existence: "it becomes a partnership not only between those who are living, but between those who are living, those who are dead, and those who are to be born."[98] This conservatism, with the weight it accords history, was fundamental to Burke's liberalism, and it defined individual freedom instrumentally, making it accessible for a government's use. Establishing a free government—that is, a government capable of deriving through the free play of institutions the mix of freedoms and restraints necessary for the maintenance of society—served the cause of the rights of man better than vain metaphysical proclamations, which could only be harmful by raising the people's hopes. Burke's undeniable attachment to constitutional monarchy was based on the time-proven continuity of institutions, and his obviously strong distaste for popular insurrection impelled him to subordinate *political freedom* to *public utility*. This utilitarianism gave his political philosophy an opportunistic quality. Though it had once been useful for him to advocate maintaining honorable relations between England and revolutionary America,[99] now, faced with the threat of political disorganization as embodied in the French Revolution, it was expedient to advocate a conditional liberalism that limited to restricted groups the exercise of political and social rights.

It was in response to Burke's *Reflections on the Revolution in France* that an obscure collaborator on Johnson's journal,[100] Mary Wollstonecraft, made her entrance on the political stage. The young woman maintained a privileged relationship with the pastor Richard Price, who earlier had helped her finance her school at Newington Green.[101] Burke's criticism stung, not only because of her friendship for the Unitarian pastor, but also because her dignity as a woman would not suffer being reduced to paternalistic stereotypes. Her book, *A Vindication of the Rights of Men*,[102] foreshadowed in many respects her famous *Vindication of the Rights of Woman*,[103] which made her one of the first British feminists.

Wollstonecraft leveled her first attack against Burke's *Reflections* in the name of reason, in opposition to imagination and "sensibility,"[104] and also in opposition to tradition and custom. She wrote:

> It is necessary emphatically to repeat, that there are rights which men inherit at their birth, as rational creatures, who were raised above the brute creation by their improvable faculties; and that, in receiving these, not from their forefathers but, from God, prescription can never undermine natural rights.[105]

Thus both sexes inherited reason from a divine lineage, and it is this faculty that legitimates the rights of man. Her faith in reason led Wollstonecraft to an evangelical interrogation of the legacy of history, a legacy that considerably darkened the social and political horizon of her country. Could English freedoms have derived from other origins than personal ambition, the barons' revolt, or the specious requests of Parliament? What credit should be given to a government which, to the detriment of its peasant population, maintained laws as barbarous as the "Game Laws"?[106]

England at the time was indeed subject to the punitive Game Laws which took away hunting rights from men with no fortunes, even from the smallest landowners on their own properties. Poachers were sentenced to forced labor, or even to death. Such feudal laws revolted Wollstonecraft, who referred to them on several occasions in her text. But what was one to expect from an institution such as Parliament, the majority of whose members, including those of the House of Commons, were on the Crown's payroll?[107] Venality and corruption in Parliament had turned the people's confidence away from their legal representatives who could no longer fulfill their duties disinterestedly. Wasn't Burke himself a representative of these "rotten boroughs"!

The law of primogeniture,[108] giving first-born sons inheritance rights at the expense of the other children, brought conflict to families and led to shady dealings that perverted the natural harmony of the relationship between parents and children. In order to preserve their titles and wealth, families resorted to trafficking in their own children. Girls suffered more than boys from this subordination of their personal lives to the family's interests.

Wollstonecraft's denunciation of tradition in the name of constitutional, penal, and personal rights led her to question the freedom/property relationship pivotal to Burke's argument. Despite his statements to the contrary, Burke was more the "champion of property" than a "friend of freedom."[109] The notion of a stable social and political order based on property, an idea whose benefits Burke touted, provoked wholly different thoughts in Wollstonecraft. For her, property did not engender civil security, but only the insecurity of the poor, exposed as they were to brutal laws according to which a man's life counted very little. Due perhaps to her evangelical inclinations, Wollstonecraft showed infinite benevolence with regard to the hard life of the people. What place should property have in this general restructuring of humanity inaugurated by the "Declaration of the Rights of Man"? By setting a limit to the acquisition of property—beyond which private property was no longer serving the individual's needs but was usurping others'—Wollstonecraft sought a new basis for property ownership that was founded as little as possible on economic grounds. The contradictory forces besetting the individual under liberalism posed a threat to social cohesion, which for Wollstonecraft was the ultimate guarantor of the rights of man. Her demand for equity and harmony in the allocation of property placed her at the center of the debate on the foundations of democracy.

As we have seen, it was Wollstonecraft's critical evangelism that led her to denounce tradition. Though she herself was an Anglican, she frequented dissident milieus, and was sensitized there to a religious fundamentalism that pointed an accusing finger at established hierarchies. In order for the rights of man to extend to every member of society, from the humblest to the most powerful, there had to be a social and political change—which did, after all, have a precedent in religious history: it was in the name of the law that the Jews crucified Christ.[110] The general abandonment of the old Judaic law and the broad dissemination of the Christian message of peace contributed to an interpretation of history as progress. In his time, Christ too had been a dangerous innovator. Patterned after a Christianity which had compassion for the poor, the Rights of Man would not sanction the exclusion of anyone. Richard Price had singled out Truth, Virtue, and Liberty as the principles that could restore the country. Mary Wollstonecraft adopted these same values. She clearly agreed with many philosophers that if a society's constitutive principles remained simple, the society could function justly.

The fundamentalist orientation of her "vindication of the rights of man" did not prevent her from taking particular interest in women's condition. She noted that Burke shared in the general suspicion surrounding the women of the people; for concerning their role in the events on 6 October 1789, Burke had written: "whilst the royal captives who followed in the train were slowly moved along, amidst the horrid yells, and shrilling screams, and frantic dances, and infamous contumelies, and all the unutterable abominations of the furies of hell, in the abused shape of the vilest of women."[111] The tears of the Queen of France seemed to move Burke the aesthete more powerfully than the sufferings of these common women anxious from hunger and worn out by endless child-bearing. In this instance, at least, the author of the *Treatise on the Sublime* was no different from most French male revolutionaries. Because nature made women into *"little, smooth, delicate, fair* creatures,"[112] they were ill-suited for political life. Writing the *Vindication of the Rights of Men* allowed Wollstonecraft to reveal the intellectual abilities and political instincts of one independent woman, who rose above the conventional images of her sex.

Critical of patriarchal liberalism, and yet still a liberal feminist, Wollstonecraft can be identified with a growing trend toward democratic individualism. Her analysis recognized the philosophic and political entity of the individual, but at the same time it examined the concrete means which the collectivity placed at the individual's disposal for self-improvement. This notion of human per-fectability, also dear to Price, was central to Wollstonecraft's *Vindication of the Rights of Woman*. Women up to that time had received little more than a me-diocre education aimed at preparing them for marriage. For Wollstonecraft, an educational system should also develop women's moral and intellectual skills.

A Vindication of the Rights of Woman opened with a dedication to Talleyrand-Périgord, the former bishop from Autun who was responsible for providing the National Assembly with a report on public education.[113] Talleyrand's report—demonstrating his consummate skill in the dialectical subtleties of reasoning—remained ambiguous on the question of girls' education. His first argument: public education is everyone's right; it is a universal principle, and nobody can be excluded based on sex or age: we must create schools for both sexes. His second point:

> If the goal of all institutions is the happiness of the greatest number, anything that diverges from this is erroneous . . . if excluding women from public em-ployment is for both sexes a way of augmenting the sum of their mutual hap-piness . . . it seems incontestable that the general welfare, and especially that of women, requires that women not aspire to exercise political rights and func-tions.[114]

Talleyrand's third statement defended the specifically feminine roles of mater-nity and household work, in order to conclude that "the paternal household is better for the education of women; they have less need of learning how to deal with the interests of others than to become accustomed to a calm and retired life. . . . taking the terms of the Constitution as our guide, we recommend a domestic education for women."[115] Was Mary Wollstonecraft really duped by Talleyrand's intentions? Did she think that his work could give women back their rights?

At the end of the eighteenth century, there was much criticism of the pre-vailing system of women's education.[116] The Saint-Cyr tradition had had its day and Rousseau's pedagogical theories were also losing their influence. Woll-stonecraft's position on women's education was part of her conception of the democratic contract, which united individual and collectivity. As Martha Storr has noted, the dialectic of rights and duties was not just a rhetorical effect in Wollstonecraft's writing: all members of a nation organized under a common government with common laws "must contribute to the correct functioning of that organization—whence emerges their duties as citizens, in exchange for which the State grants them support and protection; whence emerges their rights as citizens."[117] As a duty of the collectivity and a right of the individual, public education offered the necessary means for creating an educational space common to both sexes. Wollstonecraft maintained that boys and girls should pursue the same studies together; this model would lead to equality between adult men and women. She noted that Rousseau's pedagogy recommended private education for children of each sex. In *Emile,* he let his personal tastes on the subject of women rule his thinking;[118] and his advocacy of strictly domestic training for girls contributed toward the creation of a race of a "fanciful kind of *half* being[s]"[119] whose physical and moral weaknesses are detectable in the very actions of his fictionalized characters: Sophie, the victim of a superficial education, could not withstand life's difficulties; one could have predicted her infidelity. As Wollstonecraft writes: "Besides, how could Rousseau expect [women] to be virtuous and constant when reason is neither allowed to be the foundation of their virtue, nor truth the object of their inquiries?"[120]

Mary Wollstonecraft's evangelical rationalism was hardly compatible with the Genevan philosopher's dubious complacency toward girls. For Rousseau, girls were "by nature concerned about their person." Wollstonecraft writes: "And that a little miss should have such a correct taste as to neglect the pleasing amusement of making O's, merely because she perceived that it was an ungraceful attitude, should be selected with the anecdotes of the learned pig."[121] Wollstonecraft devoted two long sections of her book to critiquing this *philosophe,* because in her eyes, the popularity of Rousseau's ideas on education constituted a real danger to society. The state of moral infirmity in which women were kept posed a threat to social welfare: "Weak, artificial beings, raised above the common wants and affections of their race, in a premature unnatural manner, undermine the very foundation of virtue, and spread corruption through the whole mass of society!"[122] Women's subordinate status in the masculine world forced them to take oblique routes in order to participate in the life of society that was officially closed to them—and the result was that women's sense of solidarity with the other "half" of the population suffered. Wollstonecraft justified her emphasis on women's education by invoking that notion so characteristic of her period, the happiness of society and its members. But her understanding of the link between happiness and liberty was profoundly different from that evoked in Talleyrand's report. For the latter, the happiness of the couple guaranteed the true unity of society on the microcosmic level of the household. The complementary roles of men and women, distributed along the lines of the public and private life, would assure happiness. Wollstonecraft, on the other hand, saw the *individual* as the author of his or her own social happiness. Conjugal life did not in the least guarantee stability to women. The difficulties and upheavals that characteristically befell marriage conspicuously exposed the fragility of this institution. Women should be prepared to face such a situation; and the moral strength to do it would come only from within. To this extent, at least, Wollstonecraft was completely in agreement with the century's liberal thought: society's progress as a whole would occur as the sum of the individual progress of each of its members. This society could not, without compromising future progress, allow an enclave of domination. Her rationalism allowed her to conceive of a common good, directed by the interests of each man and woman, and thus distributed equally.

In her *Vindication of the Rights of Men*, Wollstonecraft pointed out the specifically monarchical character of the family's power over daughters. In her *Vindication of the Rights of Woman*, the reader's attention was redirected: "if she be not prepared by education to become the companion of man, she will stop the progress of knowledge and virtue; for truth must be common to all, or it will be inefficacious with respect to its influence on general practice."[123] Thus her argument, which began by noting the indignities of existing legislation, culminated in stating that improving women's condition would be in the national interest. The question of women's emancipation concerned everyone, not just women.

Wollstonecraft's all-embracing feminism seemed more occupied with asserting general principles than with formulating precise demands. The modalities of women's participation in public life remained undefined. Public education was for society a responsibility, and for *citoyennes*, a right; its role was to develop women and men on an equal basis. But Wollstonecraft did not specify how to extend this "improvement" into public life, as if the thought were too alien to the social reality of her period. She barely concedes the possibility of political careers for a minority of women with "superior personalities": "for I really think that women ought to have representatives, instead of being arbitrarily governed without having any direct share allowed them in the deliberations of government."[124] Medicine, which administered multiple services to women at childbirth, seemed to her another profession to which women could legitimately aspire. Wollstonecraft was not concerned with how enriching a profession might be for the individual; rather, she emphasized that the expansion of women's participation in the professions would act as a brake to the prostitution of the female population. Admittedly, her *Vindication of the Rights of Woman* was only the first part of a two-volume work; would the second volume have elaborated the more practical propositions? In her discussion of principles for regenerating the nation there is no direct evidence of any awareness on her part of the revolutionary women's political demands, nor even of Condorcet's writings on this matter. This is surprising for a woman who, as far as circumstances permitted, assiduously followed the proceedings of the National Assembly.

A Vindication of the Rights of Woman was translated into French, German, and Italian, and had several American editions. After the book was published, Wollstonecraft left for Paris in December of 1792, to see for herself the applications of the revolutionary ideas that had inspired her. Her ensuing work on the events of 1789 in France did not devote any special treatment to the question of women's political inequality.[125] Perhaps again responding to Burke's work, she carefully described the activity of women during the *journées* of October— noting, however, that among the female masses there were men dressed in women's clothes.[126] Thus, for her the historical consequences of these events were not solely the responsibility of women.

Mary Wollstonecraft died while giving birth to her daughter, the future Mary Shelley; her premature death interrupted the process of elaboration of this liberal and democratic feminism that had been set in motion by the French Revolution. At a point of overlap between two political philosophies—Locke's English liberalism and French democratic ideas—her feminism was *not* the expression of an isolated demand, as it has all too often been portrayed. Surely polemical, Wollstonecraft's work is deeply interwoven with the events of her time. Her penchant for abstract formulations might explain her inability to articulate practical statements that could assign women a precise place in the life of the polity and of the nation.

VI

AFTER THE REVOLUTION
WOMEN AND THE INCONSEQUENTIAL
LEGACY OF MODERN LIBERALISM

> Women's existence in society is still
> precarious in many ways . . . , someday, I
> believe, philosopher-lawmakers will give
> serious attention to the education that
> women ought to have, to the civil laws that
> protect them, to the duties they must assume,
> to the happiness that can be guaranteed
> them; but as things currently are, women
> belong for the most part neither to the
> natural order, nor to the social order.[1]

Madame de Staël published the above statement shortly after the Constitution
of Year VIII had abandoned the ambiguously universalist wording of the
"Rights of Man," and four years before the Napoleonic Civil Code inscribed
women's inferior status into law. The Consulate, preoccupied by making republican ideals operable on the scale of a country with many millions of inhabitants, sought to resolve "the democratic aporia caused by the mistaken
identification of the nation with its government."[2] Napoleon solved this problem in his own fashion by crowning himself emperor, thus bringing the French
Revolution to an end. Succeeding where both the monarchy and the Revolution had failed, the legal rationalism of this period definitively relegated
women to social obscurity. It was in 1801, after all, that Babeuf's[3] friend, the
lawyer Sylvain Maréchal, published a work advocating that teaching girls how
to read be outlawed!

To attribute the Code's harshness concerning women, with its institution-
alization of marital tyranny (which it would take more than a century to undo),
solely to Napoleon's personal influence would not be quite accurate. A new
system of political representation had replaced that of national sovereignty
founded on natural rights; and unlike the latter, which involved the whole social
body in political life, the new system claimed an authority independent of the
people. The Code's legalization of women's inferiority is intimately bound up

with this shift in France's political history. Of course, the Code's misogyny reflected its authors' prejudices and, more broadly, the prejudices of the Revolution's beneficiaries. But it was equally a response to moderate republican desires to contain the undeniable threat posed by "the people's power," in which women played no small part. Women's contributions to the popular insurrections of the Revolution remained deeply etched in the memories of the ex-revolutionaries. In their efforts to ensure stability of the family—investing it with an unassailable masculine authority—they moved to relegate women to a legal non-status, making it impossible for women to act politically. The Code was thus an instrument of revenge, and it ended any claim to political power formerly advanced by the masses in the name of individual rights.

Immanuel Kant's political writings created a stir in this period, as shown by the *Moniteur's* enthusiastic praises for his proposal for "Perpetual Peace":

> the famous Kant, this man who produced in Germany a revolution in minds equal to that which the vices of France's *Ancien Régime* permitted to occur in things, has just lent the stature of his name to the cause of the Republican Constitution. After having established the solid and scientific foundations for reforming philosophy, he believed it possible to state a few consequences of this reform: " . . . any legal constitution, as far as the persons who live under it are concerned, will conform to one of the three following types:
>
> (1) a constitution based on the *civil right* of individuals within a nation;
>
> (2) a constitution based on the *international right* of states in their relationships with one another;
>
> (3) a constitution based on *cosmopolitan right*. . . . "[4]

The levels of constitutional legitimacy which Kant distinguishes reflected a certain type of political liberalism.[5] The male/female opposition that he affirmed, as well as the distinction between the active and passive citizen, both restrict the scope of popular sovereignty in his theories to women's disadvantage.[6] Although it is hardly likely that the authors of the Code (Portalis, Tronchet, and Bigot de Préameneu) were influenced directly by Kant's juridical doctrine,[7] Kantian philosophy still seems to represent a general impulse to evacuate women from the political arena, as though they were trespassers there. Behind his arguments seem to be the same presuppositions held by those who attempted to implement a moderate republicanism. Kant's originality lay in his ability to systematize the view of women already prevalent among his contemporaries. Like a mirror, then, his work reflects the "European crisis of conscience"[8] that crowned Enlightenment philosophy. How did Kant treat the question of sexual difference in his circumscription of popular sovereignty?

For Kant, there existed moral, rational beings who attain freedom through willing submission to morally compelling laws, and yet who are not allowed full legal personhood. Women, due to their "natural" aspect, belong to this category.[9] This division separating women from men develops from Kant's radical distinction between, on the one hand, the rational "Idea" of moral freedom and, on the other, the actual conditions for realizing freedom, requiring "external" legal and political intervention. Without explicitly invoking a doctrine of natural right, Kant still implied that women belonged to a state of nature in that they were incapable of understanding or contributing to society's general welfare. Nor were women any more capable of exercising rights of constraint over others in a relation of mutual recognition. Finally, they were seen as incapable of socioeconomic independence. Concerning this last deficiency, we should point out that Kant never mentioned unmarried women or property-owning widows, though even these examples would not have led him to reexamine the hierarchy of principles defining civil society. Kant's definition of woman through her "inadequacies" proceeded from the trend in his political doctrine that assured the establishment of natural rights by institutionalizing civil society's public rights. But from this point of view, one can legitimately ask whether or not the category "woman" has simply become a rational fiction.

In his section on private or natural law, Kant located marriage under the rubric of "personal right," defining it as a reciprocal possession that man and woman take of each other.[10] The proprietary symmetry between husband and wife is offset, however, by "the natural superiority of the faculties of the husband compared to the wife" in the "common interest of the family."[11] The man's superiority takes the form of an authoritarian power that provides no reciprocity of rights and duties to the woman for her vassalage. The conflation of family and marriage interests privatizes family law,[12] violates the contractual relations of community life, and oversimplifies one of the rare social institutions where Kant does acknowledge women. Was this oversimplification part and parcel of the political ideology of the time, which assigned women to the private sphere of the household and men to the public sphere of civil society?

For Kant, conjugal right institutes a sexual community freely agreed to by man and woman as morally autonomous agents, the condition that renders both rights and ethics possible. It is this legal institution that rescues human sexual relations from the debasing animal state.[13] In opposition to this "private law," civil law unifies the social body, but only by limiting the status of subjects and citizens to its male elements. As Michèle Jalley-Crampe-Casnabet notes, the authority of "public law" in Kant's conception of the state shatters the linearity of a political order that begins with the individual "as the origin of power" and builds from there to the totality of the state.[14] The fluidity of liberal political theory had given women in France reason to hope for complete access to the political sphere, due solely to their innate qualities as "rational beings." However, the relationship between private and public law as conceived by Kant abandoned this linear construct. For Kant, it is the cohesiveness of civil society that protects the precarious existence of individual agreements. Even though Kant affirmed marriage as the only permissible means of expressing human sexuality, the state still relegates civil society and its institutions to a secondary existence. The distinction between private law and public law is not based on the interior/exterior division which, although used frequently by Kant,[15] is inadequate here to describe the civil condition. Rather, the public/private division arises out of a constraint that the state imposes on society. In his essay "Perpetual Peace,"[16] Kant criticized the despotism of democracy, favoring instead a representative republican constitution. Once again, he demonstrated his desire to subordinate society to the state, this time through the traditional categories of political science. Even though Kant evinced little confidence in the ethics of deputies or representatives, the profound limitations of the human species made a representative system necessary: "Man was not meant to belong to a herd, like cattle, but to a hive, like bees."[17] Despite this insect-like public law, which Kant claimed to derive from the life of bees, our recluse of Königsberg did not feel compelled to integrate women into his definition of civil society! The relationship that Kant set up between civil society and a republican constitution should be considered in light of his brief but explicit critique of the French Revolution, which can be found scattered here and there. His brand of republicanism, in fact, allows neither tyrannicide, nor insurrection (and hence prohibits revolution). Concerning national psychologies, he remarked: "it is still noteworthy that in revolutionary periods, when public injustice is established and declared lawful (as, for example, under the Committee of Public Safety in the French Republic), honor-loving men (such as Roland) have sought to anticipate by suicide their execution under the law."[18]

Where does our detour through Kant's political thought lead us in our analysis of women's civil and political equality? Theodor von Hippel—commentator on French politics and skillful rhetorician—wrote a treatise in 1792 advocating a greater role for women in French civil society.[19] Why is his work, therefore, not given a corresponding significance in this study of women's fluctuating political status in the modern age?

The question of women's political status can be traced to a dual genesis: an abstract philosophical genesis, and an empirical/factual one gleaned from the history of [Western] societies and states. In taking the approach of the history of ideas—taking into account the contradictions of the erudite humanism of the fifteenth and sixteenth centuries regarding the "woman question," the Reformation and Counter-Reformation, the Cartesian intellectual revolution, and the political anthropology of the eighteenth-century *philosophes*—we should not neglect the actual consequences of Protestantism in resisting the power of the state, nor of women's political protests during the Revolution. Histories of feminism generally limit themselves to noting the political silence that befell women after the Revolution.[20] This silence, however, requires interpretation. In view of the extensive social and political restrictions spawned by the French Civil Code, it is imperative that we explore the shifting meanings of the word "reason." Once the vehicle to which women attached their hopes for political equality during the struggle against the power and authority of tradition, it later became the principle on which their exclusion was based.

From this perspective, Kant's political doctrine enriches our understanding of the complex relationship that existed between feminism and liberalism. (His political views informed the actions of the revolutionary Directory; and it is only due to Kant's distaste for worldly affairs that he did not play a more direct political role himself.)[21] To the question, "What is Enlightenment?" Kant replied that it is "man's emergence from his self-incurred immaturity. Immaturity is the inability to use one's own understanding without the guidance of another."[22] The place he assigned for women, however, remained outside this general emancipation of the understanding and the individual will. Nineteenth-century political liberalism could be seen as a direct extension of Kant's definition of Enlightenment; it would take a sharp turn toward misogyny, as the exclusions of this philosophy of progress became identified with the prejudices of the bourgeois social order.

Kant, generally perceived as a liberal, indeed assimilated certain elements into his political philosophy that were traditionally found in the liberal philosophy of preceding centuries. His theory of private contract stems from a conception of subjective rights that was first formulated in humanist jurisprudence. His principle of equality, as it regulates civil society for men, still allows for the distinction of individuals based on their differing abilities and possessions; similar ideas had already been suggested by the French *philosophes*. And finally, his penchant for constitutional monarchy brings him closer than is generally recognized to the views expressed in Montesquieu's *Spirit of the Laws*. These influences and reinterpretations, however, are only of secondary interest.

Rousseau had identified national sovereignty with the people's will. Though this helped to justify the Revolution, it also allowed a handful of men to capture and misuse political power in the name of the people. Wary of the perverse dangers of democratic sovereignty, Kant constructed a legal system that prohibited any reneging on the initial contract between individual and society. The state's constraints upon civil society—legitimated by a moral law that is no less constraining and external—gives shape to a law that is both natural and international, and establishes history as an irreversible progression. Henceforth, the legitimacy of individual contracts is founded solely on the relation of the individual to the totality. Kant's description of the modalities for acquiring these civil rights reflected a shift in the location of the origin of political autonomy and power toward a representative system: thus the natural social body could not claim unmediated political power, nor the individual unmediated rights. The preeminence of the whole over its parts[23] announced a new normative rationalism that ignores inequalities between the sexes. The alliance of law and power, symbolized for women by the French Civil Code, flushed this "immature" population into the infrapolitical backwaters, where they "belong for the most part neither to the natural order, nor to the social order."

Madame de Staël's literary works bear the scars of this philosophical and political setback. Her novel *Delphine*,[24] though set in the revolutionary period, does not treat the Revolution itself; instead, the heroine's deeper interests lie elsewhere. Except for her shady dealings involving Napoleon's succession, Madame de Staël's personal life also revealed a disaffection with politics. What had happened to the confidence displayed by women in their actions of 1789 and 1793? Madame de Staël's posthumously published work, "Les Principaux Evénements de la Révolution française" [The Principal Elements of the Revolution],[25] was little more than an elaborate defense of the actions of her father, Jacques Necker, passing silently over women's participation in the Revolution. What was the cause of this suicidal woman's melancholy?

In the wake of the French Revolution and its subsequent commentary, modern forms of political liberalism began to emerge in France during the period around the Revolution of 1830. It is quite remarkable that for women this period would become synonymous with a new type of servitude. For Benjamin Constant, a friend to both Madame de Staël and Madame Récamier, the cause for this was clear. His discussion of the limits to the people's sovereignty gave no quarter to a possible female electorate. According to Constant, the great majority of women lacked both the intellectual—"enlightened"—independence and the financial, landowning independence required to form an electorate that would be free from influence.

For Alexis de Tocqueville, American society offered the unique example of a democratic state still in its early stage, and its institutions provided a concrete instructive example of how equality in a natural democracy could form the basis for social relations without violent upheavals. Compared to this new world, the much older France, with its stubbornly persistent aristocratic social structures, had much to learn! The author of *Democracy in America* attributed a decisive role to the morals and popular attitudes as guarantors of American democratic institutions. With the incisive observation that "morals are the work of women,"[26] he acknowledged the importance of women in defining social practices, and thus also acknowledged their political significance. But what he said about the austerity and regularity of American morality, and about the individual freedom enjoyed by women before and in marriage, still in no way led Tocqueville to advocate equality between the sexes. Women's social role is immense, he wrote, and it should be accorded respect and esteem comparable to men's. But the differentiation of functions between the sexes in American democratic society allowed him to maintain the traditional divisions between private life and public life. "In America," he wrote, "the independence of woman is irrecoverably lost in the bonds of matrimony."[27] Their apprenticeship in freedom did not induce women to leave the family home, even though from an early age they had this democratic education, which would allow them to face the perils of life in society. In his praise of the American woman, Tocqueville pointedly criticized the feminist demands that had again surfaced in Europe during the revolutionary upheavals of the 1830s: "and in the United States it is not the practice for a guilty wife to clamor for the rights of women while she is trampling on her own holiest duties."[28] Though democracy declared all people to be equal, it did not declare them to be the same: "There are people in Europe who, confounding together the different characteristics of the sexes, would make man and woman into beings not only equal but alike."[29] Tocqueville's distinction between equality and sameness allowed him to avoid questioning the legitimacy of men's domination over women, common to both aristocratic and democratic societies.

Modern forms of government, whether constitutional monarchy or republic, allowed individuals of both sexes to think about and act out their emancipation with reference to an undifferentiated royal power whose superior will alone had determined the constitution of society. The theological and political convulsions caused by the Reformation in the sixteenth century established the demand for equal relations between human beings. From that time on, the monarchy had to take into account not only two religions, but two categories of beings—men and women. Representation of a pacified social body became the birth certificate for national sovereignty because it introduced a principle of alternation in the exercise of political power.

The role of the Reformation (following Christian humanism) in shaping the question of sexual equality in France was crucial in having pointed the need for reintegrating spiritual and moral values into the individual. Well after Mary Wollstonecraft's death, the militant moralism of the Protestant Eugénie Niboyet, head of the socialist newspaper *La Voix des femmes* in 1848, indicated that Calvinist thought in favor of women's rights was still very much alive: "Equal to man before God, before the law woman is in a state of dependence from which she alone can extricate herself."[30]

The scenarios projected by the various theories of natural rights, of whatever stamp, share a common desire to restore full human dignity. However, all of them failed to deal with woman's condition, or to advance women's causes, except to the extent that they were influenced in France by Protestant "radicalism," the kind of radicalism that sometimes arises among religious and social minority positions. While the ostracized Poullain de la Barre sought to free women from their oppression, the Huguenot philosopher Jean-Jacques Rousseau, zealous Genevan that he was, contrived new shackles for them.

The establishment of universal manhood suffrage in 1848 excluded women, in an era in which the political and social spheres were sharply separated. The Revolution of 1848 did not accomplish the political reenfranchisement of all society that women of the French Revolution and the rest of the population had sought. Women's attempts to reoccupy the political sphere remained too respectful of the law, too attached to the values of the family and the couple. For them, the "social individual" was represented by the union of man and woman. This interpretation of one of the key concepts of political liberalism reflects the legal submission forced on women in turn by the Civil Code, the Charter of 1830, and the 1848 Constitution. The addition of a republican ideal of equality and demands for improved working conditions did not suffice to overcome the jealously guarded prerogatives of men. The workers' movement as a social avant-garde maintained the same sexual division of the public and private; the movement's leaders only reaffirmed women's absolute subordination to the family's requirements. Throughout the nineteenth century, the fragmentary laws dealing with women's condition, and specifically with their work, hardly altered this state of subordination. The constitution of 19 April 1946 finally gave women in France complete legal equality; more recently, further legislation has worked toward erasing all traces of their past subjugation. However, between the universalizing requirements of democracy on one hand, and the necessity for modern legislators to clear a legal space capable of encompassing the specific types of discrimination that are still aimed against women, there remains a contradiction. And it is this contradiction that the increasing number of women in France's political structure will have to resolve.

NOTES

Foreword

1. For a fascinating account of this generation in France, see Hervé Hamon and Patrick Rotman, *Génération*, 2 vols. (Paris: Le Seuil, 1987, 1988).

2. Christine Fauré, editor, *Quatre femmes terroristes contre le tsar: Textes réunis et présentés par Christine Fauré*, trans. from Russian by Hélène Chatelain (Paris: Maspéro, 1978); Christine Fauré, *Terre, terreur, liberté* (Paris: Maspéro, 1979).

3. Christine Fauré, "The Utopia of the New Woman in the Work of Alexandra Kollontai and Its Impact on the French Feminist and Communist Press," *Women in Culture and Politics: A Century of Change*, trans. D. Irving, ed. J. Friedlander, B. Wiesen Cook, A. Kessler-Harris, and C. Smith-Rosenberg (Bloomington: Indiana University Press, 1986), 376–89.

4. See, for example, Alison M. Jaggar, *Feminist Politics and Human Nature* (Sussex: The Harvester Press Ltd., 1983); and Teresa Brennan and Carole Pateman, "More Auxiliaries to the Commonwealth: Women and the Origins of Liberalism," *Political Studies* 27 (June 1979): 183–200.

5. Since publishing the French edition of *Democracy without Women*, Christine Fauré has edited and presented the debates and texts concerned with the 1789 Declarations of the Rights of Man: *Les Déclarations des droits de l'homme de 1789* (Paris: Payot, 1988).

Introduction

1. J. Michelet, *Les Femmes de la Révolution* (Paris, 1854), but also more recent works by, for example, historian Edith Thomas, *Les Femmes en 1848* (Paris: PUF, 1948) and *Les Pétroleuses* (Paris: Gallimard, 1963).

2. Cf. *Histoire sans qualités*, collectively edited essays (Paris: Galilée, 1979).

3. "Les Vésuviennes": an organization of women workers established in 1848 to demand the emancipation of women. "Why this name? It was the first derisive label applied to us in ridicule, and we take pride in reappropriating it. Also it marvelously depicts our position, and more than any other term it expresses our ideas—only the lava flow, held in so long that it finally has to pour out all around us, is by no means incendiary, but regenerative." Quoted in Maïté Albistur and Daniel Armogathe, eds., *Le Grief des femmes: Anthologie de textes féministes du Moyen âge à 1848* (Poitiers: Hier et Demain, 1978), p. 296.

4. The feminist Maria Cheliga writes on the word's origin, "Here it would take too long to give the names of men whose writing contributed to the development of 'feminism'; we owe this term to Fourier, who, in his theory of the four movements, posited the equality of the sexes as a basic principle of social renewal" "Les Hommes féministes," (*Revue encyclopédique Larousse*, 1896). This reference does in fact reflect Fourier's statement on the social necessity of a transformation of the feminine condition; but the term "feminism" itself is not in the text. Should we then date the appearance of the word to the "Congress of Feminist Organizations," held in 1892? [See also Karen Offen, "On the French Origin of the Words *Feminism* and *Feminist*," *Feminist Issues* 8, no. 2 (Fall 1988): 45–51 —Trans.]

5. See Michelle Perrot, "L'Eloge de la ménagère dans le discours des ouvriers français au XIXe siècle," *Romantisme: Revue du XIXe siècle*, issue "Mythe et représentation de la femme," February 1977: 13–14.

6. Irénée Dauthier, *Séance du Congrès ouvrier de France, session de 1876, tenue à Paris du 2 au 10 octobre* (Paris: Sandoz et Fischbacher, 1877).

7. [See Charles Sowerwine, "Workers and Women in France before 1914: The Debate over the Couriau Affair," *Journal of Modern History* 55, no. 3 (Sept. 1983): 411–41.—Trans.]

8. See, for example, Arlette Farge, *Le Miroir des femmes* (Paris: Montalba, 1982).

9. Charles Sowerwine, *Les Femmes et le socialisme* (Paris: Presses de la Fondation Nationale des Sciences Politiques, 1978). Revised English edition: *Sisters or Citizens? Women and Socialism in France since 1876* (New York: Cambridge University Press, 1982).

10. Ibid., p. 227.

11. Suzon (Suzanne Lacore), "Féminisme et Socialisme," *L'Equité*, 15 Oct. 1913.

12. Since she never abandoned her socialist pacifism from pre-1914, certain policies she supported during WWII were close to the positions of the Vichy government.

13. Louise Saumoneau, Speech to the International Women's Rights Congress, 1900; cited by Sowerwine, *Les Femmes et le Socialisme*, p. 82.

14. [SFIO: French section of the Workers' International, France's unified socialist party, founded in 1905.—Trans.]

15. In 1880 she founded L'Union des Femmes Socialistes [Union of Socialist Women]; in 1889, a short-lived Ligue Socialiste des Femmes [Socialist Women's League]; in 1891, Le Groupe de la Solidarité des Femmes [Women's Solidarity Group].

16. [Secretary of the Fédération du Livre (the federation of printers' unions), 1885–1919.—Trans.]

17. Maurice Duverger, "La Participation des femmes à la vie politique," Unesco, 1955, p. 17.

18. [Formed at the Congress of Tours (21 Dec. 1920); as a result of a split in the SFIO, the SFIC, which would later become the PCF or Parti Communiste Français, was born.—Trans.]

19. The question of women was a central focus of the Bolshevization of the French Communist Party. As the French Party was being Bolshevized in 1924–25, the *Cahiers du Bolchevisme* (the theoretical arm of the French section of the International) wrote:

> The broadened executive branch has held, in its statements on the bolshevization of parties, that work among women in capitalist countries was still entirely too rare. Comrade Zinoviev has declared several times that "a party that cannot mobilize women workers for the proletarian Revolution cannot be considered a truly Bolshevik party."

Marie Dubois, "Organisons le prolétariat féminin," *Cahiers du bolchevisme* 1, no. 19 (15 May 1925): 1220.

20. Frederick Engels, *The Origin of the Family, Private Property and the State* (New York: International Publishers, 1942) [no trans.], p. 58.

21. [For two English-language biographies of Kollontai, see Barbara Evans Clements, *Bolshevik Feminist: The Life of Aleksandra Kollontai* (Bloomington: Indiana University Press, 1979); and Beatrice Farnsworth, *Aleksandra Kollontai: Socialism, Feminism, and the Bolshevik Revolution* (Stanford: Stanford University Press, 1980).—Trans.]

22. "Cinq semaines à Moscou," pub. L. Weiss in *L'Europe nouvelle* (17 Dec. 1921), a weekly covering foreign economic and literary issues. The articles were published first in the newspaper *Le petit parisien* (2 Nov.–8 Dec. 1921).

23. Madeleine Pelletier, *Mon voyage aventureux en Russie communiste* (Paris: Giard, 1922).

24. Second family code, 1926; New family code, 1936.

25. *L'Humanité* (2 May 1956).

26. The newspaper *La Fronde* was one of the greatest successes of this press; it published daily for six years (1897–1903).

27. Maria Deraismes, *Ce que veulent les femmes*, articles and speeches from 1869–94, with preface, notes, and comments by O. Krakovitch (Paris: Syros, 1980).

28. After numerous attempts, she was examined for the baccalaureate by the jury of Lyon's Faculty of Letters in 1862, and passed; she took the License in Letters in 1871. Author of (among other works) *La Femme pauvre au XIXe siècle* (1866) and *L'Emancipation de la femme* (1871).

29. "Intellectuals in the world of workers and underpaid, they were predisposed to critical reflection." Anne-Marie Sohn, "Féminisme et syndicalisme," doctoral thesis (Paris: Paris Audiovisuel, Hachette, 1973), p. 295.

30. E.g., Hubertine Auclert, who resumed her activism after the death of her husband in 1892.

31. In 1914, Noëlie Drous (anagram of Sourd ["deaf"]) married an architect; they divorced in 1922. In 1924 she became editor of the newspaper *La Voix des femmes* [Women's voice]. Also, Marguerite Durand, who married the Boulangist parliamentary deputy George Laguerre, divorced, and then in 1897 founded the feminist journal *La Fronde*.

32. This was the case with the schoolteacher Lucie Colliard, who was married to a peasant, then separated in 1918. She lived afterward with her two children, one son and one daughter (who also became a teacher).

33. *La Libre Parole* (4 Apr. 1894).

34. The motto of the newspaper *La Libre Parole* was "France for the French!"

35. An example of a publication claiming roots in Christian feminism: an article on the council of Mâcon and the soul of women, *Revue du féminisme chrétien* (10 Apr. 1896): 33.

36. For me the idea of defining feminism as a "phenomenon of the Third Republic" seems too narrow. See Anne-Marie Sohn, "Féminisme et syndicalisme."

37. In this overview we cite the main points of the work directed by Marc Ancel on the status of women, *La Condition de la femme dans la société contemporaine* (Paris: Librairie du Recueil Sirey, 1938). The article on France was edited by Suzanne Grinberg, pp. 265–75. [See also Steven Hause, *Woman's Suffrage and Social Politics in the French Third Republic* (Princeton: Princeton University Press, 1984).—Trans.]

38. In 1919, on the proposition sponsored by Aristide Briand and René Viviani, the Chamber of Deputies endorsed women's right to vote, but the Senate rejected the bill.

Between 1919 and 1929:

(a) 20 May 1919—Jean Bon's proposal granted women over thirty years old the vote for, and eligibility to, municipal councils and general councils. The bill passed by the Chamber, 344 to 94, was rejected by the Senate on 21 Nov., 156 to 134.

(b) 15 Apr. 1925—The Chamber approved municipal and cantonal suffrage for women, 390–183. Debate adjourned indefinitely by the Senate.

(c) 1929—The Chamber again endorsed the female vote as in 1919; the Senate rejected this bill.

Between 1929 and 1939:

(a) The Chamber's Commission on Universal Suffrage endorsed a text establishing political equality of the sexes. On 30 July 1936, the Chamber, by 95 yes votes to 46 abstentions, passed the Marin bill on this issue. But the proposal, like its predecessor, ran up against the radical socialist bloc in the Senate.

(b) July 1936—the Chamber declared in favor (488–1) of political equality of men and women. Once more in 1937, the Senate rejected the Chamber's bill.

—Albert Brimo, *Les Femmes françaises face au pouvoir politique* (Paris: Montchrétien, 1975), pp. 53–55.

39. Cf. especially Louise A. Tilly and Joan W. Scott, *Women, Work and Family* (New York: Holt, Rinehart & Winston, 1978).

40. Law of 23 Apr. 1919: workday fixed at 8 hours per day.

Article 55, book II of the Labor Code. Ban on women's work in the mines.

Law of 30 June 1928 and decree of 5 May 1928: ban on night shifts in factories, mines, quarries, and workshops.

Decrees of 21 Mar. 1914, 24 Sept. 1926, and 8 Aug. 1930: ban on certain dangerous kinds of labor.

Law of 30 June 1928: women's right not to work in factories on Sundays.

Decree of 28 Dec. 1909 and 26 Oct. 1912: the weight limit of loads that women are required to carry, pull, or push.

Article 76, book II of Labor Code: the obligation to install in shops a number of seats equal to the number of women employed, and so on.

41. A partial list:

Law of 4 Jan. 1928: the right to suspend work for twelve consecutive weeks in the period before and after childbirth.

Law of 5 Aug. 1917, concerning the nursing mother:

(a) the right to one free hour per working day for a year after childbirth;

(b) the right to nurse the child in the workplace;

(c) the obligation of the director of a company employing more than 100 women to set aside nursing rooms.

Law of 17 June 1913: the right, for the woman deprived of sufficient resources before and after childbirth, to a daily payment.

42. The law of 13 July 1907 gave the married woman the right over revenues from her employment without her husband's authorization, and even the right to lodge a legal complaint in court if her business so demanded.

43. In the event of the husband's opposition, the courts evaluated the reasons for this opposition. Legal precedent shows little but cases involving husbands preventing their wives from working in theaters, vaudeville houses, and movie theaters.

44. Article 4 of the Commercial Code.

45. The law of 9 Apr. 1881, complemented by the law of 20 July 1895, allowed for issuance of a savings bank passbook to married women without the husband's authorization, and also their right to withdraw funds from their accounts on their own.

The law of 20 July 1886 allowed married women to make deposits into the National Retirement Fund independently of their husbands.

The law of 6 Feb. 1893 restored full civil capacity to legally separated women.

The law of 7 Dec. 1897, fulfilling a feminist demand dating from 1830, gave women the right to be witnesses for birth, marriage, and death certificates, and the right to be witnesses to deeds.

The law of 13 July 1907 (see above), giving married women free disposition over revenues from their employment and spelling out spousal financial household obligations, constituted a significant dispensation from inequities of the civil code.

The law of 12 July 1909, on family property, granted married women legal recourse regarding this property in the event of contestation.

The law of 20 Mar. 1917, regarding women's guardianship and their admission into family councils, granted them certain new rights.

The law of 31 Mar. 1919 allowed married women to act without husbands' authorization in matters pertaining to their own inheritance benefits.

The law of 28 Dec. 1922 did the same for the collection of arrears of pensions they held.

The law of 10 Aug. 1927 on nationality affirmed the principle of independent nationality for married women.

This legislative inventory is taken from Marc Ancel, *Traité de la capacité civile de la femme mariée dans la loi du 18 février 1938* (Paris: Librarie du Recueil Sirey, 1938), pp. 22–25.

46. Law of 22 Sept. 1942.

47. See Odile Dhavernas, *Droits des femmes, pouvoir des hommes* (Paris: Seuil, 1978), p. 92.

48. "The Revolution reintroduced divorce into France with the law of 20 Sept. 1792, which instituted an egalitarian and liberal system with respect to which the Civil Code marks a definite regression. In 1816, divorce was eliminated because of reaction by royalists and clergy, and it would not be reinstated until the Naquet Law of 27 July 1884." Odile Dhavernas, *Droits des femmes*, p. 29.

49. Law of 4 June 1970, pertaining to parental authority.

50. Law of 16 Nov. 1912 (art. 340 of the Civil Code).

51. See the article by F. Picq, "Par delà la loi du père: Le débat sur la recherche de la paternité au Congrès féministe de 1900," *Les Temps modernes* 34, no. 391 (Feb. 1979): 1199–1212.

52. Hélène Brion, *La Voie féministe 1916*, preface and commentary by Huguette Bouchardeau (Paris: Syros, 1978), p. 87.

53. Art. 317 of the 1810 Penal Code; Law of 31 July 1920, complemented by the Law of 27 Mar. 1923; statutory order of 29 July 1939. See Odile Dhavernas, *Droits des femmes*, pp. 137–48.

54. *Journal Officiel*, Document A-1, 18 Jan. 1975, p. 739.

55. Yvette Roudy, *La Femme en marge* (Paris: Flammarion, 1975), p. 133.

56. Georges Burdeau, *Le Libéralisme* (Paris: Points-Seuil, 1979), Introduction, p. 7.

57. *L'Esprit du socialisme: Féministes françaises* (Paris: Editions du Parti Socialiste, 1978).

1. Christine de Pizan and the Paradox of an Origin

1. Léon Abensour, *La Femme et le féminisme avant la Révolution* (Paris: E. Leroux, 1923); Maïté Albistur and Daniel Armogathe, *Histoire du féminisme français*, 2 vols. (Paris: Edition des femmes, 1977). J. Rabaut, *Histoire des féminismes français* (Paris: Stock, 1978).

2. "Christine de Pizan was the first to elaborate a feminist doctrine in the same spirit and method as the modern defenders of women's rights," Léon Abensour, *La Femme et le féminisme*, p. 6. "This woman may rightly be considered the first feminist in the modern sense of the word. As the first professional woman of letters, she struggled hard to conquer her economic freedom and devoted the majority of her work to rehabilitating her ridiculed sex," M. Albistur and D. Armogathe, *Le Grief des femmes: Anthologie de textes féministes du Moyen Age à 1848* (Poitiers: Hier et Demain, 1978).

3. Yves Badel, *Le Roman de la Rose au XIVe siècle: Etude de la réception de l'oeuvre* (Geneva: Droz, 1980), p. 9.

4. Eric Hicks, *Le Débat sur le Roman de la Rose* (Paris: Honoré Champion, 1977), pp. 102, 103, 104.

5. Gontier Col, a close friend of Jean de Montreuil, and secretary to the king. Pierre Col, Canon of Notre-Dame and Tournay, was the younger brother of Gontier. Cf. Alfred Coville, *Gonthier et Pierre Col et l'humanisme en France au temps de Charles VI* (Paris: Droz, 1934).

6. "L'Epistre Christine au Prévost de Lisle envoyé par la dicte contre le *Romant de la Rose*," in Hicks, *Débat*, p. 56. [All translations of Pizan's texts are the translators'.]

7. The order of the texts in the first manuscript edition of Pizan's work is as follows: the debate of two lovers, epistle to the God of Love, the tale of the Rose, the tale of the three judgments of love, the tale of Passy, the epistles on the *Roman de la Rose*; see Hicks, *Débat*, p. 32.

8. Cf. Marie-Josèphe Pinet, *Christine de Pisan, 1364–1430* (Paris: Champion, 1927), pp. 66–67.

9. Cited by Daniel Poirion, *Le Poète et le prince: L'Evolution du lyrisme courtois de Guillaume de Machaut à Charles d'Orléans* (Paris: Presses universitaires de France, 1965), p. 241.

10. Hicks, *Débat*, p. 9.

11. Jean de Montreuil's treatise was not in the collection, but only the letters exchanged between Gonthier Col, Jean de Montreuil, and Christine de Pizan.

12. Yves Badel, *Le* Roman de la Rose *au XIVe siècle*, p. 431.

13. "While Deschamps addressed his petitions and sermons to the King, it was to the Queen that Christine sent her letters on the *Roman de la Rose*, the debate which made her famous as the 'champion' of woman's cause. It is to the 'high' and all-powerful lady that she dedicated one of her first New Year's ballads. No doubt we find somewhat disturbing her allusions to Pallas, Juno, and Lucrèce when speaking of Queen Isabeau, but this was probably voluntary blindness," Daniel Poirion, *Poète*, p. 244.

14. Hicks, *Débat*, p. xlix.

15. Poirion, *Poète*, p. 253.

16. M. M. Gorce, "Le *Roman de la Rose* de Jean de Meun et son caractère universitaire," in *Mélanges Mandonnet*, vol. 1 (Paris: Librairie Vrin, 1930), p. 242.

17. Averroës (c. 1126–c. 1198) was a Spanish Muslim philosopher best known for his commentaries on Aristotle. Averroism was very influential in Western Latin philosophy at the end of the thirteenth century.

18. Georges de Lagarde, *La Naissance de l'esprit laïque au déclin du Moyen Age*, vol. 2 (Louvain-Paris: Nauwelaerts, 1958), p. 35.

19. Jacques Le Goff, *Les Intellectuels au Moyen Age* (Paris: Le Seuil, 1957), p. 118.

20. Norman Cohn, *The Pursuit of the Millennium* (New York: Harper and Row, 1961).

21. Roland Hissette, *Enquêtes sur les 219 articles condamnés à Paris le 7 mars 1277* (Louvain: Publications universitaires, 1977).

22. For example, 207: "Quod delectatio in artibus venereis non impedit actum seu usum intellectus" (172; 20, 4). The author of the condemned thesis is probably rebelling against a theological conception inspired by Saint Augustine, who considered the sexual act disrupting because it permitted sensuality to dominate reason. The critics no doubt found it to be an encouragement to sexual abandon. 208: "Quod continentia non est essentialiter virtus" (168; 20, 5).

(1) Continence is not essentially a virtue.

(2) The opposition of this thesis with Christian thought is manifest, continence having been identified by Saint Paul with the virtue of chastity.

23. Cf. Etienne Gilson, *La Philosophie au Moyen Age: Des origines patristiques à la fin du XIVe siècle* (Paris: Payot, 1944), p. 558.

24. "Is it true that it was on Pope Alexander's request around 1257 that Thomas Aquinas undertook the work we call *Summa against the Gentiles*? In this case, one could easily connect the Pope's initiative with one several months previously which led him to entrust a document devoted to a more specific point on the same subject to Albert the Great." M. M. Gorce, "La Lutte *contra gentiles* à Paris au XIIIe siècle," in *Mélanges Mandonnet*, vol. 1 (Paris, 1930), p. 228.

25. Hissette, *Enquêtes*, p. 7.

26. Hicks, *Débat*, p. 11.

27. André Combes, *Jean de Montreuil et le Chancelier Gerson* (Paris: Vrin, 1942), p. 16.

28. André Combes, *Etudes Gersoniennes* (Paris: Archives d'histoire doctrinale et littéraire du Moyen Age, 1939), p. 294.

29. "Le Traité d'une vision faite contre le *Roumant de la Roze* par le Chancelier de Paris," in Hicks, *Débat*, p. 77.

30. Ibid., p. 87.

31. "While the Aristotelians accepted the battle on purely philosophical grounds, the

Augustinians intended to remain within the domain of Christian wisdom and check the progress of Averroism by denying the very principle of a separate philosophy." Etienne Gilson, *La Philosophie de Saint Bonaventure* (Paris: Vrin, 1924), p. 33.

32. "Quod simplex fornicatio ut Pote soluti cum soluta, non est peccatum" (183; 20, 2). Hissette, *Enquêtes*, p. 294.

33. "La Response Maistre Pierre Col, Chanoine de Paris aux deux traités precedens," Hicks, *Débat*, p. 100.

34. Saint Augustine's interpreters debated whether concupiscence was the original sin or only a result of this sin. Cf. Gilson, *La Philosophie de Saint Augustin* (Paris: Vrin, 1929), p. 189.

35. Cf. F. J. Thonnard, "La Notion de nature chez Augustin," *Revue des études augustiniennes* (Paris, 1965).

36. Jean Gerson, "Responsion ad scripta cuiusdam," Hicks, *Débat*, p. 165.

37. Cf. Gilson, *Philosophie de Saint Bonaventure*, pp. 424–26.

38. Cf. M. J. Pinet, *Christine de Pisan, 1364–1430* (Paris: Champion, 1927), p. 423.

39. For Saint Augustine, the "Good of Marriage" tempers the evil of carnal concupiscence which makes man, engendered by this vice, contract original sin. Cf. *Traitez de morale de Saint Augustin*, chap. 4 "Du bien du Mariage," chap. 5 "Du mariage et de la concupiscence pour les personnes mariées" (Paris, 1680).

40. Hicks, *Débat*, p. 22.

41. Ibid., p. 125.

42. Ibid., pp. 138–39.

43. Cf. Maria Daraki, "L'Emergence du sujet singulier dans les confessions d'Augustin," *Esprit* (Feb. 1981).

44. Louis Dumont, "La Conception moderne de l'individu: Notes sur la Genèse, en relation avec les conceptions de la poétique et de l'Etat à partir du XIIIe siècle," *Esprit* (Feb. 1978).

45. Maria Daraki, "L'Emergence," p. 115.

46. André Vachet, *L'Idéologie libérale* (Paris: Anthropos, 1970), p. 44.

II. The Sixteenth Century

1. Jacob Burckhardt, *The Civilization of the Renaissance in Italy* (1860), trans. S. G. C. Middlemore, 4th rev. ed. (London: Phaidon Press, 1951), p. 240.

2. Ibid., p. 241.

3. René de Maulde la Clavière, *Les Femmes et la Renaissance* (Paris: Perrin, 1898); trans. G. H. Ely, *The Women of the Renaissance: A Study of Feminism* (New York: Putnam, 1901).

4. Emmanuel Rodocanachi, *La Femme italienne à l'époque de la Renaissance: Sa vie privée et mondaine, son influence sociale* (Paris: Hachette, 1907).

5. W. K. Ferguson, *The Renaissance in Historical Thought: Five Centuries of Interpretation* (Boston: Houghton Mifflin Co., 1948), p. 182.

6. J. Michelet, "Le Seizième siècle est un héros," *Histoire de France*, complete works (Paris: Flammarion, 1978), p. 54.

7. Francis Bacon's tree of knowledge is reproduced in the *Encyclopédie* as a diagram of the structure of the arts and sciences.

8. Maurice de Gandillac, "Histoire de la philosophie; Philosophie de la Renaissance," *Encyclopédie de la Pléiade* (Paris: Gallimard), vol. 2, p. 3.

9. Cited by Augustin Renaudet from Hauser's article "Humanisme et Réforme en France," in a commemorative volume to Henri Hauser, *Humanisme et Renaissance* (Geneva: Librairie Droz, 1958), p. 12.

10. G. Ascoli, "Essai sur l'histoire des idées féministes en France du XVIe siècle à la Révolution," *Revue de synthèse historique* (1906): 29.

11. Henri Hauser, *La Modernité du XVIe siècle* (Paris: Alcan, 1930). "Four great events at the end of the 15th and beginning of the 16th centuries signal a new era in European politics:
(1) the formation of modern States, and the birth of the idea of nationality;
(2) the elaboration of the democratic ideal;
(3) the secularization of politics;
(4) the transformation of international relations."

12. Ruth Kelso, *Doctrine for the Lady of the Renaissance* (Urbana: University of Illinois Press, 1956, new ed. 1978).

13. Jean Delumeau, *La Civilisation de la Renaissance* (Paris: Arthaud, 1967), p. 435.

14. *De l'institution du Prince*, "a book containing several teachings and wise sayings of the Greek and also Latin ancients, made and composed by Guillaume Budé," 1547.

15. *Annotationes ad libros pandectarum* (1527), p. 186. [Altera editio Annotationum in Pandectas.] "Philological research drew attention to Celtic; it did not take long to remark relationships between Celtic and Greek," Claude Gilbert Dubois, *Celtes et Gaulois au XVIe siècle: Le Développement littéraire d'un mythe nationaliste* (Paris: Vrin, 1972), p. 27.

16. We only know that Budé complained to Erasmus about hindrances to his intellectual activity caused by domestic worries. He also had frequent contacts with the Spanish Erasmian Juan Luis Vivès (1492–1540), author of *The Instruction of a Christian Woman* (French translation: 1579; English, 1557).

17. *Correspondance d'Erasme de Rotterdam et de Guillaume Budé*, ed. Marie-Madeleine de la Garanderie (Paris: J. Vrin, 1967), p. 230.

18. Erasmus, *La Civilité puérile* [*De Civilitate morum puerilium*, Good manners for children], with prefatory notes by Alcide Bonneau on books of manners since the sixteenth century (Paris: Éditions Ramsay, 1977) p. 89.

19. "A first question inevitably posed itself: to what extent is she the pupil of humanism and what does she owe to it? She did not know Greek; she probably did not know Latin very well. . . . Attracted early on by the Bible and Christian spirituality, she does not appear to have acquainted herself thoroughly with classical art or philosophy. She only came into contact with Platonism fairly late, via the intermediary of the mystic glossers of Alexandria or Florence." Augustin Renaudet, *Humanisme et Renaissance*, p. 219.

20. Castiglione cites Anne de Bretagne among the most remarkable women of his time. See *The Courtier*, book 3, chap. 34.

21. In the index of his complete works the word "mulier" is mentioned only once: "Correspondance de officiis Marsilius fecimus de Cherubino Quasqualio vero doctissimo," *Omnio opera*, vol. 1, p. 744. The conviviality he established between his disciples and himself did not include women. Unlike Urbino of Ferrara where, at the beginning of the sixteenth century, great ladies surrounded by their courtiers would make Platonism fashionable, the Florentine academy was a circle impenetrable by women. See André Chastel, *Marsile Ficin et l'art* (Geneva: Droz, 1954), p. 13.

22. M. Ficino, *Commentary on Plato's Symposium on Love*, trans. with intro. and notes by Sears Jayne (Dallas: Spring Publishers, 1985), p. 136.

23. Raymond Marcel, *Marsile Ficin sur le Banquet de Platon: Ou De l'amour*, thesis in Letters (Paris: Ed. les Belles Lettres, 1956), p. 97.

24. Jean Festugière, *La Philosophie de l'amour de Marsile Ficin et son influence sur la littérature française au XVIe siècle* (Paris: J. Vrin, 1941), p. 124.

25. Ibid., p. 45: "There were at least sixteen Italian editions from 1526 to 1587; one of these was printed in Lyon by Guillaume in 1562. It was translated into French by 1537, and six French editions appeared by 1592."

26. Erwin Panofsky, *Studies in Iconology: Humanistic Themes in the Art of the Renaissance* (1939, New York: Harper & Row, 1962), p. 144.

27. M. Spanneut, *Permanence du stoïcisme de Zénon à Malraux* (Paris: Ed. Duculot,

1973), p. 222: "References to Cicero are frequent; he embodied the perfect orator who defined the perfect courtier's rules for living."

28. Louise Labé, in Maïté Albistur and Daniel Armogathe, "Le Grief des femmes," *Anthologie de textes féminins du Moyen Age à 1848* (Poitiers: Hier et Demain, 1978), p. 49.

29. André Tiraqueau, *De legibus connubialibus.*

30. Emile Telle, *Erasme de Rotterdam et le septième sacrement: Etude d'évangelisme matrimonial au XVIe siècle et contribution à la biographie intellectuelle d'Erasme* (Geneva: Droz, 1954), p. 296.

31. The first edition of the *Encomium Matrimonii* appeared in Louvain on 30 March 1518.

32. German translation: 1542; English: 1532–53.

33. In 1518 and 1519, Lefèvre d'Etaples became one of the first victims of this persecution. He was attacked by the Sorbonne because of his book on "the three Marys," wherein he proved that Mary Magdalene, Lazarus's sister Mary, and the sinful woman were actually three separate women, and not one as the church had long maintained.

34. On this subject, see the facsimile edition of *La Déclamation des louanges de mariage,* notes and comments by Emile Telle (1525; Geneva: Droz, 1976), pp. 44–45.

35. Ibid., pp. 206–7.

36. Ibid., p. 174.

37. "I would hope that women read the Gospel, the Epistles of St. Paul, and that the plowman and the weaver sing them at their work." Quoted by A. Renaudet, *Préréforme et humanisme à Paris pendant les premières guerres d'Italie, 1494–1517,* p. 675.

38. Max Weber, *The Protestant Ethic and the Spirit of Capitalism* (New York: Scribner, 1930).

39. *Institutio christianae religionis,* 1536; French trans. 1541–44. This book was burned by order of the Sorbonne, 1544.

40. *Calvin et l'éloquence française: Epitre au roi* (Paris: Ed. critique J. Pannier, Fischbacher, 1934).

41. At the end of 1530, in answer to the Protestant assembly of Smalkalde, François published letters obliging the Courts of Parliament, the Bailiffs, Seneschals, Provosts, and other officers of royal justice to lend their aid, manpower, and prison facilities to the judges delegated by Antoine Duprat, the Cardinal Archbishop of Sens and papal legate in France, to initiate proceedings against the Lutherans, in cooperation with the inquisitors of faith. See W. H. Guiton, *La Réforme à Paris: XVIe et XVIIe siècles* (Asnières: 1931), p. 29.

42. E. Doumergue, *Jean Calvin et les choses de son temps: La pensée ecclésiastique et la pensée politique,* vol. 5 (Lausanne, 1917).

43. [A trivializing term: little women, or silly women.—Trans.]

44. Jean Calvin, "Sermon 20, sur la seconde épitre de St. Paul à Timothée" (Geneva, 1563), p. 446.

45. Ibid., p. 448.

46. André Bieler, *L'Homme et la femme dans la morale calviniste* (Geneva: Ed. Labor et Fides, 1963), p. 89.

47. John Calvin, *Calvin's New Testament Commentaries,* ed. David and Thomas Torrance, trans. T. H. L. Parker (Grand Rapids, Mich.: Wm. B. Eerdmans Publishing Co., 1965), vol. 10, *The First and Second Epistles of Paul the Apostle to Timothy,* p. 219.

48. Bieler, *L'Homme et la femme,* pp. 147–48.

49. *Calvin's New Testament Commentaries,* vol. 11, *The Epistles of Paul the Apostle to the Galatians, Ephesians, Philippians and Colossians,* pp. 204–205.

50. Bieler's interpretation: "It is important to emphasize that in Calvin's thinking, social inequality of husband and wife is a result of historical phenomena." *L'Homme et la femme,* p. 148.

51. Bieler, *L'Homme et la femme*, p. 37.

52. "There is only one religious domain. There are not two separate realms in human life, the realm of relations with God and the realm of relations with nature. There is only one realm in nature and civil society, as in religion and in the Church." Emile Doumergue, *Jean Calvin*, vol. 4, *La Pensée religieuse de Calvin* (Lausanne, 1910), p. 49.

53. Jean Calvin, *Commentaires sur l'Ancien Testament*, vol. 1, *Le Livre de la Genèse* (Geneva: Labor et Fides, 1961), p. 55. "It is not good that the man should be alone. That sacred bond is especially conspicuous, by which the husband and the wife are combined in one body, and one soul; as nature itself taught Plato, and others of the sounder class of philosophers, to speak," Calvin, *Commentaries on the Book of Genesis*, vol. 1, trans. Rev. John King (Edinburgh, 1847), p. 128.

54. René Metz, "Le Statut de la femme en droit canonique médiéval," in *Recueils de la société Jean Bodin pour l'histoire comparative des institutions*, vol. 12, *La Femme* (Brussels, 1962), pp. 61 and 66: First Epistle to the Corinthians, Epistle to the Ephesians, Epistle to the Colossians, in the Epistles to Timothy.

55. Emile Doumergue, *Jean Calvin*, vol. 2 (Lausanne: G. Bridel, 1902), p. 79. Also cited in Emmanuel Rodocanachi, *Renée de France, duchesse de Ferrare* (Paris: P. Ollendorff, 1896), p. 385.

56. Ibid.

57. The Calvinist ecclesiastical system assigns the governing of the church to a mixed body (pastors and laity) called, at its various levels, the presbytery, presbyterial council of the parish, consistory, provincial synod, and national synod.

58. *Calvin's New Testament Commentaries*, vol. 10, p. 259.

59. "Sermon 39, sur la première épître de St. Paul à Timothée, 7:13" (Geneva, 1563), p. 236.

60. This is suggested by Doumergue: "The synod of Middelbourg speaks only of possible problems. They were acting according to the morality of the time and a certain idea of the role of women. Thus Sandeman, in juxtaposing the two dates 1609 and 1610—the last appointments of deaconesses and the definitive reallocation of funds for the poor, respectively—feels the needs to add: 'the male-dominated bureaucracy viewed women's most delicate functions with disfavor.' " *Jean Calvin*, vol. 5, p. 307.

61. Joseph Lecler, *Histoire de la tolérance au siècle de la Réforme* (Paris: Ed. Aubier, 1955), vol. 2, pp. 22–24.

62. "The king does not want you to disagree over which opinion is the better one, . . . for it is not a matter here of *constituenda religione, sed de constituenda republica*; even he who is excommunicated is still a citizen. . . . And we can live peaceably with those of diverse opinions, as we see in a family, or those who are Catholics do not allow to live in peace, love those of the new religion, as it is said that *vita uxoris aut sunt tollenda, aut toleranda.*" *Oeuvres complètes de Michel de l'Hospital*, vol. 1 (Paris, 1824), p. 452.

63. There existed a discourse on women's *courage* which still, however, found no echo in the consideration of their political rights. "The heroic fidelity to the group and to the family of Huguenot women, martyred for their faith, overrides personal affirmation." Cf. R. Gout, *Le Miroir des dames chrétiennes*, vol. 2, *Pages féminines de la Réforme française* (Paris, 1937).

64. See P. Mealy, *Les Origines des idées politiques en France: Les Publicistes de la Réforme sous François II et Charles IX* (Paris: Fischbacher, 1903).

65. Cf. Miguel Abensour and Marcel Gauchet's foreword to La Boétie's *Discours de la servitude volontaire*: "It seems that the Discourse was forgotten by most of the public, but had an underground following among the 'dangerous' groups of the period—libertines and republicans" (Paris: Ed. Payot, 1978), p. 11.

66. C. Labitte, *De la démocratie chez les prédicateurs de la Ligue* (Paris, 1841).

67. Trans. Harry Kurz (New York: Columbia University Press, 1942), p. 6.

68. Nicole Loraux, *Les Enfants d'Athéna: Idées athéniennes sur la citoyenneté et la division des sexes* (Paris: Maspéro, Textes à l'appui, 1981), p. 14.

69. "Besides, to tell the truth, the ordinary capacity of women is inadequate for that communion and fellowship which is the nurse of this sacred bond; nor does their soul seem firm enough to endure the strain of so tight and durable a knot." Michel de Montaigne, "On Friendship," *Essays*, trans. Donald Frame (Stanford: Stanford University Press, 1965), p. 138.

70. Delaruelle, "L'Inspiration antique dans le discours de la servitude volontaire," *Revue d'histoire littéraire de la France* 17 (1910): 61. Embedded citation is taken from Kurz's translation (cf. note 67), p. 50.

71. [Trans. ours. Jean Bodin, *Les six livres de la République* (Paris: Jacques du Puys, 1577) book 1, chap. 1, p. 1. For the entire original English translation, see Jean Bodin, *The Six Bookes of a Commonweale*, trans. Richard Knolles (1606), reprint ed. Kenneth D. McRae (Cambridge: Harvard University Press, 1962). For clarity, most of the following passages from Bodin are our translations. When possible, we have based our translations on the abridged version of Bodin's book translated by M. J. Tooley (Oxford: Basil Blackwell, [1955] 1967). In most cases we will give the corresponding reference to the Knolles translation within brackets, followed by the original French text cited by Fauré.]

72. [Knolles, book 2, chap. 1, p. 193.] Bodin, *République*, p. 228.

73. Jean Ceard, "Le modèle de la République de Platon et la pensée politique au XVIe siècle," in *Platon et Aristote à la Renaissance*, XVIe colloque international de Tours (Paris: Vrin, 1976), p. 178.

74. Michel Villey, "Aristote, Vitona et Grotius," in *Platon et Aristote à la Renaissance*, p. 214.

75. [Trans. ours. See Knolles, book 1, chap. 1, p. 4.] Bodin, *République*, p. 4.

76. [Trans. ours. See Knolles, book 1, chap. 3, p. 15.]

77. [Trans. ours. See Knolles, book 6, chap. 5, pp. 752–53.] Bodin, *République*, p. 726.

78. Antoine Loisel, *La Guyenne qui sont huict remonstrances faictes en la Chambre de Justice de Guyenne sur le subject des edicts de pacification* (Paris: Abel l'Angelier, 1605), p. 336.

79. See R. Chauviré's summary of the points of convergence between the texts of the Republic and the minutes of these Estates, in *Jean Bodin, auteur de la République* (Paris: La Flèche, 1914), p. 249.

80. Bodin's participation in the Estates General is recounted by Pierre Bayle in the *Dictionnaire historique et critique* (1620): "At the Estates of Blois, he showed himself to be sympathetic to the rights of the people; he proclaimed with Gallic independence that the funds of the royal domain belonged to the provinces and that the king could only use them. . . . He advised also that the deputies of the two bodies could decide nothing without the support of the third, and on his admonition, the deputies of the ecclesiastical order and the deputies of the nobility who had been of a contrary opinion, changed their feelings—which told Henri III that on that day, Jean Bodin had been the Leader of the Estates." Quoted in Jean Bodin, *Oeuvres philosophiques* (Paris: Presses universitaires de France, 1951), p. xxviii.

81. [Trans. ours. Knolles, book 4, chap. 7, p. 397.] Bodin, *République*, book 3, chap. 7, p. 382.

82. Albert Jarrin, *Un économiste libéral au XVIe siècle, Jean Bodin*, from his larger work, *Rehaussement et diminution des monnayes* (Chambéry: Imprimerie Savoisienne, 1904). Remarks on "Le discours de J. Bodin sur le fait des monnaies et réponse aux paradoxes de M. de Malestroit touchant l'enrichissement de toutes choses et le moyen d'y remédier" (Paris: Jacques du Puys, 1568).

83. Michel Villey, *La Formation de la pensée juridique moderne*, Cours d'Histoire de la Philosophie du Droit (Paris: Montchrestien, 1975), p. 544.

84. [Trans. ours.] Bodin, *République*, book 1, chap. 9, pp. 150–51.

85. "Let us limit ourselves to private law, and state that in the eyes of this customary

law as a whole, woman is solely an object. During childhood she lives like other *alieni juris* under the *patria potestas* of her father who can alienate her and reclaim her." R. Villiers, "Le Statut de la femme à Rome jusqu'à la fin de la République," *Recueils de la Société Jean Bodin*, vol. ii, (Brussels, 1959).

86. Roman women strongly resisted the sumptuary laws aimed at them. In 195 B.C. they overcame Cato's opposition, and obtained the repeal of the Oppian law that curbed external manifestations of wealth in women. See Michel Villey, "Que Sais-je?" *Le Droit Romain* (Paris: Presses universitaires de France, 1972), p. 55.

87. Jean Gaudemet, "Le Statut de la femme dans l'Empire romain," *Recueils de la Société Jean Bodin*, vol. ii, p. 191.

88. Michel Villey, *Leçons d'histoire de la philosophie du droit* (Paris: Dalloz, 1962), pp. 172–73.

89. Jean Bodin, *Tableau du droit universel* (1580), ed. Pierre Mesnard (Paris: Presses universitaires de France, 1951), pp. 83–84.

90. Etienne Pasquier, *L'Interprétation des Institutes de Justinian* (Paris, 1847).

91. Pasquier devoted an important work to this subject: *Les Recherches de la France* (Paris, 1560). The first five chapters of the *Recherches* cover various historical points about the Gauls; through these chapters Pasquier is paving the way for a rehabilitation of the Gauls. He is the first to classify would-be racial characteristics under living conditions. See Claude-Gilbert Dubois, *Celtes et Gaulois au XVIe siècle*, p. 116: "For him, Roman law's only authority is moral and doctrinal. Etienne Pasquier recognizes in it only its character of written argument; judges should apply Roman principles and texts only when they are harmonious with the spirit of existing custom."

92. Pasquier, *Institutes de Justinian*, p. 74.

93. Etienne Pasquier, "Le Mauvais traitement": "In the case when the husband employs horrible cruelties against her, she may appear not before the church judge but before the royal judge, so that a separation of bodies may be ordered. The other cause for divorce is when the husband accuses his wife of adultery. And although according to God's law there must be reciprocal justice, women's modesty has never permitted them to take action for this against their husbands, thus only husbands against wives. Ordinarily the judgment given is to establish the wife in certain convents, for the rest of her life, unless her husband wishes to take her back and reconcile with her." *Institutes de Justinian*, p. 96.

94. Robert Muchembled, *La Sorcière au village, XVIe et XVIIe siècles* (Paris: Gallimard/Julliard, Coll. Archives, 1979), p. 73.

95. Sydney Anglo, "Melancholia and Witchcraft: The Debate Between Wier, Bodin, and Scott," in *Folie et déraison à la Renaissance* (Brussels: University of Brussels, 1976), p. 211. "Modern estimates of Wier's work have, in general, been very high . . . to praise his common sense, his humanity and his skillful deployment of medical evidence; to enthuse over his allegedly liberal minded skepticism."

96. "And since Wier is a physician, he must know that the woman's humor is directly contrary to adjust melancholy . . . as doctors all agree . . . as Galen says in his book *De atrabile*. Women are naturally cold and humid." Bodin, *De la démonomanie des sorciers* (J. du Puys, 1580), p. 226. Galen's medical authority was important until the Renaissance—the finalism of his system was appreciated by medical clerics of the Middle Ages. Cf. Yvonne Knibiehler and Catherine Fouquet, *La Femme et les médecins: Analyse historique* (Paris: Hachette, 1983), p. 38.

97. "Whoever casts spells upon men, or beasts or plants, as well as those who rise up in the air, or make a dog talk, or sever limbs with outpouring of blood and then reassemble them, this is evident proof. The second means of establishing clear and certain proof is when there are several reliable witnesses to give evidence of concrete things directly, and non-concrete things through speech and believable argument. The evidence of a notable fact must be apparent to judges and others present." Bodin, *La Démonomanie des sorciers*, book 4, chap. 2, p. 174.

98. Robert Muchembled, *Culture populaire et culture des élites* (Paris: Flammarion, 1978), p. 90.

99. Muchembled, *La Sorcière au village*. "The king's men were few: in 1554, 600 provosts, 86 bailiffs and seneschals, and 10 parliaments composed the monarchy's entire judiciary apparatus—while at the same time France had twenty or thirty thousand seigneurial justice courts."

100. Muchembled, *La Sorcière au village*, p. 125.

101. Jean Wier, Médecin du duc de Clèves, *Histoires, disputes et discours des illusions et impostures des diables, des magiciens infâmes, sorcières et empoisonneurs des ensorcellez démoniaques et de la guérison d'iceux: Item de la punition que méritent les magiciens, les empoisonneurs et les sorciers*, vol. 1 (Paris, 1885, chap. 4), p. 300.

102. R. Mandrou, *Magistrats et sorciers en France au XVIIe siècle: Une analyse de psychologie historique* (Paris: Plon, 1968), p. 133.

103. Very systematically, Bodin analyzed the implications of his position against women: "If under gynocracy natural law is violated, civil law and the law of the land are violated all the more." *La République*, book 6, chap. 5, p. 725.

104. She died around the age of eighty.

105. "Mlle. de Gournay, who made the mistake of living too long...also mistaken in having the aggressive and surly attitude of an old pedant." Maurice Rat, *Oeuvres complètes de Montaigne* (Paris: Gallimard, Bibliothèque de la Pléïade, 1962), p. 3.

106. 1588, 1595, 1598, 1600, 1602, 1604, 1611, 1617, 1625, 1635.

107. Mario Schiff, *La Fille d'alliance de Montaigne, Marie de Gournay*, essay followed by *L'Egalité des hommes et des femmes* and the *Grief des dames* (Paris: Champion, 1910).

108. Emile Telle, *L'Oeuvre de Marguerite d'Angoulême, reine de Navarre, et la querelle des femmes* (Toulouse, 1937), p. 299.

109. See note 69 above.

110. Montaigne, *Oeuvres complètes*, p. 502.

111. This same letter (25 Apr. 1593) reveals that a missive from Marie to Lipsius had been lost, along with a brief treatise on the alliance between her father and herself.

112. "Justi Lispsii epistolarum selectarum centuriae ad Belgas XV," cited by Mario Schiff, *La Fille d'alliance*, p. 11.

113. Ascoli, "Essai sur l'histoire des idées féministes en France . . . ," *Revue de synthèse historique* (Paris, 1906): 43.

114. *Egalité des hommes et des femmes*, 1622.

115. Ibid., edition introduced by Mario Schiff (Paris, 1910), p. 61.

116. Léontine Zanta, *La Renaissance du stoïcisme au XVI siècle* (Paris: Champion, 1914).

117. Mlle. de Gournay herself took part in this debate and defended the Spanish Jesuit Mariana, who authored a work called *De rege, et regis institutione*, and whose theories were accused of inspiring Henri IV's assassination. "Adieu de l'âme du roy de France et de Navarre, Henry le Grand à la Reyne avec la defense des pères jésuites par la Damoiselle de Gournay" (Paris, 1610).

118. Bayle, *Dictionnaire historique et critique*, vol. 2, p. 1294. "She would have done well not to write against the Jansenist partisans in the Coton debate. A person of her sex should carefully avoid this sort of controversy."

119. Eugenio Garin, *L'Education de l'homme moderne, 1400–1600* (Paris: Fayard, 1968), pp. 94–95.

120. While she seems to have a good knowledge of Plato, her references to Aristotle are more tenuous; thus she advanced the claim: "as for the philosopher Aristotle, while moving heaven and earth [i.e., while he touched on all subjects], he did not contradict in any large measure, as far as I know, the opinion which favors women, but rather he confirmed it." Her misunderstanding of Aristotle is not an isolated case: Montaigne declared that he felt no attraction for him, as did Erasmus and, later, Bacon and Gassendi.

121. Three variants of the 1622 text exist in the following collections: *L'Ombre de la*

demoiselle de Gournay (1626), *Les Advis ou les presens de la demoiselle de Gournay* (1634), and the second edition of the latter, 1641.

122. Anna Maria van Schurman settled in Utrecht after her father's death. She was considered a true prodigy by her contemporaries. Her biographers inform us that she knew the following languages fluently: Hebrew, Chaldean, Assyrian, Arabic, Turkish, Greek, Latin, French, Italian, Spanish, English, German, Flemish, and Dutch.

123. "If ladies achieve degrees of excellence less often than men, it is not surprising, because of their lack of good education." Cited in Schiff, *La Fille d'alliance*, p. 65.

124. "Is there more difference between men and women than between women . . . raised in city and countryside, or in different nations?" Ibid., p. 65.

125. "French women, and even English women, have a special advantage on those of other nations in wit and politeness over those of Italy, where the cleverest people in Europe are born. And this advantage could not arise . . . if French women were not well instructed, polite, and refined by conversation; the others are not: they are recluses . . . not mixing much in the world."

126. *Grief des dames*, ed. Mario Schiff, p. 89.

III. Female Education and Feminist Humanism under Absolute Monarchy

1. Albert Thibaudet, *Histoire de la littérature française de 1789 à nos jours* (Paris: Stock, 1936), p. 458.

2. Daniel Mornet, *Histoire de la clarté française* (Paris: Payot, 1929), p. 39.

3. Paul Bénichou, *Man and Ethics: Studies in French Classicism*, trans. Elizabeth Hughes (Garden City: Anchor Books, 1971), p. 245.

4. Ibid., p. 245.

5. Ibid., p. 206.

6. Gilles Deleuze, *Spinoza et le problème de l'expression* (Paris: Minuit, 1968), pp. 137–38.

7. Michel Foucault, *Madness and Civilization: A History of Insanity in the Age of Reason*, trans. Richard Howard (New York: Pantheon Books, 1965), p. 38.

8. Bénichou, *Man and Ethics*, p. 119.

9. Cardin le Bret, *De la souveraineté du Roy* (Paris: Chez Toussaincts du Bray, 1632), p. 31.

10. "We should nevertheless note that in the seventeenth century it was more easily accepted than before that a woman could serve as regent not only during the absence of the King, but also during his minority (minority of Louis XIII and Edict of April 1643). The conflicts between the king and the aristocracy led at times to designating the queen 'overseer of the seas' (appointment letters from 9 July 1646), gave them a princess as governor (Marie-Louise de Gonzague), governor and lieutenant-general of the land, and duchy of Nivernois and Donziois." See Jean Portemer, "La Femme dans la législation royale," in *Etudes d'histoire du droit privé, offertes à Pierre Petot* (Dalloz, Librairie du Recueil Sirey, 1959), p. 9.

11. Jean Portemer, "Le Statut de la femme en France depuis la réformation des coutumes jusqu'à la rédaction du code civil," *Recueils de la Société Jean Bodin*, vol. 12 (Brussels, 1959), p. 451.

12. Jean Domat, "Des personnes," *Les Lois civiles dans leur ordre naturel: Le Droit public et legum delectus* (Paris, 1623), sect. 1, p. 11.

13. René de Lespinasse, *Histoire générale de Paris: Les Métiers et corporations de la ville de Paris XIV, XVIII ordonnances générales*, vol. 1, *Métiers de l'alimentation* (Paris: Imprimerie nationale, 1886), p. 11.

14. Letters of 23 Mar. 1673.

15. Lespinasse, *Histoire générale de Paris*, vol. 3, p. 62.

16. Ibid., p. 64. "There were six linen maids among the *métiers* that traveled with the court; an edict of 1694 named as a matter of course 34 new official cloth measurers."

17. Ibid., vol. 3, p. 45.

18. By letters patent of November 1595, they are elevated to the status of sworn trades.

19. 21 Aug. 1677.

20. Ibid., vol. 3, pp. 616–17.

21. Ibid., vol. 1, p. 489.

22. Emile Coornaert, *Les Corporations en France avant 1789* (Paris: Gallimard, 1941), p. 190. "It was considered appropriate for the decency and modesty of women and girls to permit them to be dressed by people of their own sex whenever they deemed it appropriate."

23. A. R. J. Turgot, "Eloge de Monsieur de Gournay," in *Oeuvres de Turgot, Ministre d'Etat* (1808), vol. 3, p. 333.

24. —Order of King Henry III, published in the court of Parliament, the 25th day of January 1580, arts. 40, 44;
—Order of King Louis XIII, published in Parliament 15 Jan. 1629, arts. 39, 40, 169;
—Order of King Louis XIV—April 1667, for civil matters, Title XX;
—Edict of the King, March 1697, concerning the formalities that should be observed in marriage;
—Declaration of the king on 9 Apr. 1736, concerning the formalities for registering baptisms, marriages, burials, the donning of the habit, novitiates and professions, and the certificates that should be delivered.

25. Order of King Henry III, published in the court of Parliament, 25 Jan. 1580, chap. 1, 40, 42.

26. Henri Rollet, *La Condition de la femme dans l'Eglise* (Paris: Fayard, 1975), p. 132.

27. "Tametsi" chapter of the Conciliar Decree concerning marriage reform, cited by François Lebrun, *La Vie conjugale sous l'Ancien Régime* (Paris: Armand Colin, 1975), p. 16.

28. Roger Chartier, Marie-Madeleine Compère, Dominique Julia, *L'Education en France du XVIe au XVIIe siècle* (Paris: Sedes, 1976), p. 233.

29. Text noted in the bull accorded to the Toulouse Ursulines 9 Apr. 1615. The different pontifical bulls contained other such texts. Cited by Mother Marie de Chantal Gueudré, *Les Monastères d'Ursulines sous l'ancien régime, 1612–1788* (Paris: S. Paul), pp. 229–30.

30. Ibid., p. 87. The author provides a detailed chronology of these creations.

31. Ibid.

32. Abbé Reneault, *Les Ursulines de Rouen, 1619–1906* (Fécamp, 1919), p. 6.

33. Chartier, et al., *L'Education en France*, p. 236.

34. Reneault, *Les Ursulines*, pp. 168–71.

35. Gustave Fagniez, *La Femme et la société française dans la première moité du XVIIe siècle* (Paris, 1929), p. 343.

36. *Conseils de Saint Jérôme sur l'éducation d'une jeune fille, adressés à Laeta, mère de Paula, pouvant servir à toutes les mères chrétiennes* (n.d.).

37. Mother Marie de Chantal Gueudré, "La Femme et la vie spirituelle," in *Revue XVIIe siècle* 62–63 (1964): 70. [Pierre de Berulle, the French cardinal who helped Mme. Acarie to establish the Carmelite order, was a key figure in the French spiritual movement of the seventeenth century. Saint Theresa was an influential Spanish Carmelite whose mysticism is best known through her *Le Château Intérieur*. —Trans.]

38. Cited by Gueudré, ibid., p. 71.

39. Georges Snyders, *La Pédagogie en France au XVIIe siècle* (Paris: PUF, 1965), p. 164.

40. "Historians of French religion have shown that the Counter-Reformation, during the reigns of Henry IV and Louis XIII, relied on Augustinism. Berulle and others were behind the great reaction against stoicism that constitutes one of the most significant developments of the spiritual renaissance during the seventeenth century." Antoine Adam, *Sur le problème religieux dans la première moitié du XVIIe siècle* (Oxford: Clarendon Press, 1959), p. 7.

41. Jean Palmero, *Histoires des institutions et des doctrines pédagogiques par les textes* (Paris: Sudel, 1951), p. 186.

42. Jacqueline Pascal, *Les constitutions du Monastère de Port-Royal du sacrement* (1665), p. 426.

43. Adam, *Sur le problème religieux*, p. 13.

44. Antoine Adam, *Les Jansénistes du XVIIe siècle* (Paris: Fayard, 1968), p. 58.

45. Robert Dequenne, *La Femme et l'éducation à travers la littérature du XVII siècle*, doctoral thesis (Université de Paris, 1970), p. 72.

46. Henriette Houillon came up with the following figures: in 1680, there were 334 primary schools in Paris of which 167 were for girls; in Normandy, out of 1160 parishes, there were 1160 schools of which 306 were for girls. From "La femme en France au XVIIe et XVIIIe siècles," in *Histoire mondiale de la femme*, ed. Pierre Grimal, vol. 4 (Paris: Nouvelle Librairie de France, 1966), p. 19. Georges Mongrédien came up with similar figures in *La Vie quotidienne sous Louis XIV* (Paris: Hachette, 1948).

47. A list of these organizations was drawn up by Chartier et al., *L'Education en France*, p. 237.

48. Some Ursulines went out to spread the gospel in the New World. The establishment of the Rouen Ursulines in Louisiana took place in 1625. Cf. Abbé Reneault, *Les Ursulines de Rouen*, p. 199.

49. "Toward this end I have found it necessary to order that all schools for boys be run by men . . . and that all schools for girls be run by women or girls, without allowing boys or girls ever to attend the same schools." Excerpted in Palermo, *Histoire des institutions*, p. 208.

50. [RPR: Religion Prétendue Réformée, or alleged reformed religion, was used by French Catholics to refer to Protestants. —Trans.]

51. Article from the register of Parliament, 13 Dec. 1698, vol. 7, p. 472.

52. "You are to train excellent virgins for the cloisters and pious mothers for society; in thus sanctifying the two principal states of your sex, you will contribute to establishing the true reign of God for all orders and for all conditions, because we know how much a mother is concerned for the proper education of her children, how a prudent and virtuous wife can instill religion into her husband's heart." Cited by Théophile Lavallée, *Histoire de la maison royale de Saint-Cyr* (Paris, 1856), pp. 134–35.

53. Chartier et al., *L'Education en France*, pp. 242–43.

54. 1688 and 1691.

55. Cited by Yves Poutet, *Le XVIIe siècle: Recherches sur la genèse de l'oeuvre scolaire et religieuse de Jean-Baptiste de la Salle—1651–1719*, vol. 1, 1970, p. 17.

56. Languet, *Mémoires de Saint-Cyr*, chap. 18, cited by Yves Poutet, *Le XVIIe siècle*, p. 101.

57. *Lettres de Madame de Sévigné, de sa famille et de ses amis* (Paris, 1813), vol. 9, p. 252, letter 1026, Paris, 21 Jan. 1689.

58. Gustave Reynier, *La Femme au XVIIe siècle* (Paris: Plon, 1933), p. 168.

59. *Historia mulierum philosopharum scriptore Aegigio Menago.*

60. Anne Lefebvre, Madame Dacier, later engaged in the "querelle des anciens et des modernes" that divided the intellectual world at the end of the seventeenth century.

61. "Because caring for the poor was the first purpose of this establishment." Article II, "Sommaire des chapitres de l'inventaire des adresses du bureau ou table de rencontre," *Inventaire des adresses du bureau de rencontre.*

62. Ibid., pp. 26–27.

63. *Recueil général des questions traitées et conférences du Bureau d'adresses, sur toutes sortes de matières, par les beaux esprits de ce temps à Paris* (1656), p. 449.

64. *Recueil général*, p. 456.

65. "All of the conferences, but especially these on demonology, astrology, and the occult, indicate a general and persistent skepticism. The weekly sessions did not aim at

a conclusion, permitting as a result an extravagant free-for-all of opinions, from the slavishly orthodox to the most rational, secular, or radical. Throughout there remained an invigorating flavor of skeptical questioning of these subjects." Howard Solomon, *Public Welfare, Science, and Propaganda in 17th Century France: The Innovations of Théophraste Renaudot* (Princeton: Princeton University Press, 1972), p. 81.

66. "The entire summer of 1638 was devoted to a discussion of the French economy, the pressures of a war economy were overwhelming, for the monarchy and Richelieu seemed eager to act decisively and broadly at this time; his 'reglement des finances' for example was promulgated in July 1638. Renaudot's Academy met informally throughout the summer of 1638 and prepared a report for the crown on ways of reestablishing commerce in France—the summarized recommendations ran the gamut of mercantile ideas: currency stabilization, encouraging nobles to enter commerce, supporting retail." Ibid., p. 89.

67. The expansion of religious communities reached such an extent that the general assembly of the clergy appealed to the king for the financial aid indispensable to their survival (19 Apr. 1727).

68. Guillaume Postel, 1553, "Les Très Merveilleuses Victoires des femmes du nouveau monde, et comme elles doivent à tout le monde, par raison, commander et même à ceux qui auront la monarchie du monde vieil."

69. Paul Hoffmann, "Précosité et féminisme dans le roman de Michel de Pure," *Travaux de linguistique et de littérature publiées par le Centre de Philosophie et de Littérature romanes de l'Université de Strasbourg* (Strasbourg, 1967), vol. 2, p. 2.

70. Alice de Payer, *Au temps de la Fronde* (Paris: Société des Editions Fast, 1922).

71. Budeau de Somaize, *Le Grand Dictionnaire des Précieuses* (1660; reprint, Paris: Ch. L. Livet, 1856), p. 158.

72. "One of those two old henchmen of the University, named Horacien, who, as soon as he started talking, quoted all of Cicero and Quintilian and then concluded that it was a terrible thing, very indicative of the century's evils, for women to know the rules of discourse and the value of things of knowledge," *op. cit.*, vol. 1., p. 165.

73. [*ruelle*: originally, the space between a bed and the wall; with the *Précieuses*, this came to designate the room in which the literary salon was held. —Trans.]

74. Hoffmann, "Précosité et feminisme," p. 27.

75. L'Abbé de Pure, *La Précieuse ou les mystères de la ruelle*, vol. 1, p. 169.

76. Madame de Maintenon did not hesitate to circulate the moral conversations of Mlle. de Scudéry at Saint-Cyr; and in her "new moral conversations" Mlle. de Scudéry devoted a chapter to Saint-Cyr, as a haven for Christian morality. See her *Nouvelles Conversations de morale dédiées au roi*, vol. 1 (Paris: 1688), pp. 247–79.

77. Louis de Lesclache, *Les Avantages que les femmes peuvent recevoir de la Philosophie et principalement de la morale ou l'abrégé de cette science* (Paris: 1667), p. 11.

78. It is interesting to note, however, that "the salon women, under the patronage of the one who started the 'Palais précieux,' were hardly anxious to respond to the invitation." Reynier, *La Femme au XVIIe siècle*, p. 153.

79. Portemer, "Le Statut de la femme," *Recueils de la Société Jean Bodin* (1962), p. 454.

80. Ibid., p. 458.

81. De Somaize, *La Grand Dictionnaire*, p. 156.

82. Claude Dulong, *L'Amour au XVIIe siècle* (Paris: Hachette, 1969), p. 128.

83. Roger La Thuillère, *La Préciosité: Etude historique et linguistique* (Geneva: Droz, 1966), p. 654.

84. Poullain de la Barre, *De l'égalité des deux sexes: Discours physique et moral où l'on voit l'importance de se défaire des préjugés* (Paris, 1673); *De l'éducation des Dames pour la conduite de l'esprit dans les sciences et dans les moeurs, entretiens* (Paris, 1674); *De l'excellence des hommes contre l'égalité des sexes, avec une dissertation qui sert de réponse aux objections tirées de l'Ecriture sainte contre le sentiment de l'Egalité* (Paris, 1675).

85. Henri Piéron, "De l'influence sociale des principes cartésiens, un précurseur inconnu du féminisme et de la révolution: Poullain de la Barre," *Revue de synthèse historique* 5 (1902): 10–11.

86. This information comes from the published thesis of Marie-Louise Stock, *Poullain de la Barre: A 17th-Century Feminist* (New York: Columbia University Press, 1961).

87. Bernard Magné, *Le Féminisme de Poullain de la Barre: Origine et signification*, doctoral thesis (Université de Toulouse, 1964), p. 152.

88. Henri Grappin, "Note sur un féministe oublié, le cartésien Poullain de la Barre," *Revue d'Histoire de la France* 20, (1913): 865.

89. De la Barre, *De l'égalité des deux sexes*, p. 17.

90. "The authority of the legal theorists on the subject of women . . . was given great weight, in the eyes of many people. They place women under the power of their husbands, like children under their father, and say that it is nature which has assigned them the smallest roles in society and which has separated them from public authority." Ibid., p. 94.

91. Ibid., p. 19.

92. Ibid., p. 28.

93. Ibid., p. 33, "How many people are there lying in the dust who would have made something of themselves if they had only been encouraged? And peasants who would make great scholars if given the chance to study?"

94. De la Barre, *De l'éducation des Dâmes*, p. 268.

95. De la Barre, *De l'égalité des deux sexes*, p. 42.

96. Paul Hoffmann, *La Femme dans la pensée des lumières* (Paris: Ophrys), p. 55.

97. Descartes, *Oeuvres complètes*, ed. Charles Adam and Paul Tannery, vol. 11 (Paris, 1909), p. 516.

98. Cf. Descartes's analysis between real distinction and modal distinction, paragraphs 60–61 of *Les Principes de la Philosophie* (Paris: Pléiade/Gallimard, 1953), p. 599.

99. Poullain's first book was well received by the *Précieuses*. However, he rejected any assimilation of his approach to the differences between the sexes with the more aristocratic approach of the *Précieuses*. Cf. De la Barre, *De l'éducation des Dâmes*, pp. 7–8.

100. "And even if we suppose that God had united a body to a soul so closely that it was impossible to bring them together more closely, and made a single thing out of the two, they would yet remain really distinct one from the other notwithstanding the union; because however closely God connected them He could not set aside the power which He possessed of separating them, or conserving them one apart from the other, and those things which God can separate, or conceive in separation, are really distinct." From *The Philosophical Works of Descartes*, trans. Elizabeth S. Haldane and G. R. T. Ross (Cambridge: Cambridge University Press, 1911), vol. 1, p. 244.

101. "It is the means by which commerce is maintained between us and nature; in a word, it is the channel and the instrument of all knowledge and of all actions," De la Barre, *De l'éducation des Dâmes*, p. 218.

102. In a letter to Mersenne, 23 Nov. 1646.

103. Ferdinand Alquié, *La Découverte métaphysique de l'homme chez Descartes* (Paris: PUF, 1966), p. 167.

104. *Nouvelles de la République des Lettres*, Oct. 1685, pp. 1145–46.

105. Joseph-François Michaud, *Biographie universelle ancienne et moderne*, vol. 32: Parisot, Jean Patrocle.

106. "I have established the order of my principles . . . which teach us that religion is founded on Holy Scripture, which contains Christian faith and knowledge of nature which is founded on resolvent philosophy that constitutes reason; all things of this world are expressions of this knowledge that God established, on which the entire reasoning of this book is based as if on two poles, of which one is the Gospels that God said, and the other is the work of nature which God made." Jean Patrocle Parisot, *La Foi dévoilée*

par la raison dans la connaissance de Dieu et de ses mystères et de la nature (Paris, 1681), preface.

107. *Oeuvres complètes de Michel de Montaigne,* "La Théologie naturelle de Raymond Sebond," (Paris, 1932), preface, p. 6.

108. "Finally, Stasimaque concluded, only self-knowledge can save us from a major error that has ruled over the entire earth since the beginning of the world." De la Barre, *De l'éducation des Dâmes,* p. 293.

109. "After 1689, he applied the method of rationalist exegesis to sacred texts, which was to be, at the outset of his work, the doctrine of the Protestants" Maïté Albistur and Daniel Armogathe, *Histoire du Féminisme français,* vol. 1 (Paris: Edition des Femmes, 1977), p. 226.

110. De la Barre, *De l'excellence des hommes contre l'égalité des sexes* (Paris, 1675), pp. 17–18.

111. Bayle, *Dictionnaire historique et critique,* vol. 3, p. 1937, note B: to Marinella or Marinelli Lucrece: "She carried the prejudices of her sex not only to equality, as other authors have done."

112. Michel Foucault, *Histoire de la folie à l'âge classique* (Paris: Gallimard, 1972), p. 175.

113. "How can one reasonably object to a woman with common sense, and enlightened intelligence, presiding at parliament or any other gathering?" De la Barre, *De l'égalité des deux sexes,* p. 170.

114. André Vachet, *L'Idéologie libérale* (Paris: Anthropos, 1970), p. 84.

115. Suchon alludes to Poullain de la Barre's "Traités" but never names them.

116. Gabrielle Suchon, *Traité de la morale et de la politique divisé en trois parties, scavoir: la liberté, la science et l'autorité où l'on voit que les personnes du sexe, pour en être privées, ne laissent pas d'avoir une capacité naturelle qui les en peut rendre participantes . . . avec un petit traité de la faiblesse, de la légèreté et de l'inconstance qu'on leur attribue mal à propos* (Lyon: J. Certe, 1693).

117. Suchon, "Traité de la morale," p. 118, chap. 19, "La Liberté rend l'exécution de nos entreprises aisée et facile."

118. "Bourgeois": "Collective noun, group of people who live in a city, also said of each inhabitant of the city, also said to designate people of the Third Estate as distinct from gentlemen or ecclesiastics, who enjoy several rights not enjoyed by people in the Third Estate." Furetière, *Dictionnaire universel de Furetière,* vol. 1 (The Hague and Rotterdam, 1960).

119. Ibid., p. 45.

120. Julien Eymard d'Angers, *Recherches sur le stoïcisme aux XVIe et XVIIe siècles* (G. Olms Verlag, Hildesheim, 1976), p. 464.

121. Ernst Cassirer, *Descartes, Corneille, Christine de Suède* (Paris: Vrin, 1942).

IV. Liberal Individualism, Natural Right, and Sexual Equality in the Political Philosophy of Montesquieu, Rousseau, and Condorcet

1. Thomas L. Pangle, *Montesquieu's Philosophy of Liberalism: A Commentary on the Spirit of the Laws* (Chicago: University of Chicago Press, 1973).

2. Charles Eisenmann, "L'Esprit des Lois et la séparation des pouvoirs," in *Mélanges Raymond Carré de Malberg* (Paris, 1933), p. 192. (See Bibliography for further references to Eisenmann's criticism.)

3. Author's source: *De L'Esprit des Lois, Oeuvres complètes,* Bibliothèque de la Pléiade (Paris: Gallimard, 1951). English translations are from *The Spirit of the Laws,* trans. Thomas Nugent (New York: Hafner, 1966). [All subsequent references to this work are to Nugent's translation, unless otherwise noted.] Nugent, Book 11, chap. 3, p. 150.

4. ["*Droit subjectif:* Prérogative appartenant à une personne en lui permettant d'exiger d'une autre soit des prestations ou des abstentions (droits personnels), soit le respect

d'une situation dont elle profite (droits réels, droits individuels)." *Trésor de la langue française* (CNRS, 1979), v. 7 p. 517. —Trans.]

5. Jeannette Geffriaud Rosso, *Montesquieu et la féminité* (Pisa: Libreria Goliardica editrice, 1977), p. 359.

6. *The Spirit of the Laws*, Book 11, chap. 6, p. 155 [trans. amended].

7. Ibid., book 1, chap. 3, p. 6.

8. "Levellers": label for the most diehard republicans in England during the Civil War. They were radicals in the Parliamentary Army. Their petition of January 1648 demanded suffrage for all Englishmen, "except those who are or will be legally deprived of their right to vote because of common law offences, as well as servants and indigents." Quoted in C. B. MacPherson, *La Théorie politique de l'individualisme possessif de Hobbes à Locke* (Paris: NRF, Gallimard, 1971), p. 122.

9. "One naturally follows the other: the despotic power of the prince is connected with the servitude of women; the liberty of women with the spirit of monarchy." *The Spirit of the Laws*, book 19, chap. 15, p. 300.

10. "The Salic law had not in view a preference of one sex to the other, much less had it a regard to the perpetuity of a family, a name, or the transmission of land. These things did not enter into the heads of the Germans; it was purely an economical law, which made the house and the land dependent thereon to the males who should dwell in it, and to whom it consequently was of most service." Ibid., book 18, chap. 22, p. 283.

11. Ibid., book 7, chap. 17, p. 108.

12. Ibid., book 2, chap. 1, p. 8.

13. "An essential element in understanding and interpreting *L'Esprit des Lois* is the combat against despotism, and against the *ancien régime's* arbitrariness; the doctrine of separation of powers is simply a form of revolt against tyranny." Boris Mirkine-Guetzevitch, "De la séparation des pouvoirs," *Recueil Sirey du bicentenaire de L'Esprit des Lois, 1748–1948* (Paris: Librairie du Recueil Sirey, 1952) p. 161.

14. *The Spirit of the Laws*, Book 9, chap. 7, p. 131.

15. "At Venice the legislative power is in the council, the executive in the *pregadi*, and the judiciary in the *quarantia*. But the mischief is, that these different tribunals are composed of magistrates all belonging to the same body." Ibid., book 11, chap. 6, p. 153.

16. Ibid., book 2, chap. 5, p. 18.

17. "When the savages of Louisiana wish to have fruit, they cut the tree at the bottom and gather the fruit. That is despotic government." Ibid., book 5, chap. 13, p. 57.

18. Ibid., book 16, chap. 6, p. 254.

19. Ibid., book 1, chap. 3, p. 7.

20. "Everything depends on establishing [the love of laws and of our country] in a republic . . . and to inspire it ought to be the principal business of education: but the surest way of instilling it into children is for parents to set them an example. People have it generally in their power to communicate their ideas to their children; but they are still better able to transfuse their passions." Ibid., book 4, chap. 5, p. 34.

21. Ibid., vol. 2, book 26, chap. 8, pp. 64–65.

22. "For every man who has any post at court, in Paris, or in the country, there is a woman through whose hands pass all the favours and sometimes the injustices that he does. These women are all in touch with one another, and compose a sort of commonwealth whose members are always busy giving each other mutual help and support." *Persian Letters*, trans. C. J. Betts (London: Penguin, 1973), letter 107, p. 197.

23. Jean Starobinski, *L'Invention de la liberté* (Geneva: Skira, 1964), p. 55.

24. John Locke, *Second Treatise of Government* (New York: Dutton, [n.d.]), chapter 6, p. 141. My argument here draws on the broad outlines of Susan Moller Okin's *Women in Western Political Thought* (Princeton: Princeton University Press, 1979), p. 200.

25. Locke, *Second Treatise of Government*, p. 147.

26. Ibid., chap. 7, p. 156–57.

27. Locke, "Some Thoughts Concerning Education," in Howard Penniman, ed., *John Locke on Politics and Education* (New York: Van Nostrand, 1947), p. 213.

28. *The Spirit of the Laws*, book 7, chap. 9, p. 102.

29. *The Spirit of the Laws*, Book 19, chap. 9, p. 295.

30. *L'Esprit des lois, Oeuvres Complètes* (Gallimard), book 7, chap. 4, p. 337.

31. Starobinski, *L'Invention de la liberté*, p. 13.

32. *Encyclopédie ou dictionnaire raisonné des sciences, des arts et des métiers par une Société des gens de Lettres*, vol. 7 (Paris, 1757), p. 766.

33. *The Spirit of the Laws*, vol. 2, book 28, chap. 22, p. 119. [Trans. amended.]

34. Geffriaud Rosso, *Montesquieu et la féminité*, p. 522.

35. *L'Idée du bonheur dans la littérature et la pensée française au XVIIIe siècle* (Paris: Armand Colin, 1960).

36. Jean-Jacques Rousseau, *Emile*, trans. Barbara Foxley (New York: Dutton, 1972), book 5, p. 422. [Trans. amended].

37. *The Spirit of the Laws*, book 1, chap. 2, p. 4.

38. M. le Baron de Pufendorf, *Le Droit de la nature et des gens, ou Système général des principes les plus importans de la morale de la jurisprudence et de la politique*, trans. from Latin by J. Barbeyrac (Amsterdam, 1706), vol. 1, book 1, chap. 1, p. 12. *The Law of Nature and Nations*, trans. from the 1688 ed. by C. H. and W. A. Oldfather (Oxford: Clarendon Press, 1934), p. 12.

39. Oldfather trans. vol. 1, book 1, chap. 1, par. 7, p. 8.

40. Preface to "Poème sur la loi naturelle" (1752), in Voltaire, *Mélanges*, Bibliothèque de la Pléiade (Paris: Gallimard, 1961), p. 272.

41. Michèle Duchet, *Anthropologie et histoire au siècle des lumières* (Paris: Maspero, 1971). Chapter on Voltaire's anthropology, p. 306.

42. Attributed to Ch. M. de la Condamine, *Histoire d'une jeune fille sauvage trouvée dans les bois, à l'âge de 10 ans, publiée par Madame H.* (Paris, 1755; Ducros, 1970), preface, p. 30.

43. G. D. H. Cole, "A Discourse on the Arts and Sciences," intro. to Jean-Jacques Rousseau, *The Social Contract and Discourses* (New York: E. P. Dutton, 1950). See esp. pp. 161–64.

44. "Such Luxury, which does no one any good, is the true bane of society; it brings poverty and death to the countryside, and it devastates the earth and wipes out humankind." *Fragments pour Emile, Oeuvres complètes* (Paris: Gallimard/Bibliothèque de la Pléiade, 1969), vol. 4, p. 872.

45. "Dedication to the Republic of Geneva," *Discourse on Inequality*, in *The Social Contract and Discourses*, p. 187.

46. For the important events of which women were the secret cause, see "Sur les femmes," in *Oeuvres Complètes*, vol. 2 (Paris: Gallimard/Bibliothèque de la Pléiade, 1961), pp. 1254–59.

47. Count Gaston de Villeneuve-Guibert, ed., *Le Portefeuille de Madame Dupin, Dame de Chenonceaux* (Paris, Calmann-Levy, 1884), pp. 16–17.

48. Rousseau, *Confessions*, book 8. ["L'homme de l'homme" implies "social man"; natural man would be man stripped of all that society confers on him. —Trans.]

49. *Discourse on Inequality*, in *The Social Contract and Discourses*, pp. 214–218, n. 12.

50. *The Social Contract and Discourses*, p. 239.

51. Ibid.

52. *Du Contrat social*, 1st version, chap. 5, *Oeuvres complètes*, vol. 3, p. 299. Also in *Discourse on Political Economy* in *The Social Contract and Discourses*, p. 287. Note that Rousseau does not develop this point of view in the definitive version of the Social Contract.

53. Pufendorf, *Le Droit de la nature*, vol. 2, book 6, chap. 2, par. 5; trans., p. 915.

54. "The condition of man does not permit him . . . to direct his actions by uncertain

impulse and without respect to any rule[.] [O]ur next task is to inquire into the common standard of human action, according to which every man, as a rational animal, should order his conduct. It has become the custom to designate this standard as the rule [ius] or law of nature." *Le Droit de la nature*, vol. 1, book 2, chap. 3, par. 1; trans., p. 179.

55. J. Morel, *Recherches sur les sources du Discours de l'inégalité*, vol. 5, (*Annales de la Société Jean-Jacques Rousseau*, 1909), p. 170.

56. Jean-Jacques Rousseau, *Politics and the Arts: Letter to M. D'Alembert on the Theatre*, trans. and ed. Allan Bloom (Ithaca: Cornell University Press, 1960), pp. 82–83. [Trans. slightly amended.]

57. "I expect the following question: savage women are not chaste, for they go naked? I answer that ours are even less so, for they are dressed." Ibid., p. 86n.

58. Ibid., p. 134.

59. "Whoever sang or danced best, whoever was the handsomest, the strongest, the most dexterous, or the most eloquent, came to be of most consideration; and this was the first step towards inequality, and at the same time towards vice." *Discourse on Inequality*, p. 241.

60. Jean Calvin, "Sermon où il est montré quelle doit être la modestie des femmes," (Geneva: Kundig, 1945).

61. Rousseau, "Lettres à Christophe de Beaumont, archevêque de Paris," *Oeuvres complètes*, vol. 4, p. 938. See also Ernst Cassirer, *La Philosophie des Lumières* (1932; Gérard Monford, 1982), pp. 171–72.

62. Calvin, "Sermon," p. 39.

63. "Emile is an orphan. No matter whether he has father or mother, having undertaken their duties I am invested with their rights." *Emile*, book 1, p. 20.

64. "There is all the difference in the world between a natural man living in a state of nature, and a natural man living in society. Emile is no savage to be banished to the desert, he is a savage who has to live in the town. He must know how to get his living in a town, how to use its inhabitants, and how to live among them, if not of them." Ibid., book 3, p. 167.

65. Ibid., book 4, p. 254.

66. *Du Contrat social*, book 1, chap. 1, 351–52.

67. *Emile*, book 5, p. 325.

68. "She never opens her mouth to answer him without first casting her eyes on those of her mother." *Emile, Oeuvres complètes*, vol. 4, book 5, p. 785.

69. *Emile*, book 5, Foxley trans., p. 348.

. 70. "Sophie is fond of dress, and she knows how to dress . . . Her dress is very modest in appearance and very coquettish in reality; she does not display her charms, she conceals them, but in such a way as to enhance them," book 5, Foxley trans., p. 356.

71. Ibid., p. 364. [Trans. slightly amended.]

72. Ibid., pp. 42–43.

73. *Fragments pour Emile*, 3, p. 872.

74. This threat resurfaces throughout Rousseau's writing. In the letters forming a sequel to *Emile*, Sophie betrays her husband, and sullies the conjugal bed with a bastard child ("Emile et Sophie ou les solitaires"). Was this the only logical consequence of what Rousseau considered to be female independence? The liberation of morals could produce nothing but solitude and unhappiness.

75. Pierre Burgelin, "L'Education de Sophie," *Annales de la Société Jean-Jacques Rousseau*, 1959–62, vol. 35, p. 126. [*Télémaque* was a didactic novel by Fénelon, published in 1699.—Trans.]

76. *Emile, Oeuvres complètes*, vol. 4, book 4, p. 585.

77. "An individual of whatever species is nothing in the universe. The species are Nature's only beings." Buffon, "La nature," "Seconde vue," *Oeuvres philosophiques de Buffon*, vol. 41 (Paris: PUF, 1954), p. 35.

78. Cf. *La Nouvelle Héloïse*.

79. Condorcet, "Lettres d'un bourgeois de Newhaven à un citoyen de Virginie sur l'inutilité de partager le pouvoir législatif entre plusieurs corps" (1787), added in 1788 to the historical and political research on the United States by Mazzey, in Condorcet, *Oeuvres complètes* (Paris: Ed. O'Connor et M. F. Arago, 1847), vol. 9, pp. 14–15.

80. Condorcet, "Lettres," p. 18.

81. Ibid.

82. Choderlos de Laclos, "Des femmes et de leur éducation," *Oeuvres complètes* (Paris: Bibliothèque de la Pléiade, Ed. Gallimard, 1979), pp. 389–443.

83. Condorcet, "Essai sur la constitution et les fonctions des Assemblées provinciales" (1788), *Oeuvres complètes*, vol. 8, p. 128.

84. Condorcet, *La Vie de Turgot*, in *Oeuvres complètes*, vol. 5, pp. 179–80.

85. Condorcet, "Idées sur le despotisme à l'usage de ceux qui prononcent ce mot sans l'entendre" (1787), *Oeuvres complètes*, vol. 9, p. 166.

86. Condorcet, "Que toutes les classes de la société n'ont qu'un même intérêt," *Journal d'instruction sociale*, *Oeuvres complètes*, vol. 12, p. 650, 8 June 1793.

87. Condorcet, "Réponse au premier plaidoyer de M. d'Epremesnil dans l'affaire du Comte de Lally" (1781), *Oeuvres complètes*, vol. 7, p. 42.

88. Sophie Grouchy, Veuve Condorcet, "Huit lettres sur la sympathie," in *Théorie des sentiments moraux*, by Adam Smith (Paris, 1798), vol. 2, p. 485.

89. Louis Léon Saint-Just, *Esprit de la Révolution et de la Constitution de France* (Paris, 1791), p. 65.

90. Saint-Just, "Fragments sur les institutions républicaines" (posthumously published in Paris, 1831), p. 61.

91. Condorcet, "Essai sur la constitution," p. 141.

92. When in November and December 1789 the decrees stipulated, "In order to be eligible for the National Assembly, a direct tax must be paid, equivalent to one silver mark; in addition one must own some sort of landed property," Condorcet on 12 December 1789, demanded revocation of the decree on the silver mark. Franck Alengry, *Condorcet: Guide de la Révolution française, théoricien du droit constitutionnel* (Paris, 1904; Geneva: Slatkine reprints, 1971), p. 59.

93. "We fail to see why knowledge useful to all sentient beings capable of reason should not be equally taught to everyone." Condorcet, *Essai sur la constitution*," p. 474.

94. Diderot's essay "Sur les femmes" [On women] offers a good example of this assimilation process. Based on their physiology, women's social lot is unfortunate. "It is in discomfort that Nature has ordained them to become mothers; it is by a long and dangerous illness that She takes away their power of being mothers. What, then, is a woman? Neglected by her husband, abandoned by her children, nonexistent in society." Diderot, *Oeuvres complètes* (Paris: Bibliothèque de la Pléiade, Gallimard, 1951), p. 955.

95. Condorcet, "On the Admission of Women to the Rights of Citizenship," in *Selected Writings*, ed. Keith Michael Baker (New YorK: Noonday Press, 1955), p.98.

96. Condorcet, "Essai sur l'admission des femmes au droit de cité," *Oeuvres complètes*, vol. 10, p. 123. Catherine Macaulay-Graham, 1733–91. During a voyage to Paris in 1777, she met Franklin, Turgot, Marmontel, and Mme. Dubocage. Her principal works are: a history of England (in 8 vols., 1763–83), "Reflections on the Causes of the Current Unhappiness" (1770), "Treatise on the Immutability of Moral Truth" (1773), and "Letters on Education" (1790).

97. Condorcet, *On the Admission of Women*, p. 102.

98. Ibid., p. 98.

99. Gilles-Gaston Granger, *La Mathématique sociale du marquis de Condorcet* (Paris: PUF, 1956).

100. Condorcet, *La Vie de Voltaire* (1789), *Oeuvres complètes*, vol. 4 (Paris, 1847), "Note sur Voltaire," p. 577.

101. According to Condorcet, the natural rights are: (1) the individual's personal safety and freedom, (2) the safety and freedom of his property, and (3) equality. In "Idées sur

le despotisme à l'usage de ceux qui prononcent ce mot sans l'entendre" (1789), *Oeuvres complètes*, vol. 9 (Paris, 1847), p. 166.

102. Vol. 4, "Note sur Voltaire," p. 561.

103. Léon Cahen, *Condorcet et la Révolution française* (Paris, 1904; Geneva: Slatkine reprints, 1970), p. 3.

104. Condorcet, *Recueils de pièces sur l'état des protestants en France* (1781), *Oeuvres complètes*, vol. 5 (Paris, 1847), p. 420.

105. Condorcet, *Sketch for a Historical Picture of the Progress of the Human Mind*, trans. June Barraclough (New York: Noonday Press, 1955), p. 190.

106. Destutt de Tracy, *Commentaire sur L'Esprit des Lois de Montesquieu, suivi d'observations inédites de Condorcet* (Paris, 1819).

107. Ibid., p. 401.

108. Condorcet, "Sketch," pp. 134–35.

109. Condorcet, "Idées sur le despotisme," p. 166.

110. Condorcet, "Sketch," p. 193.

111. Alengry, *Condorcet*, p. 450.

112. Condorcet, *Déclaration des droits*, section 5, division 1, article 4, *Oeuvres complètes*, vol. 9 (Paris, 1847), p. 207.

113. This is also the opinion of Florence Brugidou-Waetcher, in her thesis in legal history, "Condorcet et les droits des femmes," Paris, 1971.

114. Quoted by F. Alengry, *Condorcet*, p. 291.

115. Convention, 29 Apr. 1793.

116. [i.e., between whether "man" means males or all of humanity. —Trans.]

117. Pierre Guyomar, "Le Partisan de l'égalité politique entre les individus ou problème très important de l'égalité des droits et de l'inégalité en fait," Convention, 29 Apr. 1793, p. 3.

118. J. L. Talmon, in the introduction of his *Origines de la démocratie totalitaire* (Paris: Calmann-Lévy, 1952), oriented his study in a direction very close to our reading. "At the same time as liberal-type democracy and based on the same premises, a totalitarian tendency of democratic type appeared in the eighteenth century."

V. Women and the French Revolution

1. Marie-Charlotte-Pauline Robert de Lézardière, *Théorie des lois politiques de la Monarchie française* (published and sold in 1792) (Paris, 1844). De Lézardière was born on 25 Mar. 1754 in Vendée and died in 1835.

2. [The *parlements* were the "sovereign" courts of justice for the thirteen juridical districts into which the country was divided. The twenty-three hundred magistrates that filled these courts constituted the "noblesse de robe," whose power to oppose the king Maupéou greatly reduced. —Trans.]

3. Silvia Burian-Schweinzer, *Mademoiselle de Lézardière: Leben, Werk und Zeit einer Schülerin Montesquieus*, thesis (Vienna, 1976).

4. Elie Carcassonne, *Montesquieu et le problème de la Constitution française au XVIIIe siècle* (Paris: PUF, 1927).

5. Ibid., also Octave Demartial, *Essai sur la Théorie des lois politiques de la Monarchie française* (Poitiers, 1864).

6. [The Estates General was a national representative body with vaguely defined powers that met at irregular intervals, sometimes serving as protection against the king's abuse of power. In 1789 the Estates General would be convoked by the king for the first time since 1614. —Trans.]

7. Lézardière, *Théorie*, vol. 1, book 9, chap. 6, p. 61.

8. [Portrait of the monarchy's and subjects' real and respective rights from the beginnings of French monarchy to the present] in *Ecrits inédits de Mlle de Lézardière*, with an introduction and notes by Elie Carcassonne (Paris: PUF, 1927), p. 117.

9. Lézardière, *Ecrits inédits*, p. 117.

10. Montesquieu, *The Spirit of the Laws*, trans. Thomas Nugent, vol. 2, 4th ed. (Nourse, Vaillant in the Strand, 1766), book 31, chap. 1, p. 443.

11. Lézardière, "Idée générale de la Constitution politique de la Monarchie, ou précis d'un ouvrage ayant pour titre, 'Théorie des lois politiques de la Monarchie française,' " in *Ecrits inédits*, p.471.

12. Lézardière, "Idée générale," p. 440.

13. *Très humbles et très respectueuses remontrances de la Cour des Aydes de Paris sur l'Edit de décembre 1770 et l'état actuel du Parlement de Paris: Un recueil des réclamations, re-montrances, lettres, arrêts, arrêtés, protestations au sujet de l'Edit de décembre 1770, l'éviction des conseils supérieurs, la suppression des Parlements* (London, 1773), vol. 1, p. 16.

14. The physiocrats and later Condorcet argued against this division into orders and promoted a uniform organization through the creation of Provincial Assemblies. Pierre Renouvin, *Les Assemblées provinciales de 1787* (Paris, 1921), p. 318.

15. Lézardière, *Ecrits inédits*, p. 399.

16. "Lettre du Roi pour la convocation des Etats Généraux à Versailles," 27 Apr. 1789 (Paris, 1789), art. XI, XX.

17. [A *bailliage* was an administrative district over which the *bailli* or bailiff exercised vice-regal power. —Trans.]

18. Jacques Cadart, *Le Régime électoral des Etats Généraux de 1789 et ses origines, 1302–1614* (Paris: Librairie du Recueil Sirey, 1952), p. 43.

19. Cadart, *Régime électoral*, p. 90.

20. "Doléance des marchandes de mode, plumassières, fleuristes de Paris," in *Cahiers de doléances des femmes et autres textes*, (1789), preface by Paule-Marie Duhet (Paris: Ed. des Femmes, 1981), p. 39.

21. "Doléances des dames religieuses de la ville d'Aups," "Plaintes et remontrances des Soeurs pénitentes d'Hondtschoote," and "Doléances des Soeurs grises d'Hondt-schoote," in *Cahiers de doléances*, pp. 59–71.

22. "Cahier des doléances et réclamations des femmes par Madame B . . . , 1789. Pays de Caux," in *Cahiers de doléances*, pp. 47–59.

23. "Pétition des femmes du Tiers Etat au Roi," 1 Jan. 1789, in *Cahiers de doléances*, pp. 25–29.

24. Such is Paule-Marie Duhet's opinion of this text. See *Les Femmes dans la Révo-lution, 1789–1794*, ed. P.-M. Duhet (Collection Archives, Julliard, 1971), p. 33.

25. [The *Ferme Générale* was the tax-collectors'; the Hôtel-Dieu was the hospital, where so many poor Parisians went to die. —Trans.]

26. Mlle. de Coicy, *Les Femmes comme il convient de les voir* (London and Paris, 1785).

27. *Mémoire pour le sexe féminin contre le sexe masculin* (London, 1787). This essay responds to a publication by the Chevalier d'Artaize, also known as the Chevalier de Feucher.

28. "Lettre au peuple ou projet d'une caisse patriotique par une citoyenne à Vienne" (1788).

29. "Let us go and offer the voluntary tribute of these useless ornaments to the august National Assembly." From "Motion à faire," Sept. 1789, in *Cahiers de doléances*, pp. 76–77.

30. "Grief et plaintes des femmes mal mariées" (1790); "Motions adressées à l'As-semblée Nationale en faveur du sexe" (1789), etc. [Grievances and complaints of ill-married women; Motions addressed to the National Assembly in favor of women.]

31. In "Motion à faire," "the majority of women citizens, not constituted in guilds and having no status but that of their husbands, will meet and form associations ac-cording to these statuses, each one in her respective class." *Cahiers de doléances*, p. 75.

32. "Vues législatives, pour les femmes, adressées à L'Assemblée Nationale, par Mlle Jodin, fille d'un citoyen de Genève" (Angers, 1790), in *Cahiers de doléances*, pp. 183–99.

33. *Archives parlementaires de 1787 à 1860, recueil complet des débats législatifs et politiques*

des chambres parlementaires, ed. Madival, Laurent, and Clavel, series 1, vol. 8, pp. 284 and 504. See also Christine Fauré, *Les Déclarations des droits de l'homme de 1789* (Paris: Payot, 1988), p. 116.

34. George Rudé, "La Composition sociale des insurrections parisiennes de 1789 à 1791," *Annales historiques de la Révolution française* 127 (July-August 1952): 271–73.

35. "The Revolution of July 14 came, but I did not witness the main events. Therefore I can only tell you what I saw, because I remember only very vaguely what I heard from others. . . . on the evening of July 14, I was walking with a servant through the streets of Paris, all I saw were armed men and others looking for weapons. . . . Then there were the events of October 5 and 6, I was at the National Assembly the evening of the 5th when the women of Paris arrived." Quoted in Otto Ernst, *Théroigne de Méricourt, d'après des documents inédits tirés des archives secrètes de la Maison d'Autriche* (Paris: Payot, 1935), pp. 87–90.

36. F. Gerbaux, "Les femmes-soldats pendant la Révolution," in *La Révolution française* 47, no. 1 (July 1904): 47–61.

37. "Adresse individuelle à l'Assemblée nationale par des citoyennes de la capitale, le 6 mars 1791, imprimé par ordre de l'Assemblée nationale."

38. *Discours prononcé à la Société fraternelle des Minimes le 25 mars 1792, l'an quatrième de la liberté, par Mlle Théroigne, en présentant un Drapeau aux citoyennes du faubourg St. Antoine.*

39. *Théroigne aux 48 sections* (Paris, n.d. [certainly published after 10 Aug. 1792]).

40. [Formerly called the "Society of the Friends of the Rights of Man and of the Citizen," the *section* or administrative district of the Club of the Cordeliers took its name from its original meeting place in Paris, the nationalized monastery of the Cordeliers (Franciscans). It was one of the popular clubs founded after the Revolution to protect against the abuse of power. —Trans.]

41. *Révolution de France et de Brabant*, no. 14, second trimester including March, April, and May of the first year of the Constitution, p. 25.

42. Léopold Lacour, *Les Origines du féminisme contemporain: Trois femmes de la Révolution: Olympe de Gouges, Théroigne de Méricourt, Rose Lacombe* (Paris: Plon-Nourrit, 1900).

43. Olympe de Gouges, *Lettres à la Reine, aux Généraux de l'Armée, aux amis de la Constitution, et aux Françaises citoyennes: Description de la fête du 3 juin* (Paris, 1792).

44. See Olivier Blanc, *Olympe de Gouges* (Paris: Syros, 1981). This recent biography will flesh out the all-too-brief portrait of Gouges's political activity provided in this essay.

45. For English translation used in subsequent citations see "The Declaration of the Rights of Woman," in *Women in Revolutionary Paris, 1789–1795*, trans. and ed. Darline Levy et al. (Urbana: University of Illinois Press, 1979), pp. 87–96.

46. Gouges, *Lettres à la Reine.*

47. "Every female citizen can therefore freely say, 'I am the mother of a child that belongs to you,' without a barbaric prejudice forcing her to conceal the truth." Olympe de Gouges, "Déclaration des droits," p. 10.

48. "Les trois urnes ou le salut de la Patrie" (July 1793).

49. "Pronostic sur Maximilien Robespierre par un animal amphibie" 5 Nov. 1792.

50. "Do you remember this virago, this woman-man, the impudent Olympe de Gouges, who was the first to establish women's societies, and who tried to be a politician," *Journal de la Montagne* 6, day 29, month 2, Year 2 of the Republic, p. 43.

51. *Le Moniteur* 59, 29 Brumaire, Year 2 (Nov. 19, 1793), anonymous article.

52. Etta Palm d'Aelders, *Appel aux Françaises sur la régénération des moeurs, et nécessité de l'influence des femmes dans un gouvernement libre* (Paris: Imprimerie du Cercle Social), no. 4 (1791), p. 15.

53. This society formed a company in the National Guard.

54. "Lettre d'une amie de la vérité, Etta Palm née d'Aelders, hollandaise, sur les dé-

marches des ennemis extérieurs et intérieurs de la France," *Appel aux Françaises* p. 26; English trans. from *Women in Revolutionary Paris*, Levy et al., pp. 69–70.

55. "A campaign of malicious slander against her was serious enough to be taken up by *Le Moniteur*; it was even reported that she was arrested as a Prussian spy and counterrevolutionary agent." *Les Femmes et la Révolution, 1789–1794* (Paris: Julliard, 1971), ed. Paule-Marie Duhet, p. 83.

56. Albert Soboul, *Les Sans-Culottes parisiens de l'an II: Mouvement populaire et gouvernement révolutionnaire, 2 juin 1793, 9 thermidor an II* (Paris, 1958).

57. Marie Cerati, *Le Club des citoyennes républicaines révolutionnaires* (Paris: Editions sociales, 1966).

58. [The new study by Dominique Godineau, *Citoyennes Tricoteuses* (Paris: Alinea, 1988), attempts to fill this gap. —Trans.]

59. [*Le Moniteur universel* was a political journal founded in 1789 in which the debates of the National Assembly were published. In 1799 it became the government's official newspaper. —Trans.]

60. On 19 May a delegation of Cordeliers accompanied a new deputation to the Jacobins; the orator of the two combined groups read a petition which was to be taken to the Convention by a large group of people. Cerati, *Club des citoyennes*, p. 54.

61. [*Montagnard* is the name given to the deputies occupying the highest seats of the Assembly—called *la Montagne*—signaling in this way their political radicalism in relation to the Girondins. Robespierre and Marat were both members of the Montagnard faction. —Trans.]

62. "Feuille des rapports et déclarations faites au Bureau de surveillance de la police, 16 mai 1793." [Bulletin of the reports and declarations made at the Surveillance Bureau of the police, 16 May 1793.]

63. George Rudé, *La Foule dans la Révolution française* (Paris, Maspéro, 1962), pp. 140–43; English edition, *The Crowd in the French Revolution* (Oxford: Oxford University Press, 1959).

64. Département de Paris, "Les autorités constituées du département de Paris et les commissaires des sections aux Républicaines révolutionnaires" 30 June 1793.

65. The sans-culottes women citizens of the Croix-Rouge section addressed the National Convention thus: "Our mothers, our wives and our daughters come also with us to pay tribute to the acceptance of the "Rights of Man" and the Constitution; and though their sex doesn't permit them to vote, their hearts are nonetheless touched, and they joyfully participate in all the activities of their fathers, their husbands, and their sons." *Archives parlementaires*, vol. 68, 5 July 1793, p. 283.

66. Soboul, *Sans-Culottes*, p. 77.

67. "Précis de la conduite révolutionnaire, Pauline Léon, femme Leclerc, 16 Messidor, l'An II."

68. [The *Enragé* is the name given in 1792–93 to the revolutionary extremists (such as Jacques Roux) who demanded equality in social, political and economic spheres. Their socialist program was later taken over by the *hébertistes*. —Trans.]

69. *Archives parlementaires*, vol. 68, 4 July 1793, p. 254.

70. "Pétition des citoyennes républicaines révolutionnaires, lue à la tribune de la Convention nationale," signed Champion, president (Paris, n.d.).

71. "Discours prononcé à la Société des citoyennes républicaines révolutionnaires par les citoyennes de la section des Droits de l'Homme, en lui donnant un guidon sur lequel est la déclaration des Droits de l'Homme" (n.d.).

72. Soboul, *Sans-Culottes*, "While Leclerc prepared the revolutionary women's entry onto the political scene and threatened governmental authorities with popular revolt. . . . " p. 145.

73. Latour-Lamontagne, "Rapport de l'observateur de police," 20 Sept. 1793, *Archives nationales, F7 3688 3*.

74. Ibid., 22 Sept. 1793.

75. *Le Moniteur*, 30 Oct. 1793.

76. Jacques Roux, remaining loyal to the Revolutionary Women, condemned the Montagnards' opportunism in his newspaper: "But the Society of Revolutionary Women, which has given so much for liberty, has been denounced by the Jacobins themselves, by men who called on their courage and their virtue a thousand times; and the warmest republican women have been treated as schemers." *Le Publiciste de la République française par l'ombre de Marat*, Paris, no. 267. And: "Who does not see your intrigues? Who cannot see that most of those who rose to popularity since 89 and who are responsible for our destinies have planned to usurp the supreme power? They used the Revolutionary Women, the Lacombes, the Colombes, the Champions, the Ardoins . . . in order to break the tyrant's scepter." Ibid., no. 268.

77. [Jacques René Hébert (Père Duchesne) was the leader of the *hébertistes*, the name given to his ultrarevolutionary followers who took up the popular movement of the sans-culottes after the *enragés* were eliminated. —Trans.]

78. Lacombe, in *Le Moniteur*, 9 Oct. 1793.

79. *Journal de la Montagne*, no. 6 (day 29, month 2, Year 2 of the French Republic), p. 43.

80. We should note that Madame Roland herself was hostile to women's participation in politics: "I do not believe that our customs yet permit women to appear in public; they should inspire goodness, and should nurture and ignite all the useful sentiments," she wrote. *Lettres autographes de Madame Roland adressées à Bancal des Issarts* (Paris, 1835), pp. 198–99.

81. *Le Moniteur*, 19 Nov. 1793.

82. Amar, in *Le Moniteur*, 31 Oct. 1793.

83. Ibid.

84. George Rudé, *The Crowd in the French Revolution* (Oxford: Oxford University Press, 1959), p. 142.

85. *Le Moniteur*, 23 May 1795.

86. [Those moderates who, during two days in Thermidor (27–28 July) of Year II, brought about the overthrow of Robespierre and his associates. —Trans.]

87. *Le Moniteur*, 28 May 1795.

88. "A discourse on the love of our country, delivered on 4 Nov. 1789, at the meeting-house in the Old Jewry, to the Society for Commemorating the Revolution in Great Britain." French ed. trans. M. de Keralio (Paris, 1790).

89. See Henri Laboucheix, *Richard Price, théoricien de la Révolution américaine: Le philosophe et le sociologue, le pamphlétaire et l'orateur*, doctoral dissertation, presented and defended on 20 June 1969 (Didier, 1970), p. 50.

90. These principles are only three in number, while the Declaration of the Rights of Man has 17 articles. The three principles are: (1) all civil and political authority is derived from the people; (2) abuse of power is a justification for resistance; and (3) the right to private opinion, freedom of thought, trial by jury, freedom of the press, and free elections must always be upheld as sacred and inviolable.

91. *Le Moniteur*, 10 Dec. 1789.

92. Edmund Burke, *Reflections on the Revolution in France* (1790; Garden City: Anchor Press/Doubleday, 1973).

93. Burke, *Reflections*, p. 72.

94. Burke, *Reflections*, 75.

95. "Judge, Sir, of my surprise, when I found that a very great proportion of the Assembly (a majority, I believe, of the members who attended) was composed of practitioners in the law. It was composed . . . of the inferior, unlearned, mechanical, merely instrumental members of the profession," Burke, *Reflections*, p. 54.

96. Burke, *Reflections*, p. 64.

97. Burke, *Reflections*, p. 74.

98. Burke, *Reflections*, p. 110.

99. "A Letter to the sheriffs of Bristol" (1777).

100. *Analytical Review.* The majority of the articles in the *Review* are anonymous, making it difficult to determine which ones were written by Wollstonecraft. However, some articles are signed by the initials M. and W.

101. This school closed in 1786.

102. Mary Wollstonecraft, *A Vindication of the Rights of Men* (London: Johnson, 1790).

103. Mary Wollstonecraft, *A Vindication of the Rights of Woman: With Strictures on Political and Moral Subjects* (1792), a critical edition by Ulrich H. Hardt (Troy: The Whitston Publishing Company, 1982).

104. *Rights of Men*, p. 5.

105. *Rights of Men*, p. 21.

106. Paule-Marie Duhet-Penigault, *Mary Wollstonecraft-Godwin, 1759–1767*, thesis for the Doctorat d'Etat (Université de Paris III, 1975).

107. Wollstonecraft, *Rights of Men*, p. 41.

108. Ibid., p. 42.

109. Ibid., p. 19.

110. Ibid., p. 20.

111. Burke, *Reflections*, p. 85, quoted by Wollstonecraft, *Rights of Men*, p. 67.

112. Wollstonecraft, *Rights of Men*, p. 107.

113. Charles Talleyrand-Périgord, *Rapport sur l'instruction publique, fait au nom du Comité de Constitution* (Paris: Imprimerie nationale, 1791).

114. Ibid., p. 118.

115. Ibid., pp. 120–22.

116. Catherine Macaulay-Graham, *Letters on Education* (London, 1790).

117. Martha Severn Storr, *Mary Wollstonecraft et le mouvement féministe dans la littérature anglaise* (Paris: PUF, 1932), p. 343.

118. "Truly to justify to himself the affection which weakness and virtue had made him cherish for that fool Theresa, he could not raise her to the common level of her sex; and therefore he laboured to bring woman down to hers." Wollstonecraft, *Rights of Woman*, p. 369.

119. Ibid., p. 92.

120. Ibid., p. 198.

121. Ibid., p. 100.

122. Ibid., p. 33.

123. Ibid., p. 20.

124. Ibid., p. 311.

125. Mary Wollstonecraft, *An Historical and Moral View of the French Revolution* (1795), a facsimile reproduction with introduction by Janet Todd (Delmar: Scholars' Facsimiles and Reprints, 1975).

126. Wollstonecraft, *French Revolution*, p. 437.

VI. After the Revolution

1. Madame de Staël, *De la littérature considérée dans ses rapports avec les institutions sociales* (Paris: Maradam, 1800), p. 305.

2. Benjamin Constant, *De la liberté chez les modernes*, ed. Marcel Gauchet (Paris: Le Livre de Poche, 1980), preface, p. 20.

3. [François Noël "Gracchus" Babeuf was an active participant in the Revolution and an advocate of land reform. He founded the newspaper *Le Tribun du peuple* in which he disseminated his communistic theories of equality. He was condemned to death in 1797 for conspiring against the Directory. —Trans.]

4. *Le Moniteur*, 3 Jan. 1796. [The rest of the sentence explaining the third type of constitution reads, "in so far as individuals and states, coexisting in an external relationship of mutual influences, may be regarded as citizens of a universal state of man-

kind." From Immanuel Kant, "Perpetual Peace: A Philosophical Sketch," in *Kant's Political Writings*, ed. Hans Reiss, trans. H. B. Nisbet (Cambridge: Cambridge University Press, 1970), p. 98. —Trans.]

5. [" . . . one can distinguish two distinct—indeed, opposing—schools among French theorists who claim to be liberal. One is the Lockean liberalism of Voltaire, Montesquieu, and Benjamin Constant . . . —the liberalism of the minimal state, individualism, and laissez-faire. But there is a second liberalism, represented by the masters of the French Revolution and by the youthful Napoleon, which is democratic, Rousseauesque, and *étatiste*. Whereas Lockean liberalism understands freedom as being left alone by the state, the other liberalism sees freedom as ruling oneself though the medium of a state which one has made one's own." Maurice Cranston, "Liberalism," in *The Encyclopedia of Philosophy*, ed. Paul Edwards (New York: Macmillan Publishing Co. and The Free Press, 1967), vol. 4, p. 459. —Trans.]

6. ["Fitness for voting is a prerequisite of being a citizen. To be fit to vote, a person must be independent. . . . This qualification leads to the distinction between an active and a passive citizen. . . . [A]ll women, and generally anyone who must depend for his support . . . on the arrangement of others . . . all such people lack civil personality. . . . Consequently, they do not possess any civil independence." Immanuel Kant, *The Metaphysical Elements of Justice*, trans. J. Ladd (Bobbs-Merrill: New York, 1965), p. 79. —Trans.]

7. Michel Villey, "Kant dans l'histoire du Droit," *Leçons d'histoire de philosophie du droit* (Paris: Nouvelle edit., Dalloz, 1962), p. 260.

8. [The reference here is to Paul Hazard's famous work *La Crise de la conscience européenne* (Paris, 1935), an intellectual history of Europe between 1680 and 1715; English edition, *The European Mind*, trans. J. Lewis May (London: Hollis and Carter, 1953). —Trans.]

9. Kant, *Théorie et pratique* (Paris: Vrin, 1980), p. 36.

10. Immanuel Kant, *Métaphysique des moeurs: Doctrine du droit* trans. A. Philonenko (Paris: Vrin, 1971), p. 158. [For German original, see Immanuel Kant *Gesammelte Schriften* (Berlin and Leipzig: Preussische Akademie der Wissenschaften, 1902–68), vol. 4, pp. 276–78. See also Howard Williams, *Kant's Political Philosophy* (New York: St. Martin's Press, 1983), pp. 114–21, for his discussion of Kant's concept of "Marriage and the Role of Women." —Trans.]

11. Kant, *Métaphysique des moeurs*, p. 158. [English quoted from Huntington Cairns, *Legal Philosophy from Plato to Hegel* (Baltimore: Johns Hopkins University Press, 1949), p. 432. —Trans.]

12. Michel Villey, preface to Kant, *Métaphysique des moeurs*, p. 21.

13. [Kant, *Gesammelte Schriften*, vol. 19, p. 543. See also vol. 6, pp. 276–78. —Trans.]

14. Michèle Jalley-Crampe-Casnabet, *Genèse idéale et genèse empirique dans la philosophie transcendante kantienne*, thesis for the Doctorat d'Etat (1980), p. 551.

15. "It is an external duty to keep a promise made in a contract." Kant, *Métaphysique des moeurs*, p. 94.

16. Kant, "Perpetual Peace" ("Zum ewigen Frieden" [1795]).

17. Immanuel Kant, *Anthropology from a Pragmatic Point of View*, trans. Mary J. Gregor (The Hague: Martinus Nijhoff, 1974), p. 190.

18. Kant, *Anthropology*, p. 126.

19. Theodor Hippel, *Über die bürgerliche Verbesserung der Weiber* (Berlin: Vossischen Buchhandlung, 1792).

20. E.g., Maïté Albistur and Daniel Armogathe, *Histoire du féminisme français* (Paris: Ed. des Femmes, 1972), vol. 2.

21. After the peace of Basel (1795), Sieyes seems to have been disposed to exchange an "academic correspondence" with him, looking to him as a political counselor. Kant did not respond to these advances. See Maurice Boucher, *La Révolution de 1789 vue par les écrivains allemands* (Paris: Didier, 1954), p. 116.

22. Kant, *Political Writings*, p. 54.

23. Rousseau was ambiguous on this point, giving rise to contradictory interpretations that can be read as favoring either political liberalism or a "totalitarian" conception of democracy.

24. Published in 1802.

25. Madame de Staël, *Considérations sur les principaux événements de la Révolution française*, ouvrage posthume publié par le duc de Broglie et le baron A. de Staël (Paris: Delaunay, Bossange and Masson, 1818).

26. Alexis de Tocqueville, *Democracy in America*, vol. 2, book 3, chap. 9, trans. Henry Reeve (New York: Alfred Knopf, 1945), p. 198.

27. Ibid., ch. 10, p. 201.

28. Ibid., ch. 12, p. 212.

29. Ibid., p. 211.

30. Eugénie Niboyet, *Le Vrai Livre des femmes* (Paris: E. Dentu, 1863), p. 117.

BIBLIOGRAPHY

A. Primary Sources

1. Manuscripts—French State Archives

Département de Paris. Les autorités constituées du département de Paris et les commissaires des sections aux républicains révolutionnaires, 30 juin 1793. T 1001.

Feuille des rapports et déclarations faits au bureau de surveillance de la police, 16 may 1793. AF II 351.

Feuille des rapports et declarations faits au bureau de surveillance de la police, 19 may de l'an II de la République. AF IV 1470.

Lacombe, Claire [known as Rose]. T 1001.

Léon, Pauline, femme Leclerc. Précis de la conduite révolutionnaire. F⁷ 4774⁹.

Pétition à l'Assemblée nationale, en faveur d'une femme délaissée depuis douze ans par son mary. D III 361–69².

Rapport de l'observateur de police en septembre 1793. F⁷ 3688³.

Section de l'Hôtel de Ville. "La patrie est en danger. . . . " C 154 292 bis.

2. Publications

Adresse individuelle à l'Assemblée nationale par des citoyennes de la capitale le 6 mars 1791, imprimée par ordre de l'Assemblée nationale. Paris.

The Analytical Review, or History of Literature, Domestic and Foreign on an Enlarged Plan . . . , London, printed for J. Johnson, 1788–99.

André le Chapelain. Tractatus amoris et de amoris remedio. Andree Capellani, n.d.

Archives parlementaires de 1787 à 1860. Complete collection of the legislative and political debates in chambers of Parliament, printed by order of the Senate and the Chamber of Deputies under the direction of M. Mavidal and E. Laurent. Paris: Librairie administrative de P. Dupont, 1862.

St. Augustine, Sancti Aureli Augustini de Fide et symbolo, de Fide et Operibus, de Agone Christiano, de continentia, de Bono conjugali, de sancta Virginitate, de Bono viduitatis, de Adulterinis conjugüs lib II, de Mendacio, contra mendacium, de Opere monachorum, de Divinatione daemonum, de cura pro mortuis gerenda, de Patienta Recensuit Josephus Zycha. F. Tempsky, Vindobonae, 1900.

———. Traité de morale de saint Augustin pour tous les états qui composent le corps de l'Eglise, à savoir: I. De la sainte virginité, pour les vierges; II. Du bien de la viduité; III. De la manière dont on doit prier Dieu, pour les veuves; IV. Du bien du mariage; V. Du mariage et de la concupiscence, pour les personnes mariées. Fr. trans. Jean Hamon. Paris: H. Josset, 1680.

Barbantanne, Achille de [pseud. Dard du Bosco]. Le Discours sur les femmes. Avignon: Giroux, 1754.

Bayle, Pierre. Dictionnaire historique et critique. 3rd ed. Rotterdam: Michel Bohm, 1720.

———. Nouvelles de la République des Lettres. Amsterdam: H. Desbordes, 1684–1718: Sept. 1684, Apr. 1685, May 1685, Sept. 1685, Oct. 1685, Jan. 1686, May 1686, Oct. 1687.

———? Avis important aux réfugiés sur leur prochain retour en France; donné pour estrennes à l'un d'eux en 1690 par Monsieur CLA. A. P.DP. Amsterdam: J. Le Censeur, 1690.

Bebel, Auguste, La femme dans le passé, le présent et l'avenir. Fr. trans. H. Rave. Paris: Carre, 1891.

Berquin, Chevalier de. *La Déclamation des louanges du mariage*. 1525. Ed. Emile Telle. Geneva: Droz, 1976.

Bodin, Jean. *De la Démonomanie des sorciers*. Paris: J. Du Puys, 1580.

———. *Oeuvres philosophiques*. Ed. Pierre Mesnard. Paris: PUF, 1951.

———. *Sur le rehaussement et diminution des monnayes, tant d'or que d'argent, et le moyen d'y rémedier et responce aux Paradoxes de Monsieur de Malestroict; plus un recueil des principaux advis donnez en l'assemblée de Sainct-Germain-des-Prez au mois d'aoust dernier avec les paradoxes sur le faict des monnayes, par François Ganault*. Paris: J. Du Puys, 1578.

———. *Les Six Livres de la République*. Paris: J. Du Puys, 1577.

———. *Les Six Livres de la République*. Edition de Paris, 1583; Aalen: Scientia, 1977.

———. *The Six Bookes of a Commonweale*. Ed. Kenneth D. McRae. Cambridge, Mass.: Harvard University Press, 1962.

———. *Six Books of the Commonwealth*. Eng. trans. M. J. Tooley. Oxford: Basil Blackwell, [1955] 1967.

Bordeu, Théophile de, *Recherches anatomiques sur la position des glandes et sur leur action*. Paris: G. F. Guillau, 1751.

Bossuet, *Oeuvres*. Ed. l'abbé Velat and Yvonne Champailler. Paris: Bibliothèque de la Pléiade, Gallimard, 1979.

Brion, Hélène. *La Voie féministe*. Paris: Syros, 1978.

Budé, Guillaume. *Annotationes in quatuor et viginti pandectarum libros . . . ab iodoco Badio Ascensio nuper impressae*. Paris, 1508.

———. *De l'institution du prince J. de Luxembourg, l'Arrivour N.* Paris, 1547.

Buffon, Georges Louis Leclerc, comte de. *Oeuvres Philosophiques*. Ed. Jean Piveteau, with Maurice Frechet and Charles Bruneau. Paris: PUF, 1954.

Burke, Edmund. *A Letter to the Sheriffs of Bristol, London, 1777*. Ed. James Hugh Moffatt. Philadelphia and New York: Hinds, Noble and Eldredge, 1904.

———. *Reflections on the Revolution in France, and on the Proceedings in Certain Societies in London Relative to That Event: In a letter intended to have been sent to a gentleman in Paris*. London: Dodsley, 1790.

———. *Reflections on the Revolution in France*. Garden City: Anchor Press/Doubleday, 1973.

———. *Réflexions sur la Révolution française*. Trans. from the English J. d'Anglejan. Paris: Nouvelle Librairie nationale, 1912.

Burlamaqui, Jean-Jacques. *Principes du droit de la nature et des gens, et du droit public général; contenant les Principes du droit naturel, les Eléments du droit naturel, et les Principes du droit politique*. Ed. Pr Felice; revised and expanded. M. Cotelle Fils. Paris: Janet et Cotelle, 1821.

Buzot, François Nicolas Léonard. *Mémoires sur la Révolution française par Buzot, député à la Convention nationale*. Prefaced by a short biographical sketch, and historical notes on the Girondins, by M. Guadet. Paris: Béchet Aîné, 1823.

Calvin, Jean. *Christianae religionis Institutio*. Basileae, 1536.

———. *Commentaires sur l'Ancien Testament*. Ed. Andre Malet, with Pierre Marcel and Michel Reveillaud; revised ed. by the Société calviniste de France under the direction of Pierre Marcel. Geneva: Labor et Fides, 1960–68.

———. *Commentaires sur le Nouveau Testament sur la nouvelle épître à Timothée*. Toulouse, 1894.

———. *Commentaries on the Epistles of Paul to the Galatians and Ephesians*. Trans. Rev. William Pringle. Edinburgh, 1854.

———. *Epître au roi François Ier*. Preface to the first French edition of *L'institution de la religion chretienne* (1541). Ed. Jacques Pannier; first publication, from the Bibliothèque Nationale manuscript. Paris: Fischbacher, 1927.

———. *Sermons sur les deux épistres Sainct Paul à Timothée, et sur l'Epistre à Tite*. Geneva: Jean Bonnefoy, 1563.

———. *Sermon où il est montré quelle doit être la modestie des femmes en leurs habillements.* Geneva: Kundig, 1945.

Castiglione, Baldassare. *Le Courtisan de Messire Baltazar de Castillon.* Fr. trans. Jacques Colin, revised by Merlin de Sainct-Gelais, and published by Estienne Dolet. Lyon: François Juste, 1538.

Chabot, François. *Projet d'acte constitutif des Français: Droits naturels, droits civils, droits politiques.* Paris: Imprimerie nationale, 1793.

Clément, Elisabeth-Marie. *Dialogue de la princesse sçavante et de la dame de famille, contenant l'art d'élever les jeunes dames dans une belle et noble éducation.* Paris: J. B. Loyson, 1664.

Coicy, Madame de. *Les Femmes comme il convient de les voir; ou Apperçu de ce que les femmes ont été, de ce qu'elles sont, et de ce qu'elles pourroient être.* A Londres, et se trouve à Paris, chez Bacot, 1785.

Condorcet, Jean-Antoine-Nicolas de Caritat, marquis de. *Lettres d'un bourgeois de New-heaven à un citoyen de Virginie sur l'inutilité de partager le pouvoir législatif entre plusieurs corps.* A Colle et se trouve à Paris chez Froullé, 1788.

———. *Mémoires de Condorcet sur la Révolution française.* Extraits de sa correspondance et de celle de ses amis. Paris: Ponthieu, 1824.

———. *Oeuvres de Condorcet.* Pub. A. Condorcet O'Connor and M. F. Arago. Paris: Firmin Didot Frères, 1847–49.

———. [Pseud. M. Schwartz, pasteur du Saint Evangile à Bienne, membre de la Société économique de B.] *Réflexion sur l'esclavage des négres.* Neufchâtel: Société typographique, 1781.

———. *Selected Writings.* Ed. Keith Michael Baker. Indianapolis: Bobbs-Merrill, 1976.

———. *Sketch for a Historical Picture of the Progress of the Human Mind.* Trans. June Barraclough. New York: Noonday Press, 1955.

Constant de Rebecque, Benjamin. *De la liberté chez les modernes: Ecrits politiques.* Ed. Marcel Gauchet. Paris: Le Livre de Poche, 1980.

———. *Oeuvres.* Ed. Alfred Roulin. Paris: Bibliothèque de la Plèiade, Gallimard, 1957.

Daubenton, Louis Jean Marie. *Histoire naturelle, générale et particulière avec la description du Cabinet du Roy.* Paris: De l'Imprimerie royale, 1750–1804.

Daubié, Julie. *L'Emancipation de la femme en dix livraisons.* Paris: E. Thorin, 1871.

———. *La Femme pauvre au XIX siecle.* Paris: Guillaumin et Cie, 1866.

Deraismes, Maria. *Ce que veulent les femmes: Articles et discours de 1869 à 1891.* Ed. Odile Kracovitch. Paris: Syros, 1980.

Descartes, René. *Oeuvres.* Ed. Charles Adam and Paul Tannery. Paris: Cerf, 1897–1913. Reprint. Paris: Vrin, 1957–58.

———. *Oeuvres et lettres.* Ed. André Bridoux. Paris: Bibliothèque de la Pléiade, Gallimard, 1978.

———. *The Philosophical Works of Descartes.* Trans. Elizabeth S. Haldane and G. R. T. Ross. 2 vols. Cambridge: Cambridge University Press, 1911.

Destutt de Tracy, Antoine Louis Claude, comte de. *Commentaire sur l'Esprit des Lois de Montesquieu, suivi d'Observations inédites de Condorcet sur le vingt-neuvième livre du même ouvrage, et d'un mémoire sur cette question: Quels sont les moyens de fonder la morale d'un peuple? Ecrit et publié par l'auteur du commentaire de l'Esprit des Lois, en 1789 (an VI).* Paris: T. Desoer, 1819.

Diderot, Denis. *Oeuvres complètes.* Ed. A. Billy. Paris: Bibliothèque de la Pléiade, Gallimard, 1962.

———. *Encyclopédie ou Dictionnaire raisonné des sciences, des arts et des métiers par une société de gens de lettres.* Mis en ordre et publié par M. Diderot et quant à la partie mathématique par M. d'Alembert. Paris: Briasson, 1751–65.

Discours prononcé à la Société des Citoyennes républicaines révolutionnaires, par les citoyennes de la section des Droits de l'Homme en lui donnant un guidon sur lequel est la déclaration des Droits de l'Homme. N.p., n.d.

Domat, Jean. *Les Lois civiles dans leur ordre naturel, le droit public, et legum delectus.* Revised and expanded edition of the third and fourth books of the *Droit public.* Paris: Nicolas Gosselin, 1723.

Dubois, Marie. "Organisons le prolétariat féminin." *Cahiers du Bolchevisme* 1, no.19 (15 May 1925).

Duhet, Paule-Marie. *Cahiers de doléances des femmes en 1789 et autres textes.* Paris: Ed. des femmes, 1981.

Engels, Frederick. *The Origin of the Family, Private Property and the State.* New York: International Publishers, 1942.

Epinay, Louise Florence Pétronille Tardieu d'Esclavelles, marquise d'. *Les Conversations d'Emilie.* Leipzig: Siegfried Lebrecht Crusius, 1774.

Erasmus, Desiderius. *La Civilité puérile.* Preface on "livres de civilité" since the 16th century, by Alcide Bonneau; ed. Philippe Ariès. Paris: Ramsay, 1977.

———. *Les Colloques d'Erasme.* Ed. and Fr. trans. Leon E. Halkin. Québec: Presses de l'Université de Laval, 1971.

———. *Eloge de la folie* [Moriae Encomium, 1515]. 2 vols. Paris: Union latine d'Editions; Lausanne: Editions du Bibliophile, 1967.

L'Esprit du socialisme: Féministes françaises. Paris: Parti socialiste, 1978.

Les Femmes dans la Révolution. 2 vols. Facsimile. Paris: Edhis, 1982.

Fénelon, François de Salignac de la Mothe. *De l'éducation des filles.* In *Oeuvres.* Paris: Bibliothèque de la Pléiade, Gallimard, 1983.

Ficino, Marsilio. *Marsilii Ficini . . . Opera et quaehactenus existere et quae in lucem nunc primum prodiere omnia. . . .* Base: Henriepetrina, 1576.

———. *Commentary on Plato's Symposium on Love.* Trans. and ed. Sears Jayne. Dallas: Spring Publishers, 1985.

Furetière, Antoine. *Dictionnaire universel, contenant généralement tous les mots français tant vieux que modernes et les termes des sciences et des arts.* The Hague and Rotterdam: Leers, 1690.

Gacon-Dufour, Marie Armande Jeanne. *Contre le Projet de loi de Sxxx Mxxx, portant défense d'apprendre à lire aux femmes, par une femme qui ne se pique pas d'être femme de lettres.* Paris: Ouvrier et Barba, 1801.

———. *Lettre à Madame Dxxx, auteur du Mémoire pour le sexe féminin, contre le sexe masculin (par le chevalier de Feucher).* Paris: chez tous les marchands de nouveautés, 1788.

———. *Mémoire pour le sexe féminin, contre le sexe masculin, par Madame xxx.* Londres, se trouve à Paris, chez Royez, 1787.

———. *De la nécessité de l'instruction pour les femmes.* Paris, chez F. Buisson, 1805.

Gaius. *Institutes.* Ed. and Fr. trans. Julien Reinach. Paris: Belles-Lettres, 1965.

Gouges, Olympe de [known as Gouze Marie]. *Les Droits de la femme.* A la Reine, n.d.

———. *Lettre au peuple, ou projet d'une caisse patriotique; par une citoyenne.* Vienna, et se trouve à Paris: chez les marchands de nouveautés, 1788.

———. *Lettres à la Reine, aux généraux de l'armée, aux amis de la Constitution et aux Françaises citoyennes, description de la fête du 3 juin.* Paris, aux Jacobins Saint-Honoré n.d.

———. [pseud. Polyme]. *Réponse à la justification de Maximilien Robespierre, adressée à Jérôme Pétion. Pronostic sur Maximilien Robespierre par un animal amphibie.* N.p., n.d.

———. *Les Trois Urnes, ou le sabot de la patrie.* July 1793.

———. "The Declaration of the Rights of Woman," in *Women in Revolutionary Paris, 1789–1795,* ed. and trans. Darlene Levy et al., pp. 87–96. Urbana: University of Illinois Press, 1979.

Gournay, Mlle. Marie le Jars de. *Egalité des hommes et des femmes.* A la Reyne, 1622.

Guyomar, Pierre, député à la Convention. *Le Partisan de l'égalité politique entre les individus ou problème important de l'égalité en droits et de l'inégalité en fait.* Convention, 29 Apr. 1793.

Hippel, Theodor Gottlieb, von. *Über die bürgerliche Verbesserung der Weiber.* Berlin: Vossischen Buchhandlung, 1792.

St. Jérôme. *Conseils sur l'éducation d'une jeune fille adressés à Laeta, mère de Paula pouvant servir à toutes les mères chrétiennes.* Montpellier: A. Seguin, n.d.

Jodin, Mlle. *Vues législatives pour les Femmes, adressées à l'Assemblée Nationale par Mademoiselle Jodin, fille d'un citoyen de Genève.* Angers: Mame, 1790.

Journal de la Montagne. Ed.: J.-Ch. Laveaux and Th. Rousseau. Imprimerie du Journal de la Montagne et de la Société des Jacobins, Paris (daily). 1 June 1793–28 brumaire of Year 3 (18 Nov. 1794).

Kant, Emmanuel. *Anthropologie du point de vue pragmatique.* Fr. trans. Michel Foucault. Paris: Vrin, 1964.

———. *Anthropology from a Pragmatic Point of View.* Eng. trans. Mary J. Gregor. The Hague: Martinus Nijhoff, 1974.

———. *Sur l'expression courante: Il se peut que ce soit juste en théorie, mais en pratique cela ne vaut rien. . . . Sur un prétendu droit de mentir par l'humanité.* Fr. trans. L. Guillermit. Paris: Vrin, 1980.

———. *Kant's Political Writings.* Ed. Hans Reiss, trans. H. B. Nisbet. Cambridge: Cambridge University Press, 1970.

———. *Métaphysique des moeurs.* Preface by Michel Villey; introd. and Fr. trans. A. Philonenko. Paris: Vrin, 1968–71.

———. *The Metaphysical Elements of Justice.* Trans. J. Ladd. New York: Bobbs-Merrill, 1965.

———. *La Philosophie de l'histoire, opuscule.* Introd. and Fr. trans. Stéphane Piobetta. Paris: Aubier, 1947.

———. *Projet de paix perpétuelle: Esquisse philosophique* (1795). Fr. trans. J. Gibelin. Paris: Vrin, 1947.

La Boétie, Etienne de. *Le Discours de la servitude volontaire.* Ed. P. Léonard; articles by De Lamenais, P. Leroux, A. Vermorel, G. Landauer; introduction by Miguel Abensour and Marcel Gauchet. Paris: Payot, 1976.

———. *Anti-Dictator, the Discourse on Voluntary Servitude.* English trans. Harry Kurz. New York: Columbia University Press, 1942.

Laclos, Pierre Choderlos de. *Oeuvres complètes.* Ed. L. Versini. Paris: Bibliothèque de la Pléiade, Gallimard, 1979.

Lacore, Suzanne, "Feminisme et socialisme," *L'Equite,* 15 October 1913.

Laërce, Diogène. *De la vie des philosophes.* Fr. trans. "M. Bxxx" [Gilles Boileau]. Paris: J. Cochart, 1668.

La Fayette, Marie-Madeleine Pioche de la Vergne, comtesse de. *Choix de mémoires et écrits des femmes françaises aux XVIIe, XVIIIe et XIXe siècles, avec leurs biographies par Mme Carette, née Bouvet.* Paris: Ollendorff, 1897.

———. *Correspondance.* Ed. André Beaunier. Paris: Gallimard, 1942.

———. *Lettres de Mme de Villars, de Coulanges et de La Fayette, de Ninon L'Enclos et Mlle Aissé, accompagnées de notices biographiques et de la coquette vengée par Ninon de l'Enclos.* Paris: L. Collin, 1805.

———. *Lettres de Marie-Madeleine Pioche de La Vergne, comtesse de La Fayette, et de Gilles Ménage.* Pub. H. Ashton, n.d.

Lambert, Anne Thérèse de Marguenat de Courcelles, marquise de. *Avis d'une mère à son fils et à sa fille.* A Paris, chez Etienne Ganeau, libraire juré de l'Université, rue Saint-Jacques, aux Armes de Dombes, près la rue du Plâtre, 1728.

———. *Avis d'une mère à son fils et à sa fille.* Rev. ed., including reflections on women. Paris: E. Ganeau, 1745.

———. *Oeuvres morales.* Prefaced with an essay in praise of the author by Fontenelle, and an essay by Madame Louise Colet. Paris: C. Gosselin, 1843.

————. *Oeuvres morales de Madame de Lambert*. Prefaced with a critical study by M. de
Lescure. Paris: Librairie des Bibliophiles, 1883.
Le Bret, Cardin. *De la souveraineté du Roy*. Paris: chez Toussaincts du Bray, 1632.
Lefèvre d'Etaples, Jacques. *De Maria Magdalena, Triduo Christi, disceptatio*. Paris: Ex
Officina H. Stephani, 1517.
Lesclache, Louis de. *Les Avantages que les femmes peuvent recevoir de la philosophie et prin-
cipalement de la morale, ou l'Abrégé de cette science*. Paris: chez l'auteur et Laurent
Rondet, 1667.
Lettres bougrement patriotiques de la Mère Duchêne. Paris 1 [n.d., 1791]-18 [n.d., 1791].
Lettres bougrement patriotiques de la Mère Duchêne, followed by the *Journal des Femmes*.
Feb.-Apr. 1791. Ed. Ouzi Elyada. Paris: Les éditions de Paris/Edhis, 1989.
*Lettre du Roi pour la convocation des États Généraux à Versailles, le 27 avril 1789, et réglement
y annexé*. Paris: Imprimerie Royale, 1789.
Lettre écrite au Roi par les Trois Ordres de la province du Dauphiné sur les Etats Généraux.
1788.
Lézardière, Marie Charlotte Pauline Robert de. *Théorie des lois politiques de la monarchie
française*. Rev. ed. pub. under the auspices of the Ministers of Foreign Affairs
and Public Instruction, by the vicomte de Lézardière. Paris: Au Comptoir des
Imprimeurs unis, 1844.
L'Hospital, Michel de. *Oeuvres complètes*. Prefaced by an essay on his life and works, by
P. J. S. Dufey. 3 vols. Paris: Boulland, 1824–25.
La Libre Parole. Edouard Drumont. "La France aux Français." 20 Apr. 1892–7 June 1924.
Locke, John. *Deuxième traité du gouvernement civil*. Constitutions fondamentales de la
Caroline, résumé du premier "Traité du gouvernement civil." Ed. and Fr. trans.
B. Gilson. Paris: Vrin, 1967.
————. *Quelques pensées sur l'éducation*. Fr. trans. G. Compayre, ed. J. Château. Paris:
Vrin, 1966.
————. *John Locke on Politics and Education*. Ed. Howard Penniman. New York: Van
Nostrand, 1947.
————. *Two Treatises of Government*. With a supplement, *Patriarcha*, by Robert Filmer.
Ed. Thomas I. Cook. New York: Hafner Pub. Co., 1947.
————. *Second Treatise of Government*. New York: Dutton, n.d.
Loisel, Antoine. *La Guyenne de M. Antoine Loisel, qui sont huict remonstrances faictes en
la Chambre de Justice de Guyenne sur le subject des édicts de pacification. Plus une
autre remonstrance sur la réduction de la ville et restablissement du Parlement de Paris*.
Paris: chez Abel l'Angelier, au premier pilier de la grand salle du Palais, 1605.
Lorris, Guillaume de, and Jean de Meun. *Le Roman de la Rose*. Ed. Daniel Poirion. Paris:
Garnier-Flammarion, 1974.
Macaulay-Graham, Catharine. *Letters on education, with observations on religious and me-
taphysical subjects*. London: C. Dilly, 1790.
Maintenon, Françoise d'Aubigné, marquise de. *Conseils et instructions aux demoiselles pour
leur conduite dans le monde*. Paris: Charpentier, 1857.
————. *Madame de Maintenon institutrice: Extraits de ses lettres, avec entretiens, conver-
sations et proverbes sur l'éducation*. Ed. Emile Faguet. Paris: H. Gudin, 1885.
Marguerite de Navarre. *L'Heptaméron*. Ed. Michel François. Paris: Garnier, 1960.
Ménage, Gilles. *Historia mulierum philosopharum scriptore Aegidio Menagio*. Paris: Posuel
et C. Rigaud, 1690.
(La) Mère Duchêne. *Journal des femmes*. Paris: Imprimerie du véritable Père Duchêne,
mon mari, rue du Vieux-Colombier, no. 1–3 (June 1791).
Michelet, Jules. *Oeuvres complètes*. Ed. Paul Viallaneix. Paris: Flammarion, 1971–87.
(Le) *Moniteur universel*. May 5 1789–1868, Paris. From Dec. 1789 to 1810, titled *Gazette
nationale* or *Le Moniteur universel*.
Montaigne, Michel Eyquem de. *Oeuvres complètes*. Ed. A. Thibaudet and Maurice Rat.
Paris: Bibliothèque de la Pléiade, Gallimard, 1967–76.

———. *Essays*. Eng. trans. J. M. Cohen. New York: Penguin, 1958.

———. *Texte du manuscrit de Bordeaux*. Ed. Dr. Armaingaud. Paris: Conard, 1924–41.

———. *La Théologie naturelle de Raymond Sebon*. *Oeuvres complètes*, vol. 9.

Montesquieu, Charles Louis de. *Oeuvres complètes*. Paris: Bibliothèque de la Pléiade, Gallimard, 1976.

———. *Persian Letters*. Eng. trans. C. J. Betts. London: Penguin, 1973.

———. *The Spirit of the Laws*. Eng. trans. Thomas Nugent. New York: Hafner, 1966.

Morelly, Pierre François. *Code de la Nature, ou le véritable esprit de ses lois, de tout temps négligé ou méconnu*. Paris, Partout: chez le vrai sage, 1760.

Niboyet, Eugénie. *Le Vrai Livre des Femmes*. Paris: E. Dentu, 1863.

Nougarède de Fayet, André Jean Simon. *Histoire des lois sur le mariage et sur le divorce depuis leur origine dans le droit civil et coutumier jusqu'à la fin du XVIIIe siècle*. 2 vols. Paris, 1803.

Ordonnances du Roy Louis XIII sur les plaintes et les doléances. *Code Michau* rédigé par Michel de Marillac. Paris: A. Estiène, P. Mettayer et C. Prévost, 1629.

Paine, Thomas. *The Age of Reason: Being an investigation of true and of fabulous theologie*. Paris: Barrois, 1794.

———. *Déclaration des Droits de l'Homme et du Citoyen*. *Collection de livres classiques dédiée à la Convention nationale pour la nouvelle introduction publique*. Paris, 1793.

———. *Droits de l'Homme; en réponse à l'attaque de M. Burke sur la révolution française avec des notes et une nouvelle preface de l'auteur*. Paris: F. Buisson, 1793.

———. *Lettre de Thomas Paine au peuple français sur la journée du 18 fructidor*. Paris: Imprimerie du Cercle social, 1797.

———. *Théorie et pratique des Droits de l'Homme*, suivi du *Sens commun*. Fr. trans. F. Lanthenas. Rennes: R. Vator Fils, 1793.

Palme d'Aelders, Etta. *Appel aux Françaises sur la régénération des moeurs, et nécessité de l'influence des femmes dans un gouvernement libre*. Paris: Imprimerie du Cercle Social, [1791].

———. *Discours de Madame Palme d'Aelders, Hollandaise, lu à la confédération des amis de la vérité*. Caen: Imprimerie de F. Chalopin, n.d.

Parisot, Jean Patrocle. *La Foi dévoilée par la raison dans la connaissance de Dieu, de ses mystères et de la nature*. Paris: chez l'auteur, 1681.

Pascal, Jacqueline. *Les Constitutions du monastère de Port-Royal du Saint-Sacrement*. Mons: G. Migeot, 1665.

Pasquier, Etienne. *L'Interprétation des institutes de justinian avec la conférence de chasque paragraphe aux ordonnances royaux, arrestz de parlement et coutumes générales de la France*. Ouvrage inédit d'E. Pasquier. Paris: M. le duc Pasquier, 1847.

Pelletier, Madeleine. *Mon voyage aventureux en Russie communiste*. Paris: Girard, 1922.

Perrault, Charles. *L'Apologie des femmes*. Paris: chez la veuve de Jean-Baptiste Coignard et Jean-Baptiste Coignard Fils, 1694.

Pétition à l'Assemblée nationale pour lui demander une loi qui accorde aux enfants le droit d'hériter de leurs pères et mères libres, par Madame Grandval. Paris: Imprimerie de Demonville, n.d.

Pétition des citoyennes républicaines révolutionnaires, lue à la barre de la Convention nationale (signed "Champion, présidente"), n.d.

Poullain de la Barre, François ["Poulain"], *De l'Education des dames pour la conduite de l'esprit dans les sciences et dans les moeurs*. *Entretiens*. Paris: J. Du Puis, 1674.

———. *De l'égalité des deux sexes, discours physique et moral, où l'on voit l'importance de se défaire des préjugez*. Paris: chez Jean Du Puis, 1673.

———. *De l'Excellence des hommes, contre l'égalité des sexes*. Paris: chez Jean Du Puis, 1675.

Price, Richard. *Discours sur l'amour de la patrie, prononcé le 4 novembre 1789, par le Docteur Price, dans l'Assemblée de la Société formée pour célébrer la Révolution de la Grande-Bretagne*. With an appendix; Fr. trans. M. De Keralio. Paris: chez Prault, 1790.

Pufendorf, Samuel, Freiherr von. *Le Droit de la nature et des gens; ou, Système général des principes les plus importants de la morale, de la jurisprudence, et de la politique.* Ed. and Fr. trans. by Jean Barbeyrac. Amsterdam: O. Kuyper, 1706.

————. *Of the Law of Nature and Nations.* Eng. trans Basil Kennett, notes by Mr. Barbeyrac. London: J. Walthoe, R. Wilkin [etc.], 1729.

————. *The Law of Nature and Nations.* Trans. C. H. and W. A. Oldfather (from the edition of 1688). Oxford: Clarendon Press, 1934.

Recueil général des questions traictées ès conférences du Bureau d'adresses. Paris: L. Chamhoudry, 1655–56.

Renaudot, Théophraste. *Inventaire des addresses du Bureau de rencontre, où chacun peut donner et recevoir avis de toutes les nécessitez et comoditez de la vie et société humaine.* Paris: a l'Enseigne du Coq, rue de la Calandre, 1630.

Révolutions de France et de Brabant by Camille Desmoulins. Paris, 28 Nov. 1789; 12 Dec. 1791.

Revue encyclopédique. Paris: Recueil Larousse, 1896.

Roland de la Platière, Marie-Jeanne Phlipon. *Lettres autographes de Madame Roland, adressées à Bancal-des-Issarts, membre de la Convention.* Pub. by Mme. Henriette Bancal-des-Issarts, with an introduction by Sainte-Beuve. Paris: E. Renduel, 1835.

————. *Mémoires de Madame Roland.* Paris: Baudoin Frères, 1820.

Rousseau, Jean-Jacques. *Oeuvres complètes.* Ed. Bernard Gagnebin and Marcel Raymond. Paris: Bibliothèque de la Pléiade, Gallimard, 1959–79.

————. *Lettre à M. d'Alembert sur son article Genève.* Ed. Michel Launay. Paris: Garnier-Flammarion, 1967.

————. *Emile.* Trans. Barbara Foxley. New York: Dutton, 1972.

————. *The Social Contract* and *Discourses.* Trans. and ed., G. D. H. Cole. New York: Dutton, 1950.

————. *Rousseau's Political Writings.* Ed. Alan Ritter and Julia Bondanella; trans. Julia Bondanella. New York: W. W. Norton, 1988.

————. *Politics and the Arts: Letter to M. D'Alembert on the Theatre.* Trans. and ed. Allan Bloom. Ithaca: Cornell University Press, 1960.

Roux, Jacques. *(Le) Publiciste de la République française par l'ombre de Marat* (Jacques Roux). Paris, 16 July 1793-Nov. 1793.

Sainte-Marthe, Claude de; Antoine Arnauld and Pierre Nicole. *Apologie pour les religieuses de Port-Royal du Saint-Sacrement, contre les injustices et les violences du procédé dont on a usé envers ce monastère.* 1665.

Saint-Just, Antoine Louis Léon de. *Esprit de la Révolution et de la constitution en France.* Paris: Beuvin, 1791.

————. *Fragments sur les institutions républicaines.* Posthumous. Paris: Fayolle, 1800.

Schiff, Mario. *La fille d'alliance de Montaigne, Marie de Gournay*; followed by *L'Egalité des hommes et des femmes* and *Grief des Dames* with variants, notes, and appendices. Paris: Champion, 1910.

Schurman, Anna-Maria van. *Question célèbre s'il est nécessaire ou non que les filles soient sçavantes, agitées de part et d'autre par Mademoiselle Anne-Marie de Schurman et le Sr André Rivet.* Fr. trans. by "le Sr" Colletet. Paris: R. Le Duc, 1646.

Séances du Congrès ouvrier de France, session de 1876 tenue à Paris du 2 au 10 octobre. Paris: Sandoz et Fischbacher, 1877.

Sévigné, Marie de Rabutin-Chantal. *Lettres de Madame de Sévigné, de sa famille, de ses amies.* Ed. L. J. N. Momerqué; biographical note by P. Mesnard. Paris: Hachette, 1862–68.

Smith, Adam. *Théorie des sentiments moraux, un Essai analytique sur les principes des jugemens que portent naturellement les hommes, d'abord sur les actions des autres, et ensuite sur leurs propres actions, suivi d'une dissertation sur l'origine des langues.* Fr. trans., from the 7th (latest) edition, by Sophie Grouchy, veuve Condorcet. Includes eight letters on sympathy. Paris: F. Buisson, 1798.

Staël-Holstein, Germaine Necker, baronne de, known as Mme. de Staël. *Considérations sur les principaux évenements de la Révolution française.* Posthumously published by the duke of Broglie and baron A. de Staël. Paris: Delaunay, Bossange et Masson, 1818.

———. *Corinne ou l'Italie.* Feminist edition by Claudine Herrmann. Paris: Ed. des Femmes, 1979.

———. *De la littérature considérée dans ses rapports avec les institutions sociales.* Paris: Maradam, 1800.

———. *De l'influence des passions sur le bonheur des individus et des nations.* Lausanne: J. Mourer, 1796.

———. *Delphine.* Ed. Claudine Herrmann. Paris: Ed. des Femmes, 1982.

———. *Oeuvres complètes de Mme la Baronne de Staël.* Pub. by her son; prefaced by an essay on the character and writings of Mme. de Staël by Madame Necker de Saussure. V. 1, *Lettres sur J.-J. Rousseau.* Paris: Treutted et Wurtz, 1820–21.

———. *Réflexions sur le suicide.* Paris: Eds. de l'Opale, 1983.

Suchon, Gabrielle. *Du célibat volontaire, ou la vie sans engagement.* 2 vols. Paris: J. et M. Guignard, 1700.

———. *Traité de la Morale et de la politique divisé en trois parties, sçavoir, la liberté, la science et l'autorité, où l'on voit que les personnes du sexe, pour en être privées, ne laissent pas d'avoir une capacité naturelle, qui les en peut rendre participantes; avec un petit traité de la faiblesse, de la légèreté et de l'inconstance que leur attribue mal à propos par G. S. Aristophile.* Lyon: J. Certe, 1693.

———. *Traité de la morale et de la politique.* Ed. Séverine Auffret. Paris: Ed. des Femmes, 1988.

Talleyrand-Périgord, Charles Maurice. *Rapport sur l'instruction publique, fait au nom du Comité de Constitution.* Paris: Imprimerie nationale, 1791.

Théroigne de Méricourt [known as Anne Josephe Terwagne]. *Aux 48 sections.* N.p.

———. *Discours prononcé à la société fraternelle des minimes le 25 mars 1792 . . . en présentant un drapeau aux citoyennes du faubourg Saint-Antoine.* 1792.

Tiraqueau, André. *De legibus connubialibus.* Paris, 1513.

Tocqueville, Alexis Charles Clerel de. *L'Ancien Régime et la Révolution.* Ed. J.-P. Mayer, Paris: Gallimard, 1964.

———. *De la démocratie en Amérique.* Ed. François Furet. Paris: Flammarion, 1981.

———. *Democracy in America.* Trans. Henry Reeve. New York: Alfred Knopf, 1945.

Très humbles et très respectueuses remontrances de la cour des Aydes de Paris sur l'édit de décembre 1770 et l'état actuel du Parlement de Paris. London, 1773.

Turgot, Anne Robert Jacques. *Oeuvres de Turgot.* Ed. Pierre-Samuel Dupont de Nemours. 9 vols. Paris: Delance, 1808–11.

Vives, Juan Luis. *De l'Institution de la femme chrestienne, tant en son enfance que mariage et viduité aussi. De l'office du mary.* Trans. from Latin by Pierre de Changy. Paris: J. Kerver, 1543.

La Voix des femmes. Socialist and political journal (later daily). Organe des intérêts de toutes [organ of interest to all women], 19 Mar.-20 June 1848, Paris.

Voltaire, François Marie Arouet de. *Dictionnaire philosophique dans lequel sont réunies les questions sur l'encyclopédie, l'opinion en alphabet.* 14 vols. Paris: Didot, 1809.

———. *Mélanges.* Preface by Emmanuel Berl; ed. Jacques Van den Heuvel. Paris: Bibliothèque de la Pléiade, Gallimard, 1961.

Weiss, Louise. "Cinq semaines à Moscou." *L'Europe nouvelle*, revue hebdomadaire des questions extérieures économiques et littéraires (Paris), no. 51, 17 Dec. 1921.

Wier, Johann. *Histoires, disputes et discours, des illusions et impostures des diables, des magiciens infâmes, sorcières et empoisonneurs; des ensorcelez et démoniaques et de la guérison d'iceux. Item de la punition que méritent les magiciens, les empoisonneurs et les sorcières, le tout compris en six livres. . . . Deux dialogues touchant le pouvoir des sorcières et de la punition qu'elles méritent par Thomas Erastus.* Paris: Bureaux du Progrès médical, 1885.

Williams, David. *Observations sur la dernière constitution de la France, avec des vues pour la formation de la nouvelle constitution.* Fr. trans. by "le citoyen" Maudru. Paris: Imprimerie du Cercle social, 1792, An 2.

Wollstonecraft, Mary. *An Historical and Moral View of the Origin and Progress of the French Revolution; and the Effect It Has Produced in Europe.* London: J. Johnson, 1794.

———. *A Vindication of the Rights of Men, in a letter to the right honourable E. Burke; occasioned by his Reflections on the Revolution in France.* London: J. Johnson, 1790.

———. *A Vindication of the Rights of Men.* Gainesville: Scholars' Facsimiles and Reprints, 1960.

———. *A Vindication of the Rights of Women: With strictures on political and moral subjects.* London: Johnson, 1792.

———. *A Vindication of the Rights of Women: with Strictures on Political and Moral Subjects.* Ed. Ulrich H. Hardt. Troy: Whitston Publishing Co., 1982.

B. Secondary Sources

Abensour, Léon. *La Femme et le féminisme avant la Révolution.* Paris: E. Leroux, 1923.

———. *Le Féminisme sous le règne de Louis-Philippe et en 1848.* Paris: Plon-Nourrit, 1913.

———. *Histoire générale du féminisme des origines à nos jours.* Paris: Delagrave, 1921.

———. *Le Problème féministe: Un Cas d'aspiration collective vers l'égalité.* Paris: Radot, 1927.

———. *Les Vaillantes, héroïnes, martyres et remplaçantes.* Preface by Louis Barthou. Paris: Chapelot, 1927.

Actes du XVIe Colloque international de Tours, *Platon et Aristote à la Renaissance*, ed. Jean-Claude Margolin. Paris: Vrin, 1976.

Actes du Congrès Montesquieu. Proceedings of colloquium held at Bordeaux 23–26 May 1955, on the occasion of the 200th anniversary of the death of Montesquieu. Bordeaux: Delmas, 1956.

Adam, Antoine. *Les Libertins au XVIIe siècle.* Paris: Buchet-Chastel, 1964.

———. *Du mysticisme à la révolte: Les jansénistes du XVIIe siècle.* Paris: Fayard, 1968.

———. *Sur le problème religieux dans la première moitié du XIIe siècle.* Oxford: Clarendon Press, 1959.

Adam, Charles Ernest. *Descartes: Ses amitiés féminines.* Paris: Boivin, 1937.

Albistur, Maïté, and Daniel Armogathe. *Anthologie de textes féministes du Moyen Age à 1848.* Poitiers: Hier et Demain, 1978.

———. *Histoire du féminisme français: Du Moyen Age à nos jours*, Paris: Ed. des Femmes, 1977.

Alcover, Madeleine. "The Indecency of Knowledge." *Rice University Studies*, vol. 64, no.1 (Winter 1978).

———. "Poullain de la Barre, une aventure philosophique." *Papers on French Seventeenth-Century Literature*, Paris-Seattle-Tübingen, 1981.

Alengry, Franck. *Condorcet: Guide de la Révolution française, théoricien du droit constitutionnel, et précurseur de la science sociale.* Paris, 1903. Reprint. Geneva: Slatkine Reprints, 1971.

Alquié, Ferdinand. *La Découverte Métaphysique de l'homme chez Descartes.* Paris: PUF, 1966.

Amiable, Louis. *Une Loge maçonnique d'avant 1789, la R. -. L. -. les neuf soeurs.* Paris: Alcan, 1897.

Ancel, Marc. *La Condition de la femme dans la société contemporaine.* Paris: Recueil Sirey, 1938.

———. *Traité de la capacité civile de la femme mariée d'après la loi du 16 février 1938.* Paris: Sirey, 1938.

Angenot, Marc. *Les Champions des femmes: Examen du discours sur la majorité des femmes, 1400–1800.* Montréal: Presses de l'Université de Québec, 1977.

Anglo, Sydney. "Melancholia and Witchcraft: The Debate between Wier, Bodin and Scott," in *Folie et déraison à la Renaissance.* Proceedings of an international colloquium held Nov. 1973. Brussels: Université de Bruxelles, 1976.

Archambault de Monfort, Henri. *Les idées de Condorcet sur le suffrage.* Paris, 1915. Reprint. Geneva: Slatkine Reprints, 1970.

Arnaud, Jean André. *Les Origines doctrinales du Code civil français.* Preface by Michel Villey. Paris: Librairie générale de Droit et de Jurisprudence, 1969.

Ascoli, Georges. "Bibliographie pour servir à l'histoire des idées féministes depuis le milieu du XVIe siècle jusqu'à la fin du XVIIIe siècle." *Revue de Synthèse historique* (1906).

Aubertin, Charles. *L'Esprit public au XVIIIe siècle: Etude sur les mémoires et les correspondances politiques des contemporains, 1715 à 1789.* Paris: Didier et Cie, 1873.

Aulard, François-Alphonse. "Le Féminisme pendant la Révolution française." *Revue bleue, politique et littéraire* (Paris), no. 12, 4th series, vol. 9 (19 Mar. 1898).

Aulotte, Robert. *Amyot et Plutarque: La Tradition des Moralia au XVIe siècle.* Geneva: Droz, 1965.

Aymonier, Camille. "Montaigne et les femmes." *Revue philomathique de Bordeaux et du Sud-Ouest* (Apr.-June 1933).

Badel, Pierre-Yves. *Le Roman de la Rose au XIVe siècle: Etude de la réception de l'oeuvre.* Geneva: Droz, 1980.

Badinter, Elisabeth. *Emilie, Emilie: L'Ambition féminine au XVIIIe siècle.* Paris: Flammarion, 1983.

———. *Paroles d'hommes, 1790/1793.* Paris: P.O.L., 1989.

———, and Robert Badinter. *Condorcet: Un Intellectuel en politique.* Paris: Fayard, 1988.

Barbier, Antoine Alexandre. *Dictionnaire des ouvrages anonymes.* Paris: Maisonneuve et Larose, 1964.

Bauberot, Jean. *Renouveau de l'éthique, permanence du politique et changements religieux: Discours protestants et oecuméniques contemporains.* 8 pp. (mimeo). Paris, n.d.

Baudeau de Somaize, Antoine. *Le Dictionnaire des précieuses.* Ed. Ch. L. Livet. Paris: Jannet, 1856.

Baumal, Francis. *Le Féminisme au temps de Molière.* Paris: Renaissance du Livre, 1923.

Belin, Jean-Paul. *Le Mouvement philosophique de 1748 à 1789: Etude sur la diffusion des idées des philosophies à Paris d'après les documents concernant l'histoire de la librairie.* Paris: Belin Frères, 1913.

Benichou, Paul. *Morales du Grand Siècle.* Paris: Gallimard, 1948.

———. *Man and Ethics: Studies in French Classicism.* Eng. trans. Elizabeth Hughes. Garden City: Anchor Books, 1971.

Benoit, Daniel. *Marie Durand: prisonnière à la tour de Constance (1715–1768).* Dieulefit (Drôme): Nouvelles Sociétés d'Editions de France, 1938.

———. *Les Origines de la réforme à Montauban.* Montauban: Mlle. Capelle, 1910.

Benson, Mary Sumner. *Women in Eighteenth-Century America: A Study of Opinion and Social Usage.* New York: Columbia University Press, 1935.

Bieler, André. *L'Homme et la femme dans la morale calviniste: La Doctrine réformée sur l'amour, le mariage, le célibat, le divorce, l'adultère et la prostitution, considérée dans son cadre historique.* Geneva: Labor et Fides, 1963.

Blanc, Olivier. *Olympe de Gouges.* Paris: Syros, 1981.

Blanchet, Leon. *Les Antécédents historiques du je pense donc je suis.* Paris: Alcan, 1920.

Bloch, Ernst. *Droit naturel et dignité humaine.* Fr. trans. from German by Denis Authier and Jean Lacoste. Paris: Payot, 1976.

Bouchard, Marcel. *De l'humanisme à l'Encyclopédie: Essai sur l'évolution des esprits dans la bourgeoisie bourguignonne sous les règnes de Louis XIV et de Louis XV.* Thesis, University of Paris. Paris: Hachette, 1929.

Boucher, Maurice. *La Révolution de 1789 vue par les écrivains allemands, ses contemporains Klopstock, Wieland, Herder, Schiller, Kant, Fichte, Goethe.* Paris: M. Didier, 1954.

Bouillier, Francisque. *Histoire de la philosophie cartésienne.* Paris: C. Delagrave, 1868.

Bouissounouse, Janine. *Condorcet: Le Philosophe dans la Révolution.* Paris: Hachette, 1962.

Bray, René. *La Formation de la doctrine classique en France.* Paris: Hachette, 1927.

Brimo, Albert. *Les Femmes françaises face au pouvoir politique.* Paris: Montchrestien, 1975.

Brooks, Richard, ed. *A Critical Bibliography of French Literature in the Seventeenth Century.* Syracuse: Syracuse University Press, 1983.

Brown, Peter, and Robert Lamont. *La Vie de saint Augustin.* Fr. trans. from English by Jeanne Henri Marrou. Paris: Le Seuil, 1971.

Brugidou-Waetcher, Florence. *Condorcet et les droits des femmes.* Essay for "diplome superieur" in history of law. Paris, 1971.

Burckhardt, Jacob. *La Civilisation de la Renaissance en Italie.* 1860. Fr. trans. H. Schmitt, revised by R. Klein. Paris: Plon, 1958.

———. *The Civilization of the Renaissance in Italy.* English trans. S. G. C. Middlemore. 4th rev. ed. London: Phaidon Press, 1951.

Burdeau, Georges. *Le Libéralisme.* Paris: Points-Seuil, 1979.

Burgelin, Pierre. "L'Education de Sophie." *Annales de la Société Jean-Jacques Rousseau.* Geneva: A. Jullien, Bourg-de-Four, 32, vol. 35, 1959–62.

Burian-Schweinzer, Silvia. *Mademoiselle de Lézardière: Leben, Werk und Zeit einer Schulerin Montesquieus.* Thesis, Vienna, 1976.

Busson, Henri. *Les Sources et le developpement du rationalisme dans la littérature française de la Renaissance (1533–1601).* Paris, 1930.

Cabeen, David Clark, gen. ed. *A Critical Bibliography of French Literature.* Vol. 3, *The Seventeenth Century*, ed. Nathan Edelman. Syracuse: Syracuse University Press, 1961.

Cadart, Jacques. *Le Régime électoral des Etats Généraux de 1789 et ses origines (1302–1614).* Paris: Recueil Sirey, 1952.

Cahen, Léon. *Condorcet et la Révolution française.* Paris, 1904. Reprint. Geneva: Slatkine Reprints, 1970.

Callot, Emile. *La Philosophie de la vie au XVIIIe siècle, étudiée chez Fontenelle, Montesquieu, Maupertuis, La Mettrie, Diderot, d'Holbach, Linné.* Paris: M. Rivière, 1965.

Campaux, Antoine. *La Question des femmes au XVe siècle.* Paris: Berger-Levrault, 1865.

Carcassonne, Elie, ed. *Ecrits inédits de Mlle de Lézardière.* Paris: PUF, 1927.

———. *Montesquieu et le problème de la constitution française au XVIIIe siècle.* Paris: PUF, 1927.

Cassirer, Ernst. *Descartes, Corneille, Christine de Suède.* Fr. trans. M. Frances and Paul Schrecker. Paris: Vrin, 1942.

———. *La Philosophie des Lumières.* Ed. and Fr. trans. Pierre Quillet. Brionne: G. Montfort, 1982.

Ceard, Jean. "Le Modèle de la République de Platon et la pensée politique au XVIe siècle." In *Platon et Aristote à la Renaissance.* XVIe Colloque international de Tours. Paris: Vrin, 1976.

Cerati, Marie. *Le Club des citoyennes républicaines révolutionnaires.* Paris: Editions Sociales, 1966.

Cerroni, Umberto. *Kant e la fondazione della categoria giuridica.* Milan: Giuffre, 1962.

Chartier, Roger, Marie-Madeleine Compère, and Dominique Julia. *L'Education en France du XVIe au XVIIe siècle.* Paris: SEDES, 1976.

Chastel, André. *Marsile Ficin et l'art.* Geneva: Droz, 1954.

———, and Robert Klein. *L'Europe de la Renaissance: L'Age de l'humanisme.* Paris: Ed. des Deux-Mondes, 1963.

Chatelet, François. *Les lumières, le XVIIIe siècle. Histoire de la philosophie, idées, doctrines.* Paris: Hachette, 1977.

Chaunu, Pierre. *La Civilisation de l'Europe classique.* Paris: Arthaud, 1966.

Chauviré, Roger. *Jean Bodin, auteur de la République*. Paris: Champion, 1914.

Le Chevalier de Berquin. *La Déclamation des louanges du mariage*. 1525. Ed. Emile Telle. Geneva: Droz, 1976.

Cobban, Alfred. *The Social Interpretation of the French Revolution*. Cambridge: Cambridge University Press, 1964.

Cognet, Louis. *Crépuscule des mystiques: Bossuet, Fénelon*. Tournai: Desclée, 1958.

———. *La Spiritualité moderne*. Paris: Aubier, 1966.

Cohen, Gustave. *Ecrivains français en Hollande dans la première moitié du XVIIe siècle*. Paris: Champion, 1920.

Cohn, Norman Rufus Colin. *Les Fanatiques de l'Apocalypse: Courants millénaristes révolutionnaires du XIe au XVIe siècle avec une postface sur le XXe siècle*. Fr. trans. Simone Clémendot, with Michel Fuchs and Paul Rosenberg. Paris: Julliard, 1962.

———. *The Pursuit of the Millennium*. New York: Harper and Row, 1961.

Colloque international Jean Bodin. Munich, 1970.

Combes, André. *La Doctrine mariale du chancelier Jean Gerson*. Paris: Beauchesne, 1952.

———. *Etudes gersoniennes*. Paris, 1939. Extrait des archives d'histoire doctrinale et littéraire du Moyen Age, 1939.

———. *Jean de Montreuil et le chancelier Gerson. Contribution à l'histoire des rapports de l'humanisme et de la théologie en France au début du XVe siècle*. Paris: Vrin, 1942.

Comité National pour la Commémoration de Jean-Jacques Rousseau. Colloque, Paris, 1962. *Jean-Jacques Rousseau et son oeuvre: Problèmes et recherches*. Paris: Klincksieck, 1964.

Compayre, Gabriel. *Histoire critique des doctrines de l'éducation en France depuis le XVIe siècle*. Paris: Hachette, 1879.

Congrès international d'Etudes néo-latines (IIIe), septembre 1976, Tours, Université François-Rabelais. Ed. Jean-Claude Margolin. Paris: Vrin, 1980.

Conway, Moncure Daniel. *Thomas Paine (1737–1809) et la révolution dans les deux mondes*. Fr. trans. Félix Rabbé. Paris: Plon-Nourrit, 1900.

Coornaert, Emile. *Les Corporations en France avant 1789*. Paris: Gallimard, 1941.

Cousin, Victor. *Fragments littéraires: Lettres de Madame la Duchesse de Longueville, soeur du Grand Condé*. Paris: Didier, 1843.

———. *Jacqueline Pascal*. Paris: Didier, 1869.

———. *La Jeunesse de Madame de Longueville*. Paris: Didier, 1853.

———. *Madame de Longueville pendant la Fronde*. Paris: Didier, 1859.

Coville, Alfred. *Gontier et Pierre Col et l'humanisme en France au temps de Charles VI*. Paris: Droz, 1934.

———. *Recherches sur quelques écrivains du XIVe et du XVe siècle*. Paris: Droz, 1935.

Daraki, Maria. "L'Emergence du sujet singulier dans les confessions d'Augustin." *Esprit*, revue internationale (Feb. 1981).

Dedieu, Joseph. *Montesquieu: L'Homme et l'oeuvre*. Paris: Boivin, 1943.

———. *Montesquieu et la tradition politique anglaise en France: Les Sources anglaises de "L'esprit des lois"*. Paris: J. Gabalda, 1909.

———. *Le Rôle politique des protestants français (1685–1715)*. Paris: Bloud et Gay, 1920.

———. *Histoire politique des protestants français (1715–1794)*. Paris: Gabalda, 1925.

Delaruelle, Louis. *Etudes sur l'humanisme français: Guillaume Budé, les origines, les débuts, les idées maîtresses*. Paris: Champion, 1907.

———. "L'Inspiration antique dans le Discours de la servitude volontaire." *Revue de l'histoire littéraire de la France*, published by the Société d'Histoire littéraire de la France (1910).

Delaunay, Paul. *La Maternité de Paris: Port-Royal de Paris, port libre, l'hospice de la maternité, l'école des sages-femmes et ses origines (1625–1907)*. Paris: Jules Rousset, 1909.

———. *La Vie médicale aux XVIe, XVIIe et XVIIIe siècles*. Paris: Hippocrate, 1935.

Deleuze, Gilles. *Spinoza et le problème de l'expression*. Paris: Minuit, 1968.

Delpech, Jeanine. *L'Ame de la Fronde, Madame de Longueville*. Paris: Fayard, 1957.

Delsaux, Hélène. *Condorcet journaliste (1790–1794)*. Paris: Champion, 1931.

Delumeau, Jean. *La Civilisation de la Renaissance*. Paris: Arthaud, 1967.

———. *Naissance et affirmation de la Réforme*. Paris: PUF, 1965.

Demartial, Octave. *Essai sur la "théorie des lois politiques de la monarchie française" par Mlle de Lézardière*. Speech given upon the opening of the "conférences du bureau de Poitiers," 27 Jan. 1864. Poitiers: Impr. de A. Dupré, 1864.

Dequenne, Robert. *La Femme et l'éducation à travers la littérature du XVIIe siècle*. Thèse de doctorat du IIIe cycle [doctoral thesis]. Paris, 1970.

Derathe, Robert. *Jean-Jacques Rousseau et la science politique de son temps*. Paris: PUF, 1950.

———. *Le Rationalisme de Jean-Jacques Rousseau*. Paris: PUF, 1948.

Devos, Roger. *L'Origine sociale des visitandines d'Annecy aux XVIIe et XVIIIe siècles: Vie religieuse féminine et société*. Preface by Robert Mandrou. Annecy: Académie salésienne, 1973.

Dhavernas, Odile. *Droit des femmes, pouvoir des hommes*. Paris: Le Seuil, 1978.

Diesbach, Ghislain de. *Madame de Staël*. Paris: Perrin, 1983.

XVIIIe siècle. Annual publication of the Société française d'Etude du XVIIIe siècle. Paris: Garnier. No. 6 (1974), special issue: *Lumière et Révolution*; no. 10 (1978), special issue: *Qu'est-ce que les Lumières?*

Doumergue, Émile. *Jean Calvin: Les Hommes et les choses de son temps*. 7 vols. Lausanne: G. Bridel et Cie, 1899–1927.

Dubois, Claude Gilbert. *Celtes et Gaulois au XVIe siècle: Le Développement littéraire d'un mythe nationaliste, avec l'édition critique d'un traité inédit. De ce qui est premier pour réformer le monde de Guillaume Postel*. Paris: Vrin, 1972.

———. *La Conception de l'histoire en France au XVIe siècle: 1560–1610*. Thesis in letters, University of Paris IV, 1974. Paris: Nizet, 1977.

Duchet, Michèle. *Anthropologie et histoire au siècle des Lumières: Buffon, Voltaire, Rousseau, Helvetius, Diderot*. Paris: F. Maspero, 1971.

Duhet-Penigault, Paule-Marie. *Les Femmes et la Révolution, 1789–1794*. Paris: Julliard, 1971.

———. *Mary Wollstonecraft-Godwin: 1759–1767*. Dissertation for Doctorat d'Etat, University of Paris, 1975.

Dulong, Claude. *L'Amour au XVIIe siècle*. Paris: Hachette, 1969.

Dumont, Louis. "La Conception moderne de l'individu: Notes sur la genèse en relation avec les conceptions de la politique et de l'Etat à partir du XIIIe siècle." *Esprit* (Feb. 1978).

Durand, Georges. *Etats et institutions, XVIe–XVIIIe siècle*. Paris: A. Colin, 1969.

Duverger, Maurice. *La Participation des femmes à la vie politique*. Paris: Unesco, 1955.

Egret, Jean. *La Pré-Révolution française, 1787–1788*. Paris: PUF, 1962.

Ehrard, Jean. *L'Idée de Nature en France à l'aube des Lumières*. Paris: Flammarion, 1970.

Eisenmann, Charles. "L'Esprit des lois et la séparation des pouvoirs." In *Mélanges Raymond Carré de Malberg*. Paris, 1933.

———. "La Pensée constitutionnelle de Montesquieu." In *Recueil Sirey du Bicentenaire de l'Esprit des lois*. Paris, 1952.

———. "Le Système constitutionnel de Montesquieu et le temps présent," in *Actes du Congrès Montesquieu*. Bordeaux: Delmas, 1956.

Elhadad, Lydia. "Femmes prénommées: Les Prolétaires saint-simoniennes rédactrices de *La femme lue*, 1832–1834," *Les Révoltes logiques*, Cahiers du Centre de Recherches sur les idéologies de la révolte no. 4 (Winter 1977); no. 5 (Spring 1977).

Ellul, Jacques. *Histoire des institutions, XVIe–XVIIIe siècle*. Paris: PUF, 1956.

Elshtain, Jean Bethke. *Public Man, Private Woman: Women in Social and Political Thought*. Princeton: Princeton University Press, 1981.

Ernst, Otto. *Theroigne de Méricourt, d'après des documents inédits tirés des archives secrètes de la maison d'Autriche*. Fr. trans. lieut.-col. P. Waechter. Paris: Payot, 1935.

Faguet, Emile. *Le Féminisme*. Paris: Bavin, 1890.
———. *Le Libéralisme*. Paris: Société française d'Imprimerie et de Librairie, 1903.
Fagniez, Gustave. *La Femme et la société française dans la première moitié du XVIIe siècle*. Paris: Gamber, 1929.
Farge, Arlette. *Le Miroir des femmes*. Paris: Montalba, 1982.
Fauchery, Pierre. *La Destinée féminine dans le roman européen du XVIIIe siècle, 1713–1807. Essai de gynécomythie romanesque*. Paris: Colin, 1972.
Fauré, Christine. "Condorcet et la citoyenne," *Corpus, Revue de philosophie* no. 2 (Jan. 1986).
———. "Mademoiselle de Lézardière entre Jeanne d'Arc et Montesquieu." In *Les Femmes et la révolution française*. 3 vols. Proceedings of international colloquium held Apr. 12–14, 1989. Toulouse: Presses Universitaires de Mirail, 1989–90.
———. "La Pensée probabiliste de Condorcet et le suffrage féminin," in *Condorcet mathématicien, économiste, philosophe, homme politique*. Proceedings of an international colloquium. Paris: Minerve, 1989.
———. "Poullain de la Barre, sociologue et libre penseur." *Corpus, Revue de philosophie* no. 1 (May 1985).
———. "La Sauvageonne et la philosophie du droit naturel au XVIIIe siècle." *L'homme et la société*, Revue internationale de recherches et de synthèses en sciences sociales. Paris: l'Harmattan; 1–2, nos. 91, 92 (1989).
———. "L'Utopie de la femme nouvelle dans l'oeuvre d'Alexandra Kollontaï." In *Stratégies des femmes*, collectively edited. Paris: Tierce, 1984. Trans. as "The Utopia of the New Woman in the Work of Alexandra Kollontai and Its Impact on the French Feminist and Communist Press." See Friedlander et al.
———, ed. *Les Déclarations des droits de l'homme de 1789*. Paris: Payot, 1988.
Favret, Jeanne. "Sorcières et lumières." *Critique* (Jan.-June 1971).
———. *La Femme et la mort*. Groupe de Recherches interdisciplinaire d'Etudes des Femmes (GRIEF). Toulouse: Université de Toulouse-Le Mirail, 1984.
Feret, Pierre. *L'Abbaye de Sainte-Geneviève et la congrégation de France, précédées de la vie de la patronne de Paris d'après des documents inédits*. Paris: Champion, 1883.
———. *Le Droit divin et la théologie: Aperçu historico-théologique sur le pouvoir souverain en général et particulièrement en France*. Paris: V. Palme, 1874.
Ferguson, Wallace Klippert. *La Renaissance dans la pensée historique*. Paris: Payot, 1950.
———. *The Renaissance in Historical Thought: Five Centuries of Interpretation*. Boston: Houghton Mifflin, 1948.
Festugière, Jean. *La Philosophie de l'amour de Marsile Ficin et son influence dans la littérature française au XVIe siècle*. Paris: Vrin, 1941.
Feugère, Léon Jacques. *Les Femmes, poètes au XVIe siècle: Etude suivie de Mademoiselle de Gournay, Honoré d'Urfé*. Paris: Didier, 1860.
Feugère, Marius. *Les communautés de femmes dans la région d'Evreux aux XVIIe et XVIIIe siècles*. Paris: Jouve & Cie, 1927.
Flexner, Eleanor. *Mary Wollstonecraft: A Biography*. New York: Coward, McCann and Geoghegan, 1972.
Folie et déraison à la Renaissance. Université libre de Bruxelles, Institut pour l'Etude de la Renaissance et de l'Humanisme. Brussels: Editions de l'Université, 1976. Proceedings of an international colloquium in Brussels, Nov. 1973, sponsored by the Fédération internationale des instituts et sociétés pour l'étude de la Renaissance.
Forestié, Edouard. *Olympe de Gouges (1748–1793)*. Montauban, 1901.
Fosseyeux, Marcel. *Les Ecoles de charité à Paris sous l'Ancien Régime et dans la première partie du XIXe siècle*. Paris: Impr. Daupeley-Gouverneur, 1912.
Foucault, Michel. *Histoire de la folie à l'âge classique*. Paris: Gallimard, 1972.
———. *Madness and Civilization: A History of Insanity in the Age of Reason*. Trans. Richard Howard. New York: Pantheon, 1965.

Fraisse, Geneviève. "Droit naturel et question de l'origine dans la pensée féministe au XIXe siècle." In *Stratégies des femmes*.

———. "Les Femmes libres de 48: Moralisme et féminisme." *Les révoltes logiques*, Cahiers du Centre de Recherches sur les idéologies de la révolte no. 1 (Winter 1975).

———. *Muse de la raison: La Democratie exclusive et la différence des sexes*. Paris: Alinea, 1989.

Friedlander, Judith, Blanche Wiesen Cook, Alice Kessler-Harris, and Carol Smith-Rosenberg, eds. *Women in Culture and Politics: A Century of Change*. Bloomington: Indiana University Press, 1986. English trans. of collection *Stratégies des femmes* (Paris: Editions Tierce, 1984).

Furet, François. *Penser la Révolution française*. Paris: Gallimard, 1978.

Gaberel, Jean-Pierre. *Les Suisses Romands et les réfugiés de l'Edit de Nantes*. Excerpt from the report of the Academie des sciences morales et politiques. Paris, 1860.

Gagnebin, Bernard. *Burlamaqui et le droit naturel*. Geneva: La Frégate, 1944.

———. Une Vie tourmentée, excerpt from *Jean-Jacques Rousseau*. Université ouvrière et Faculté des Lettres de l'Université de Genève. Neuchâtel: Editions de La Baconnière, n.d.

Gandillac, Maurice de. *Histoire de la philosophie*. Vol. 2, *Philosophie de la Renaissance*. Paris: Encyclopédie de la Pléiade, Gallimard, 1973.

Garanderie, Marie-Madeleine de la. *Correspondance d'Erasme de Rotterdam et de Guillaume Budé*. Paris: Vrin, 1967.

Garaud, Marcel. *Histoire générale du droit privé français de 1799 à 1804*. Foreword by Georges Lefebvre. Paris: Recueil Sirey, 1953–58.

Garin, Eugenio. *L'Education de l'homme moderne, la pédagogie de la Renaissance, 1400–1600*. Paris: Fayard, 1968.

Garosci, Aldo. *Jean Bodin: politica e diritto nel rinascimento francese*. Milano: A. Corticelli, 1934.

Garrisson-Estèbe, Janine. *L'Homme protestant*. Paris: Hachette, 1980.

———. "La mort des sorcières," in *La Femme et la mort*. Groupe de Recherches interdisciplinaire d'Etudes des Femmes. Toulouse: Université de Toulouse-Le Mirail, 1984.

Geffriaud Rosso, Jeannette. *Montesquieu et la féminité*. Pisa: Libreria Goliardica, 1977.

Gerbaux, F. "Les femmes soldats pendant la Révolution." *Revue d'Histoire moderne et contemporaine* (July-Dec. 1904).

Gérold, Théodore. *Le Principe de la réforme et le passage du libéralisme*. Lecture delivered in Geneva and Paris. Geneva: A. Cherbuliez, 1882.

Gilles de la Tourette, Georges. *Théophraste Renaudot, d'après des documents inédits. La Gazette. Un essai de Faculté libre au XVIIe siècle. Le Bureau d'adresse. Les Monts-de-piété. Les consultations charitables*. Paris: Plon, Nourrit et Cie, 1884.

———. *La Vie et les oeuvres de Théophraste Renaudot, fondateur du journalisme et des consultations charitables*. Paris, rue de Beaune, 1892.

Gilmore, Myron Piper. *Le Monde, l'humanisme, 1453–1517*. Fr. trans. Anne Marie Cabrini. Paris: Payot, 1955.

Gilson, Etienne. *Introduction à l'étude de saint Augustin*. Paris: Vrin, 1929. 4th ed. Paris: Vrin, 1969.

———. *La Doctrine cartésienne de la liberté et la théologie*. Thesis in letters. Paris, 1912–13.

———. *Etudes sur le rôle de la pensée médiévale dans la formation du système cartésien*. Paris: Vrin, 1930.

———. *La Philosophie au Moyen Age, des origines patristiques à la fin du XIVe siècle*. Paris: Payot, 1944.

———. *History of Christian Philosophy in the Middle Ages*. New York: Random House, 1955.

————. *La Philosophie de saint Bonaventure*. Paris: Vrin, 1924.

————. éd. *Discours de la méthode: Texte et commentaires*, by René Descartes. Paris: Vrin, 1930.

Girard, Louis. *Le Libéralisme en France de 1814 à 1848, doctrine et mouvement*. Paris: Centre de Documentation universitaire, 1966–67.

Godineau, Dominique. *Citoyennes tricoteuses*. Paris: Alinéa, 1988.

Goldschmidt, Victor. *Anthropologie et politique: Les Principes du système de Rousseau*. Paris: Vrin, 1974.

Goncourt, Edmond de. *La Femme au XVIIIe siècle*. Preface by Elisabeth Badinter. Paris: Flammarion, 1982.

Gorce, M. M. "Le Roman de la Rose de Jean de Meun et son caractère universitaire." In *Mélanges Mandonnet*. Paris: Vrin, 1930.

Gout, Raoul. "Une Grande oeuvre protestante: L'Association des diaconesses de Paris." Lecture delivered 4 Aug. 1932 on "Radio-Paris," Carrières-Sous-Poissy, La Cause.

————. "Les Femmes de la Réforme française: Nos premières martyres," Lecture delivered 2 July 1935 on "Poste Parisien," Paris, Voix de "La Cause," 23 June 1936.

————. "Les Femmes de la Réforme française: Valeur bien française du caractère et de l'héroïsme de nos mères huguenotes." Lecture on 9 July 1935, Paris, "La Cause."

————. *Le Miroir des dames chrétiennes: Pages féminines de la Réforme française, XVIe–XVIIIe siècle*. Paris: Je Sais, 1937.

Goyard-Fabre, Simone. *Essai de critique phénoménologique du droit*. Thesis, Paris, 1970. Paris: Klincksieck, 1972.

————. *Kant et le problème du droit*. Paris: Vrin, 1975.

————. *La Philosophie du droit de Montesquieu*. Preface by Jean Carbonnier. Paris: Klincksieck, 1973.

Granger, Gilles-Gaston. *La Mathématique sociale du marquis de Condorcet*. Paris: PUF, 1956.

Grappin, Henri. "Note sur un féministe oublié, le cartésien Poullain de La Barre." *Revue d'Histoire littéraire de la France* (1913).

Greig, John Young Thomson, ed. *The Letters of David Hume*. Oxford: Clarendon Press, 1932.

Grieco, Sara F. Matthews. *Le Discours iconographique sur la femme "dangereuse" dans la gravure du XVIe siècle français*. Thesis for DEA degree, Ecole des Hautes Etudes en Sciences sociales. Paris, 1977.

————. *Mythes et iconographie de la femme dans l'estampe du XVIe siècle français: images d'un univers mental*. Doctoral dissertation. Ecole des Hautes Etudes en Sciences sociales. Paris, 1983.

Grimal, Pierre, ed. *Histoire illustrée de la femme*. Preface by Andre Maurois. Paris: Lidis, 1965.

————. *Histoire mondiale de la femme*. Paris: Nouvelle Librairie de France, 1965–69.

Groethuysen, Bernhard. *Anthropologie philosophique*. Paris: Gallimard, 1952.

————. *Jean-Jacques Rousseau*. Paris: Gallimard, 1949.

————. *Origines de l'esprit bourgeois en France*. Paris: Gallimard, 1927.

————. *Philosophie de la Révolution française*; précédé de *Motesquieu*. Paris: Gallimard, 1956.

Gueudré, Mère Marie de Chantal. *Au coeur des spiritualistes: Catherine Ranquet, mystique et éducatrice, 1602–1611*. Thesis in letters, Paris: Grasset, 1952.

————. "La Femme et la vie spirituelle." *XVIIe siècle*, journal published by the Société d'Etude du XVIIe siècle, no. 62–63 (1964).

————. *Histoire de l'ordre des Ursulines en France*. Vol. 1, *De l'institution séculière à l'ordre monastique, 1579–1650*. Vol. 2, *Sous l'Ancien Régime, 1612–1788*. Paris: Saint-Paul, 1958.

Guiton, W. H. *La Réforme à Paris, XVIe et XVIIe siècles*. Asnières, 1931.

Gusdorf, Georges. *Les Principes de la pensée au siècle des Lumières*. Paris: Payot, 1971.

Gutton, Jean-Pierre. *La Société et les pauvres en Europe, XVIe–XVIIIe siècle*. Paris: PUF, 1974.

Haag, Eugène and Emile. *La France protestante; ou, Vies des protestants français qui se sont fait un nom dans l'histoire depuis les premiers temps de la Réformation jusqu'à la reconnaissance du principe de la liberté des cultes par l'Assemblée nationale*. Geneva: Slatkine Reprints, 1966.

Hatin, Eugène. *A propos de Théophraste Renaudot: L'Histoire, la fantaisie et la fatalité*. Paris: Fechoz, 1884.

Hauser, Henri and Augustin Renaudet. *Les Débuts de l'âge moderne: La Renaissance et la Réforme*. Paris: Alcan, 1929.

———. *La Modernité du XVIe siècle*. Paris: Alcan, 1930.

Hazard, Paul. *La Crise de la conscience européenne (1680–1715)*. Paris: Boivin, 1935.

———. *The European Mind*. Trans. J. Lewis May. London: Hollis and Carter, 1953.

Hicks, Eric. *Le Débat sur le "Roman de la Rose": Christine de Pisan, Jean Gerson, Jean de Montreuil, Gontier et Pierre Col*. Ed. and trans. Eric Hicks. Paris: H. Champion, 1977.

Hissette, Roland. *Enquêtes sur les 219 articles condamnés à Paris le 7 mars 1277*. Louvain: Publications universitaires, 1977.

Histoire sans qualités. Collectively edited. Essays by Christiane Dufrancatel, Arlette Farge, Christine Fauré, Geneviève Fraisse, Michelle Perrot, Elisabeth Salvaresi, and Pascale Werner. Paris: Galilée, 1979.

Hoffmann, Paul. *Féminisme cartésien*. Centre de Philologie et de Littératures romanes, Université de Strasbourg, "Travaux de linguistique et de littérature" no. 7, 1969.

———. "Le féminisme spirituel de Gabrielle Suchon." Followed with a note by P. Ronzeaud. *XVIIe siècle*, journal published by the Société d'Etude du XVIIe siècle, no. 121 (1978).

———. *La Femme dans la pensée des lumières*. Paris: Ophrys, 1977.

———. *Préciosité et féminisme dans le roman de Michel de Pure*. Centre de Philologie et de Littératures romanes, Université de Strasbourg, "Travaux de linguistique et de littérature" no. 5 (1967).

Huizinga, Johan. *Le Déclin du Moyen Age*. Paris: Payot, 1932.

———. *Erasme*. Fr. trans. V. Bruncel. Preface by Lucien Febvre. Paris: Gallimard, 1955.

———. *Men and Ideas: History, the Middle Ages, the Renaissance*. Trans. J. S. Holmes and Hans van Marle. London: Eyre and Spottiswoode, 1959.

Hyslop, Beatrice. "Les Elections à Montargis en 1789." *Annales historiques de la Révolution française*, publication of the Société des Etudes Robespierristes, no. 103 (Apr.-June 1946).

Ilsley, Marjorie Henry. *A Daughter of the Renaissance: Marie le Jars de Gournay, Her Life and Works*. The Hague: Mouton, 1963.

Imbart de la Tour, P. *Les Origines de la Réforme*. Geneva: Slatkine Reprints, 1978.

Institoris, Henricus. *Le Marteau des sorcières*, by Jacques Sprenger and Heinrich Kramer. Fr. trans. and ed. Armand Danet. Paris: Plon, 1973.

Jalley-Crampe-Casnabet, Michèle. *Genèse idéale et genèse empirique dans la philosophie transcendante kantienne*. Thesis for the Doctorat d'Etat. Paris, 1980.

Jarrin, Albert, ed. *Un Economiste libéral au XVIe siècle: Jean Bodin*. Excerpts from his *Rehaussement et diminution des monnayes*. Chambéry: Impr. savoisienne, 1904.

Jellinek, Georg. *La Déclaration des Droits de l'Homme et du Citoyen: Contribution à l'histoire du droit constitutionnel moderne*. Fr. trans. from German by G. Fardis; preface by M. F. Larnaude. Paris: A. Fontemoing, 1902.

Julien-Eymard d'Angers. "Problèmes et difficultés de l'humanisme chrétien." *XVIIe siècle*, journal published by the Société d'Etude du XVIIe siècle, nos. 62–63 (1964).

———, ed. *Recherches sur le stoïcisme aux XVIe et XVIIe siècles*, by L. Antoine. Hildesheim and New York: O. Olm, 1976.

Kelsen, Hans, trans. *Théorie pure du droit*. Fr. trans. of the 2nd ed. of *Reine Rechtslehre* by Charles Eisenmann. Paris: Dalloz, 1962.

Kelso, Ruth. *Doctrine for the Lady of the Renaissance*. Urbana: University of Illinois Press, 1956.

Kiejman, Laurence, and Florence Rochefort. *L'Egalité en marche: Le Féminisme sous la Troisième République*. Paris: Fondation nationale des sciences politiques/Ed. des femmes, 1989.

Knibiehler, Yvonne, and Catherine Fouquet. *La Femme et les médecins: Analyse historique*. Paris: Hachette, 1983.

Kofman, Sarah. *Le Respect des femmes: Kant et Rousseau*. Paris: Galilée, 1982.

Kristeller, Paul Oskar. *Renaissance Thought: The Classic, Scholastic and Humanistic Strains*. 2 vols. New York: Harper and Row, 1961–65.

Labitte, Charles. *De la démocratie chez les prédicateurs de la Ligue*. Paris: Joubert, 1841.

Laboucheix, Henri. *Richard Price, théoricien de la révolution américaine, le philosophe et le sociologue, le pamphlétaire et l'orateur*. Thesis for Doctorat d'Etat, Paris. Montréal, Paris, and Brussels: Didier, 1970.

Labrousse, Elisabeth. *Pierre Bayle et l'instrument critique*. Critical ed., bibliography. Paris: Seghers, 1965.

———. *Pierre Bayle: Hétérodoxie et rigorisme*. The Hague: Nijhoff, 1964.

Lacour, Leopold. *Humanisme intégral: Le Duel des sexes. La Cité future*. Paris, Stock, 1897.

———. "Marat féministe." *Grande Revue*, vol. 6, no. 3 (1902).

———. *Les Origines du féminisme contemporain; trois femmes de la Révolution: Olympe de Gouges, Théroigne de Méricourt, Rose Lacombe*. Paris: Plon-Nourrit, 1900.

La Fontainerie, François de, ed. and trans. *French Liberalism and Education in the Eighteenth Century: The Writings of Chalotais, Turgot, Diderot, and Condorcet on National Education*. New York and London: McGraw-Hill, 1932.

Lagarde, Georges de. *La Naissance de l'esprit laïque, au déclin du Moyen Age*. Louvain: E. Nauwelaerts, 1956.

———. *Recherches sur l'esprit politique de la réforme*. Paris: A. Picard, 1926.

Lairtuller, E. *Les Femmes célèbres de 1789 à 1795 et leur influence dans la Révolution, pour servir de suite et de complément à toutes les histoires de la Révolution française*. Paris, 1840.

Langeron, Geneviève. "Le Club des femmes de Dijon pendant la Révolution." *La Révolution en Côte-d'Or*, publication of the Comité départemental pour l'étude de l'histoire économique de la Révolution française. Dijon, 1929.

Langlois, Ernest. *Le Traité de Gerson contre le Roman de la Rose*. Excerpts from *Romania*, Jan. 1918-Jan. 1919. Paris: Champion, n.d.

Laski, Harold. *Le Libéralisme européen, du Moyen Age à nos jours*. Paris: Emile Paul, 1950.

Lasserre, Adrien. *La Participation collective des femmes à la Révolution française: Les Antécedents du féminisme*. Toulouse: Privat. Paris: Alcan, 1906.

Lathuillère, Roger. *La Préciosité: Etude historique et linguistique*. Vol. 1, *Position du problème: Les origines*. Geneva: Droz, 1966.

Lavallée, Théophile. *Histoire de la maison royale de Saint-Cyr (1686–1793)*. Paris: Furne, 1853.

Lebrun, François. *La Vie conjugale sous l'Ancien Régime*. Paris: Colin, 1975.

Lecler, Joseph. *Histoire de la tolérance au siècle de la Réforme*. Paris: Aubier, 1955.

Le Doeuff, Michèle. *L'Imaginaire philosophique*. Paris: Payot, 1980.

Lefebvre, Georges. *Etudes sur la Révolution française*. Paris: PUF, 1954.

Le Garrec, Evelyne. *Séverine, une rebelle (1855–1929)*. Paris: Le Seuil, 1982.

Le Goff, Jacques. *Les Intellectuels au Moyen Age*. Paris: Le Seuil, 1957.

Léonard, Emile G. *Le Protestant français*. Paris: PUF, 1953.

Le Pointe, Gabriel. *Histoire des institutions et des faits sociaux*. Paris: Montchrestien, 1963.

————. *La Femme au XIVe siècle en France et dans le monde de l'Europe occidentale.* Brussels: Ed. de la Librairie encyclopédique, 1962.

Leroy, Maxime. *Histoire des idées sociales en France.* Paris: Gallimard, 1946.

————. *Les Précurseurs français du socialisme de Condorcet à Proudhon.* Paris: Ed. du Temps présent, 1948.

Lespinasse, René de. *Histoire générale de Paris: Les Métiers et corporations de la ville de Paris, XIVe–XVIIIe siècle.* Paris: Imprimerie Nationale, 1886–97.

Levy, Darlene et al., ed. and trans. *Women in Revolutionary Paris, 1789–1795.* Urbana: University of Illinois Press, 1979.

Loraux, Nicole. *Les Enfants d'Athéna: Idées athéniennes sur la citoyenneté et la division des sexes.* Paris: Maspero, 1981.

MacPherson, Crawford Brought. *The Political Theory of Possessive Individualism.* New York: Oxford University Press, 1962.

————. *La Théorie publique de l'individualisme possessif de Hobbes à Locke.* Fr. trans. Michel Fuchs. Paris: Gallimard, 1971.

Magendie, Maurice. *La Politesse mondaine et les théories de l'honnêteté en France au XVIIe siècle, de 1600 à 1660.* Paris: Alcan, 1925.

Magne, Bernard. *Crise de la littérature française sous Louis XIV: Humanisme et nationalisme.* Thesis in letters, Toulouse, 1974. Paris: Champion, 1976.

————. *Le Féminisme de Poullain de La Barre: Origine et signification.* Doctoral thesis, University of Toulouse, 1964.

Mandonnet, Pierre. *Siger de Brabant et l'averroïsme latin au XIIIe siècle: Etude critique.* Fribourg: Librairie de l'Université, 1899.

Mandrou, Robert. *Des humanistes aux hommes de science (XVIe et XVIIe siècle).* Paris: Le Seuil, 1973.

————. *Introduction à la France moderne (1500–1640): Essai de psychologie historique.* Paris: A. Michel, 1961.

————. *Magistrats et sorciers en France au XVIIe siècle: Une Analyse de psychologie historique.* Paris: Plon, 1968.

————, Janine Estèbe, Daniel Ligou, Bernard Vogler, et al., *Histoire des protestants en France.* Toulouse: Privat, 1977.

Mann, Margaret. *Erasme et les débuts de la Réforme française (1517–1536).* Paris: Champion, 1934.

Marcel, Raymond. *Marsile Ficin, 1433–1499: Commentaire sur le Banquet de Platon.* Paris: Les Belles-Lettres, 1956.

Margolin, Jean-Claude, ed. *L'Avènement des Temps modernes.* Essays by J. F. Bergier, J. Boisset, A. Châtelet, C. Verlinden. Paris: PUF, 1977.

————. *Douze années de bibliographie érasmienne (1950–1961).* Paris: Vrin, 1963.

————. "Erasme et le problème social." *Rinascimento: Rivista dell'Instituto nazionale di studi sul Rinascimento,* no. 13 (1973–74).

————. *Neuf années de bibliographie érasmienne (1962–1970).* Paris: Vrin; Toronto: University of Toronto Press, 1977.

————. *Quatorze années de bibliographie érasmienne (1936–1949).* Paris: Vrin, 1969.

————. *Recherches érasmiennes.* Geneva: Droz, 1969.

Marrou, Henri Irénée. *Saint Augustin et l'augustinisme.* With collaboration of A.-M. la Bonnardière. Paris: Le Seuil, 1955.

————. *Saint Augustin et la fin de la culture antique.* Paris: E. De Boccard, 1938.

Marseille, journal of the Centre méridional de Rencontres sur le XVIIe siècle. *Le XVIIe siècle et l'education* [papers from the 1971 Colloque de Marseille], supplement to *Marseille,* no. 88 (1972); *La Qualité de la vie au XVIIe siècle,* no. 9 (1977); "Madame De Sévigné: Molière et la médecine de son temps," no. 95 (1973).

Martin, Henri Jean. *Livre, pouvoirs et société à Paris au XVIIe siècle (1598–1701).* Geneva: Droz, 1962.

Martin, Kingsley. *The Rise of French Liberal Thought: A Study of Political Ideas from Bayle to Condorcet.* 2nd rev. ed. New York: New York University Press, 1954.
———. *Thomas Paine.* London: The Fabian Society, 1925.
Maulde la Clavière, René, *Vers le bonheur! Les femmes de la Renaissance.* Paris: Perrin, 1898.
———. *The Women of the Renaissance: A Study of Feminism.* Eng. trans. G. H. Ely. New York: Putnam, 1901.
Mauriac, François. *Blaise Pascal et sa soeur Jacqueline.* Paris: Hachette, 1931.
Mauzi, Robert. *L'idée du bonheur dans la littérature et la pensée française au XVIIIe siècle.* Paris: A. Colin, 1960.
Mealy, Paul. *Origines des idées politiques libérales en France: Les publicistes de la Réforme sous François II et Charles IX.* Paris: Fischbacher, 1903.
Mélanges Mandonnet: Etudes d'histoire littéraire et doctrinale du Moyen Age. 2 vols. Paris: Vrin, 1930.
Mélanges Raymond Carré de Malberg. Paris, 1933.
Mesnard, Pierre. *L'Essor de la philosophie politique au XVIe siècle.* Paris: Vrin, 1951.
Méthivier, Hubert. *La France de Louis XIV: Un Grand Règne?* Paris: PUF, 1975.
Metz, René. "Le statut de la femme en droit canonique médiéval," in *Recueils de la Société Jean-Bodin,* vol.12 (1962).
Michaud, Joseph François. *Biographie universelle ancienne et moderne.* Rev. ed., Paris: Mme. C. Desplaces, 1854–63.
Mirkine-Guetzevitch, Boris. "De la séparation des pouvoirs." In *Recueil Sirey du Bicentenaire de l'Esprit des lois.* Paris, 1952.
Mongredien, Georges. *Madeleine de Scudéry et son salon d'après des documents inédits.* Paris: Tallandier, 1946.
———. *Les Précieux et les précieuses: Textes choisis et présentés avec introduction et notices, suivis d'un appendice bibliographique.* Paris: Mercure de France, 1939.
———. *La Vie quotidienne sous Louis XIV.* Paris: Hachette, 1948.
Montet-Clavié, Danielle. "La Femme comme nature morte dans l'oeuvre de Jean-Jacques Rousseau." In *La Femme et la mort.* Groupe de Recherches interdisciplinaire d'étude des femmes. Toulouse: Université de Toulouse-Le Mirail, 1984.
Moreana: Bulletin Thomas More, publication of the Association Amici Thomas Mori, no. 10 (May 1966), no. 12 (Nov. 1966).
Moreau, Pierre François. *Les Racines du libéralisme.* Paris: Points/Seuil, 1978.
Morel, J. "Recherches sur les sources du discours de l'inégalité," *Annales de la Société Jean-Jacques Rousseau,* A. Jullien, Bourg-de-Four, 32, vol. 6 (1909).
Moreux, Françoise. *Elisabeth Inchbald et la revendication féminine au XVIIIe siècle.* Lille: University of Lille III, 1973.
Morgan, Betty Trebelle. *Histoire du "Journal des Sçavans" depuis 1665 jusqu'en 1701.* Thesis. Paris: PUF, 1928.
Mörikofer, Johann Caspar. *Histoire des réfugiés de la Réforme en Suisse.* Fr. trans. from German, and illustrated by G. Roux. Paris: Sandoz and Fischbacher, 1878.
Mornet, Daniel. *Histoire de la clarté française: Ses origines, son évolution, sa valeur.* Paris: Payot, 1929.
Mousnier, Roland. *L'Assassinat d'Henri IV, 14 mai 1610.* Paris: Gallimard, 1964.
———. *Etat et société en France aux XVIIe et XVIIIe siècles.* Paris: Centre de Documentation universitaire, 1968.
———. *La Famille, l'enfant et l'éducation en France et en Grande-Bretagne du XVe au XVIIIe siècle.* Paris: Centre de Documentation universitaire, 1975.
———. *Les Institutions de la France sous la monarchie absolue 1598–1789: Société et Etat.* Paris: PUF, 1974.
———. *Paris, capitale, au temps de Richelieu et de Mazarin.* Paris: Pédone, 1978.
———. *La Vénalité des offices sous Henri IV et Louis XIII.* Rouen: Maugard, 1945.
Mouy, Paul. *Le Développement de la physique cartésienne (1646–1712).* Paris: Vrin, 1934.

Muchembled, Robert. *Culture populaire et culture des élites dans la France moderne: XVe–XVIIIe siècle*. Paris: Flammarion, 1977.

———. *La Sorcière au village: XVe–XVIIIe siècle*. Paris: collection "Archives," Gallimard-Julliard, 1979.

Offen, Karen. "On the French Origin of the Words Feminism and Feminist." *Feminist Issues*, vol. 8, no. 2 (Fall 1988).

———. "Qui est Jenny d'Hericourt? Une identité retrouvée." *Bulletin de la société d'histoire de la révolution de 1848 et des révolutions du XIXe siècle*. Paris, 1987.

Okin, Susan Moller. *Women and Western Political Thought*. Princeton: Princeton University Press, 1979.

Olivier-Martin, François Jean-Marie. *La Crise du mariage dans la législation intermédiaire: 1789–1804*. Paris: A. Rousseau, 1901.

———. *Histoire du droit français des origines à la Révolution*. Paris: Domat-Montchrestien, 1948.

———. *L'Organisation corporative de la France d'Ancien Régime*. Paris: Recueil Sirey, 1938.

Palmero, Jean. *Histoire des institutions et des doctrines pédagogiques par les textes*. Paris: Société universitaire d'Editions et de Librairie, 1951.

Pangle, Thomas. *Montesquieu's Philosophy of Liberalism: A Commentary on the Spirit of the Laws*. Chicago: University of Chicago Press, 1973.

Pannier, Jacques. *Une Femme de qualité au milieu du XVIIe siècle, d'après le livre de raisons de Marguerite Mercier (Mme d'Espesses, puis Mme Du Faye de La Taillée) (1650–1661)*. Paris: Librairies-Imprimeries Réunies, n.d. Excerpt from *Bulletin de la Société de l'Histoire du protestantisme français* (Nov.-Dec. 1905).

Panofsky, Erwin. *Essai d'iconologie: Les Thèmes humanistes dans l'art de la Renaissance*. Paris: Gallimard, 1939.

———. *Studies in Iconology: Humanistic Themes in the Art of the Renaissance*. New York: Harper and Row, 1962.

Payen, Jean-Claude. *Les Origines de la courtoisie dans la littérature française médiévale*. Paris: Centre de Documentation universitaire, 1966–67.

———. *Qu'est-ce que la Renaissance?* Paris: Centre de Documentation universitaire, 1967.

———. *La Rose et l'utopie: Révolution sexuelle et communisme nostalgique chez Jean de Meung*. Paris: Editions Sociales, 1976.

Payer, Alice de. *Le Féminisme au temps de la Fronde*. Letter-preface by Admiral Degouy. Paris: Société des Editions Fast, 1922.

Perrot, Michelle. "L'Eloge de la ménagère dans le discours des ouvriers français au XIXe siècle." *Romantisme*, journal of the Société des Etudes Romantiques. Paris: Flammarion (Feb. 1977).

———. *Histoire de la vie privée, de la Révolution à la Grande Guerre*. Paris: Seuil, 1987, vol. 4.

Piaget, Arthur. "Chronologie des épîtres sur le Roman de la Rose." In *Mélanges Gaston Paris*. Paris, 1891.

Picot, Georges Marie René. *Le Droit électoral de l'ancienne France: Les Elections aux Etats généraux dans les provinces de 1302 à 1614*. Paris, 1874.

———. *Histoire des Etats généraux, considérés au point de vue de leur influence sur le gouvernement de la France de 1355 à 1614*. Paris: Hachette, 1872.

Picot, Gilbert. *Cardin le Bret, 1558–1655 et la doctrine de la souveraineté*. Nancy: Société d'Impressions typographiques, 1948.

Picq, Françoise. "Qu'est-ce que le 'féminisme bourgeois'?" In *Stratégies des femmes*. Paris: Tierce, 1984.

———. "Par-delà la loi du père, le débat sur la recherche de la paternité au congrès féministe de 1900." *Les Temps modernes*, no. 391 (Feb. 1979).

Piéron, Henri. *De l'influence sociale des principes cartésiens, un précurseur inconnu du féminisme et de la Révolution: Poullain de La Barre*. Paris: L. Cerf, n.d. From *La Revue de Synthèse historique* (1903).

Pinet, Marie-Josèphe. *Christine de Pisan 1364–1430: Etude biographique et littéraire.* Paris: Champion, 1927.

Pintard, René. "Préciosité et classicisme," *XVIIe siècle,* journal published by the Société d'Etude du XVIIe siècle, nos. 50–51.

Pire, G. "Nature et histoire dans la pensée de Jean-Jacques Rousseau; De l'influence de Sénèque sur les théories pédagogiques de J.-J. Rousseau." *Annales de la Société Jean-Jacques Rousseau,* A. Jullien, Bourg-de-Four, 32, v. 33 (1953–55).

Poirion, Daniel. *Le poète et le prince: L'Evolution du lyrisme courtois de Guillaume de Machaut à Charles d'Orléans.* Paris: PUF, 1965.

Portemer, Jean. "La Femme dans la législation royale des deux derniers siècles de l'Ancien Régime." From *Etudes d'histoire du droit privé offertes à Pierre Petat.* Paris: Dalloz, 1959.

———. "Le Statut de la femme en France depuis la réformation des coutumes jusqu'à la rédaction du Code civil." In *Recueils de la Société Jean-Bodin* (1962).

Poutet, Yves. *Le XVIIe siècle et les origines lasalliennes: Recherches sur la genèse de l'oeuvre scolaire et religieuse de Jean-Baptiste de La Salle (1651–1719).* Rennes, 1970.

Quillet, Janine. *Les Clefs du pouvoir au Moyen Age.* Paris: Flammarion, 1972.

———. *La Philosophie politique de Marsile de Padoue.* Paris: Vrin, 1970.

Rabaut, Jean. *Histoire des féminismes français.* Paris: Stock, 1978.

Recueil Sirey du bicentenaire de L'Esprit des lois. Paris: Librairie du Recueil Sirey, 1952.

Remy, Alexandre. *Les Femmes devant la guillotine.* Paris: Moutonnet, 1848.

Renaudet, Augustin. "Commémoration d'Henri Hauser." *Humanisme et Renaissance.* Geneva: Droz, 1958.

———. *Pré-réforme et humanisme à Paris pendant les premières guerres d'Italie (1494–1517).* Paris: Champion, 1916.

Renaudot, Maurice. *Le Féminisme et les droits publics de la femme.* Niort: L. Clouzot, 1902.

Reneault, Auguste. *Les Ursulines de Rouen, 1619–1906.* Fécamp: Imprimerie de L. Durand et Fils, 1919.

Rennes, Jacques. *Vie de Jacqueline Pascal.* Geneva: Roulet, 1948.

Renouvin, Pierre. *Les Assemblées provinciales de 1767: Origines, développement, résultats.* Paris: A. Picard, 1921.

Reynier, Gustave. *La Femme au XVIIe siècle: Ses ennemis et ses défenseurs.* Paris: Tallandier, 1929.

Ricard, Louis-Xavier de. *L'Esprit politique de la Réforme.* Paris: Fischbacher, 1893.

Richet, Denis. *La France moderne: L'Esprit des institutions.* Paris: Flammarion, 1973.

Rigaud, Rose. *Les Idées féministes de Christine de Pisan.* Neuchâtel, 1911. Reprint. Geneva: Slatkine Reprints, 1973.

Rodocanachi, Emmanuel. *La Femme italienne à l'époque de la Renaissance: Sa vie privée et mondaine, son influence sociale.* Paris: Hachette, 1907.

———. *Une Protectrice de la Réforme en Italie et en France, Renée de France, Duchesse de Ferrare.* Paris: Ollendorff, 1896.

Rolland, Henri. *L'Organisation corporative à la veille de la Révolution française: Essai sur l'organisation corporative et la vie économique à Blois au XVIIIe siècle.* Paris: Librarie technique et économique, 1938.

Rollet, Henri. *La Condition de la femme dans l'Eglise: Ces femmes qui ont fait l'Eglise.* Paris: Fayard, 1975.

Romier, Lucien. *Les Origines politiques des guerres de Religion.* Paris: Perrin, 1913–14.

———. *Promotion de la femme.* Paris: Hachette, 1930.

Ronzeaud, Pierre. "La Femme au pouvoir ou le monde à l'envers," *XVIIe siècle,* journal published by the Société d'Etude du XVIIe siècle, no. 108 (1975).

Roudinesco, Elisabeth. *Théroigne de Méricourt, une femme mélancolique sous la Révolution.* Paris: Seuil, 1989.

Roudy, Yvette. *La Femme en marge.* Paris: Flammarion, 1975.

Rousselot, Pierre. *Histoire de l'éducation des femmes en France*. Paris: Didier, 1883.

Roustan, Marius. *Les Philosophes et la société française au XVIIIe siècle*. Lyon: A. Rey, 1906.

Rudé, Georges. "La Composition sociale des insurrections parisiennes de 1789 à 1791." *Annales historiques de la Révolution française*, no. 127 (July-Aug. 1952).

―――. *La Foule dans la Révolution française*. Oxford University Press, 1959. Trans. Paris: Maspero, 1982.

Ruggiero, Guido de. *Storia del liberalismo europeo*. Milan: Feltrinelli, 1962.

Salomon-Bayet, Claire. *Jean-Jacques Rousseau, ou l'impossible unité*. Critical ed., bibliography. Paris: Seghers, 1967.

Schapiro, Jacob Salwyn. *Condorcet and the Rise of Liberalism*. New York: Octagon Books, 1963.

Schmidt, Albert Marie. *XIVe et XVe siècles français: Les Sources de l'humanisme*. Paris: Seghers, 1964.

Schmidt, Wilhelm Adolf. *Tableaux de la révolution française: Publiés sur les papiers inédits du département de la Police secrète de Paris*. 3 vols. Leipzig: Viet et Cie, 1867-70.

Screech, M. A. *The Rabelaisian Marriage: Aspects of Rabelais's Religion, Ethics and Comic Philosophy*. London: Arnold, 1958.

Sée, Henri. "Les Idées politiques à l'époque de la Fronde." *Revue d'Histoire moderne et contemporaine*, v. 3 (1901-2).

―――. *Les Idées politiques en France au XVIIe siècle*. Paris: Giard, 1923.

―――. *Les Idées politiques en France au XVIIIe siècle*. Paris, 1923. Reprint. Geneva: Slatkine Reprints, 1978.

Shackleton, Robert. *Montesquieu: Une Biographie critique*. French ed. by Jean Loiseau. Grenoble: PUG de Grenoble, 1977.

Simone, Franco. *Il Rinascimento francese: Studi e ricerche*. Turin: Società editrice internazionale, 1961.

―――. *Sur quelques rapports entre l'humanisme italien et l'humanisme français*. Paris: Boivin, n.d.

―――. *Pensée humaniste et tradition chrétienne aux XVe et XVIe siècles*. Publication de la Société d'Etudes italiennes. Paris: CNRS, 1950.

Snyders, Georges. *La Pédagogie en France aux XVIIe et XVIIIe siècles*. Paris: PUF, 1965.

Soboul, Albert. *Les Sans-Culottes parisiens en l'an II; mouvement populaire et gouvernement révolutionnaire, 2 juin 1793-9 thermidor an II*. Paris: Librairie Clavreuil, 1958.

Société Jean-Bodin pour l'histoire comparative des institutions. *Recueils la Société Jean-Bodin*. Vol. 10, *La Femme: Condition juridique*. Vol.11, *La Femme*. Brussels: 1959-62.

Sohn, Anne-Marie. *Féminisme et syndicalisme*. Doctoral thesis. Paris: Hachette, 1973.

Solomon, Howard. *Public Welfare, Science, and Propaganda in Seventeenth Century France: The Innovations of Théophraste Renaudot*. Princeton: Princeton University Press, 1972.

Sowerwine, Charles. *Les Femmes et le socialisme*. Paris: Presses de la Fondation des Sciences politiques, 1978.

―――. *Sisters or Citizens? Women and Socialism in France Since 1876*. New York: Cambridge University Press, 1982.

Spanneut, M. *Permanence du stoïcisme de Zénon à Malraux*. Paris: Duculot, 1973.

Spink, John Stephenson. *Jean-Jacques Rousseau et Genève: Essai sur les idées politiques et religieuses de Rousseau dans leur relation avec la pensée genevoise au XVIIIe siècle, pour servir d'introduction aux Lettres écrites de la montagne*. Paris: Boivin, 1934.

―――. *La Libre Pensée française de Gassendi à Voltaire*. Fr. trans. Paul Meier. Paris: Editions Sociales, 1966.

Starobinski, Jean. *1789: Les Emblèmes de la raison*. Paris: Flammarion, 1973.

―――. *Histoire de la médecine*. Lausanne: Rencontre, 1963.

―――. *L'Invention de la liberté*. Geneva: Skira, 1964.

———. *Jean-Jacques Rousseau: La Transparence et l'obstacle.* Paris: Plon, 1957.

Stock, Marie-Louise. *Poullain de La Barre: A Seventeenth Century Feminist.* Thesis, Columbia University, 1961.

Storr, Marthe (Miquel) Severn. *Mary Wollstonecraft et le mouvement féministe dans la littérature anglaise.* Paris: PUF, 1932.

Stratégies des femmes. Edited collectively by Marie-Claire Pasquier, Marcelle Marini, Françoise Ducrocq, Genevieve Fraisse, and Anne-Marie Sohn. Paris: Tierce, 1984.

Strauss, Léo. *Droit naturel et histoire.* Fr. trans. of *Natural Right and History* [1953] by M. Nathan and E. de Dampierre. Paris: Plon, 1954.

Sullerot, Evelyne. *Histoire de la presse féminine en France des origines à 1846.* Paris: Colin, 1966.

Talmon, Jacob Leib. *Les Origines de la démocratie totalitaire.* Paris: Calmann-Levy, 1952.

Taylor, C. V. "Les Cahiers de 1789, aspects révolutionnaires et non révolutionnaires." *Annales Economies, Sociétés, Civilisations* (Nov.-Dec. 1973).

Telle, Emile. *Erasme de Rotterdam et le septième sacrement: Etude d'évangélisme matrimonial au XVIe siècle et contribution à la biographie intellectuelle d'Erasme.* Geneva: Droz, 1954.

———. *L'Oeuvre de Marguerite d'Angoulême, reine de Navarre, et la querelle des femmes.* Doctoral thesis, University of Toulouse, 1937.

Thibaudet, Albert. *Histoire de la littérature française de 1789 a nos jours.* Paris: Stock, 1936.

———. *French Literature from 1795 to Our Era.* Eng. trans. Charles Lam Markmann. New York: Funk and Wagnalls, 1968.

Thomas, Edith. *Les Femmes en 1848.* Paris: PUF, 1948.

———. *Les Pétroleuses.* Paris: Gallimard, 1963.

Thomassy, Raymond. *Essai sur les écrits politiques de Christine de Pisan, suivi d'une notice littéraire et de pièces inédites.* Paris: Debécourt, 1838.

———. *Jean Gerson, chancelier de Notre-Dame et de l'Université de Paris.* Paris: Debécourt, 1843.

Thonnard, F. "La Notion de nature chez saint Augustin: Ses progrès dans la polémique antipélagienne." *Revue des Etudes augustiniennes* (1965).

———. "Prétendues contradictions dans la doctrine de saint Augustin sur le péché originel." *Revue des Etudes augustiniennes* (1964).

Tilly, Louise A., and Joan W. Scott. *Women, Work and Family.* New York: Holt, Rinehart and Winston, 1978.

Tinland, Franck. *Histoire d'une jeune fille sauvage trouvée dans les bois à l'âge de dix ans.* Bordeaux: Ducros, 1970.

———. *L'Homme sauvage: Homo ferus et homo sylvestris, de l'animal à l'homme.* Preface by Georges Gusdorf. Paris: Payot, 1968.

Todd, Janet M., ed. *A Wollstonecraft Anthology.* London and Bloomington: Indiana University Press, 1977.

Tomalin, Claire. *The Life and Death of Mary Wollstonecraft.* London: Weidenfeld and Nicolson, 1974.

Tourneux, Maurice. *Bibliographie de l'histoire de Paris pendant la Révolution française.* Vol. 4, *Femmes.* Paris: Imprimerie Nouvelle, 1906.

Tuetey, Alexandre. *Répertoire général des sources manuscrites de l'histoire de Paris pendant la Révolution française.* Paris: Imprimerie Nouvelle, 1890–1914.

Turbet-Delof, G. "À propos d'Emile et Sophie." *Revue d'Histoire littéraire de la France,* published by the Société d'Histoire littéraire de la France (Jan.-Mar. 1964).

Vachet, André. *L'Idéologie libérale.* Paris: Anthropos, 1970.

Vadier, Berthe, *Un Moraliste du XVIe siècle, Jean-Louis Vives et son livre sur l'éducation de la femme chrétienne.* Geneva: I. Soullier, 1892.

Valentino, Henri. *Madame de Condorcet: Ses amis et ses amours, 1764–1822.* Paris: Perrin, 1950.

————. *Madame d'Epinay, 1726–1782: Une Femme d'esprit sous Louis XV*. Paris: Perrin, 1952.

Védrine, Hélène. *Les Ruses de la raison*. Paris: Payot, 1982.

Verger, Francine. *Le Thème de la famille et de la femme chez Tocqueville*. Essay for diploma in political science, Paris, March 1979.

Villeneuve de Janti, Pierre. *Bonaparte et le Code civil*. Doctoral thesis. Paris: Loviton, 1934.

Villeneuve-Guibert, Gaston, comte de. *Le Portefeuille de Madame Dupin, Dame de Chenonceaux. Lettres et autres inédites*. Paris: Calmann-Levy, 1884.

Villey, Michel. "Aristote, Vitona et Grotius." In *Platon et Aristote à la Renaissance*. XVIe Colloque international de Tours, Paris: Vrin, 1976.

————. *La Formation de la pensée juridique moderne: Cours d'histoire de la philosophie du droit, 1961–1966*. Paris: Montchrestien, 1968.

————. *La Formation de la pensée juridique moderne: Cours d'histoire de la philosophie du droit nouvelle et corrigée*. Paris: Montchrestien, 1975.

————. *Leçons d'histoire de la philosophie du droit*. Paris: Dalloz, 1962.

Villiers du Terrage, Marc, baron de. *Histoire des clubs de femmes et des légions d'amazones, 1793, 1848, 1871*. Paris: Plon-Nourrit, 1910.

Vlachos, Georges. *La Pensée politique de Kant*. Paris: PUF, 1962.

Waddicor, Mark H. *Montesquieu and the Philosophy of Natural Law*. The Hague: Nijhoff, 1970.

Ward, Charles Frederick. *The Epistles on the Romance of the Rose and Other Documents in the Debate*. Chicago: University of Chicago Press, 1911.

Wardle, Ralph. *Mary Wollstonecraft: A Critical Biography*. Lincoln: University of Nebraska Press, 1966.

Weber, Max. *L'Ethique protestante et l'esprit du capitalisme*. Paris: Plon, 1964.

————. *The Protestant Ethic and the Spirit of Capitalism*. New York: Scribner, 1930.

Weill, Georges. *Les Théories sur le pouvoir royal en France pendant les guerres de Religion*. Paris: Hachette, 1892.

Wexler, Victor G. " 'Made for Man's Delight': Rousseau as Anti-Feminist." *American Historical Review*, vol. 81, no. 1 (1976).

Wickersheimer, E. "Sur la syphilis aux XVe et XVIe siècles," from *Humanisme et Renaissance*, vol. 1. Paris: Droz, 1937.

Wolfsgueber, Celestin. *Vie de la sainte fondatrice Angèle de Mérici (1474–1540)*. Innsbruck: Vereinsbuchhandlung, 1906.

Wormeley, Katharine Prescott. *The Correspondence of Madame, Princess Palatine, Mother of the Regent; of Marie-Adelaide Savoie, Duchess de Bourgogne; and of Madame de Maintenon, in Relation to Saint-Cyr. Preceded by introduction from C.-A. Sainte-Beuve*. Ed. Katharine Prescott Wormeley. Boston: Hardy, Pratt and Co., 1899.

Zanta, Léontine. *La Renaissance du stoïcisme au XVIe siècle*. Thesis for doctorate in letters. Paris: Champion, 1914.

Zetkin, Clara. *Bataille pour les femmes: Anthologie*. Paris: Editions Sociales, 1980.

INDEX

Author:

Christine Fauré is a sociologist with the Centre National de la Recherche Scientifique (CNRS) in Paris. Her dissertation was written under the direction of Gilles Deleuze. She is the author of *Terre, terreur et liberté* and *Les Déclarations des droits de l'homme de 1789*. Her articles on history and philosophy of women have appeared in such journals as *Cultures, Les Temps Modernes*, and *Signs*.

Translators:

Claudia Gorbman, Associate Professor of Comparative Literature and Film and Adjunct Professor of Women's Studies at Indiana University, is author of *Unheard Melodies: Narrative Film Music* and articles which have appeared in *Yale French Studies, Film Quarterly, Wide Angle*, and other journals.

John Berks, who is working toward the Ph.D. degree in Comparative Literature at Indiana University, was awarded the 1988 American Translators Association Student Grant for the translation of *La démocratie sans les femmes*.